WAR AND THE AMERICAN DIFFERENCE

WAR

AND THE

AMERICAN DIFFERENCE

Theological Reflections on Violence and National Identity

STANLEY HAUERWAS

B
Baker Academic
a division of Baker Publishing Group
Grand Rapids, Michigan

Published by Baker Academic
a division of Baker Publishing Group
P.O. Box 6287, Grand Rapids, MI 49516-6287
www.bakeracademic.com

Printed in the United States of America

Library of Congress Cataloging-in-Publication Data
Hauerwas, Stanley, 1940–
War and the American difference : theological reflections on violence and national identity / Stanley Hauerwas.
p. cm.
Includes bibliographical references and index.
ISBN 978-0-8010-3929-4 (pbk.)
1. War—Religious aspects—Christianity. 2. Nonviolence—Religious aspects—Christianity. 3. Nationalism—Religious aspects—Christianity. 4. Christianity and international relations. 5. United States—Foreign relations—2001– 6. Christianity and politics—United States. 7. Church and state—United States. I. Title.
BT736.2.H38 2011
261.8′730973—dc23 2011023834

11 12 13 14 15 16 17 7 6 5 4 3 2 1

In keeping with biblical principles of creation stewardship, Baker Publishing Group advocates the responsible use of our natural resources. As a member of the Green Press Initiative, our company uses recycled paper when possible. The text paper of this book is composed in part of post-consumer waste.

To the Ekklesia Project

Contents

Preface

Ten years and counting. America has been at war for ten years and counting. It is almost difficult to recall a time when America was not at war. The Cold War may not have seemed like war, but there can be no doubt that it was appropriately named "war." For those of us who have lived long enough to remember it, in some ways the Cold War seemed more real than the wars that ensued after September 11, 2001. The Cold War impinged on the daily lives of Americans, whereas the wars after September 11, 2001, have been fought without the general American population having to make any sacrifices. They go on, and so do we. Yet people are dying and people are killing. These wars are real.

Most Americans do not seem to be terribly bothered by the reality of the current wars. It is as if they have become but another video game. In truth, the wars themselves are increasingly shaped by technologies that make them seem gamelike. Young men and women can kill people around the world while sitting in comfortable chairs in underground bunkers in Colorado. At the end of the work day, they can go home and watch Little League baseball. I find it hard to imagine what it means to live this way.

The wars America has been fighting for ten years and counting seem so distant and vague that it is hard for any of us to deal with the reality of war. We celebrate and praise the heroism of those who fight, and we are saddened that some must make the "ultimate sacrifice" to preserve our "freedom." Those so honored, however, do not necessarily think, given the reality of war, that they should be regarded as heroes. To be sure, those who are actually engaged in combat—those who see the maimed bodies and mourning mothers—struggle more than the rest of us to make sense of the reality of war.

It is my hope that this book will in some small way help us, Christian and non-Christian alike, to confront the reality of war. I write as one committed to Christian nonviolence, but I hope that what I have written here will be an invitation for those who do not share my commitments to nevertheless join me in thinking through what a world without war might look like.

The world, for good reason, may well think it does not need another book by me, but I make no apology for putting this book together. In the face of ongoing wars it is hard to know what to say, but I am determined to continue trying to articulate what it might mean to be faithful to the gospel. Like most of my work this book is exploratory, but I hope readers will find my attempt to reframe theologically how we think about war fruitful for their own reflection. Indeed, I hope I have said some of what needs to be said if we are to have an alternative to "ten years and counting."

I'm thankful that Rodney Clapp thought these essays to be important and worthwhile. When I sent them to Rodney I did so knowing he had the editorial imagination to envision them as a whole; and he did. As usual, I am in Rodney's debt, not only for making this book possible, but for suggesting that I have some Johnny Cash in my soul.

I'm grateful to Adam Hollowell and Nathaniel Jung-Chul Lee, who proved invaluable in getting these essays ready for publication. Early on, when I first began thinking of this collection, Adam spent time reading and making insightful suggestions. That Adam has now completed his PhD and is currently a colleague at Duke is a great gift. Nate has helped with final revisions, which entailed his making substantive suggestions for the text as a whole. His determination to be a priest in the Episcopal Church is a gift to the church. Both of these young scholars are examples of what it means for the academy and the church to take seriously the realism of Christ's sacrifice.

Carole Baker was the first reader of these essays. Without her none of the chapters in this book would have been ready to be read by others. She has read and reread what I have written for so long, she is now able to say what I should have said better than me. I continue to worry that having her work for me means she cannot pursue her work as an artist as fully as I think she should. But hopefully that day is not far off.

I have dedicated this book to the Ekklesia Project because though it is a quirky group of people—and that includes me—I think it may be the kind of gathering that helps us see what it could mean for Christians to love one another.

By the time this book appears I will be seventy years old. How strange. What a wonderful life I have been given. I have been loved by many friends and I am extremely grateful. But Paula's love for me has made all the difference.

Introduction

This is a modest book with an immodest purpose: to convince Christians that war has been abolished. The grammar of that sentence is very important: the past tense is deliberate. I do not want to convince Christians to work for the abolition of war, but rather I want us to live recognizing that in the cross of Christ war has already been abolished. So I am not asking Christians to work to create a world free of war. The world has already been saved from war. The question is how Christians can and should live in a world of war as a people who believe that war has been abolished.

I am well aware that the claim that Jesus has abolished war will strike many as absurd. We live, as I just acknowledged, in a world of war. So what could it possibly mean to say that through his death and resurrection Jesus has brought an end to war? To live as if war has been abolished surely is a fool's game. Philip Bobbitt must be right to argue that we cannot and, more importantly, should not try to imagine a world without war. Rather, we ought to think hard about the wars we should have fought for political reasons so to avoid wars that lack political purpose.[1]

Bobbitt's presumption that there is no alternative to war reflects a humane and profound understanding of our common lot. He is no lover of war. He is not a cynic or a nihilist. He does not believe when all is said and done that we must live as if the bottom line is to kill or be killed. Bobbitt simply accepts the world as he finds it, that is, a world in which war, like birth and death, is simply a fact of life. He sees his task, a moral task, as helping us to understand the possibilities as well as the limits of such a world.

1. Philip Bobbitt, *The Shield of Achilles: War, Peace, and the Course of History* (New York: Anchor, 2003), 780. Although Bobbitt does not use just war categories in *The Shield of Achilles*, his analysis of war might invite a just war response if, as Paul Ramsey argued, the point of just war is to subject war to a political purpose.

The problem with Bobbitt's defense of what he considers the real world of war is that there is another world that is more real than a world determined by war: the world that has been redeemed by Christ. The world that has been redeemed by Christ has an alternative politics to the constitutional orders that Bobbitt thinks are established by war. The name for that alternative politics is "church."

The statement that there is a world without war in a war-determined world is an eschatological remark. Christians live in two ages in which, as Oliver O'Donovan puts it, "the passing age of the principalities and powers has overlapped with the coming age of God's kingdom."[2] O'Donovan calls this the "doctrine of the Two" because it expresses the Christian conviction that Christ has triumphed over the rulers of this age by making the rule of God triumphantly present through the mission of the church.[3] Accordingly the church is not at liberty to withdraw from the world but must undertake its mission in the confident hope of success.[4]

My appeal to O'Donovan's understanding of the "doctrine of the Two" may seem quite strange given my pacifism, his defense of just war, and his nuanced support of some of what we call Christendom. From O'Donovan's perspective the establishment of the church in law and practice and the development of just war reflection were appropriate expressions of the rule of Christ. One of the justifications for bringing these essays together is to suggest that my (and John Howard Yoder's) understanding of the "doctrine of the Two" shares more in common with O'Donovan than many might suspect.

My claim that Christians are called to live nonviolently, not because we think nonviolence is a strategy to rid the world of war, but rather because as faithful followers of Christ in a world of war we cannot imagine not living nonviolently, might seem quite antithetical to O'Donovan's understanding of the "doctrine of the Two." But I do not think that to be the case. Like O'Donovan, I believe that after the ascension, everything, including those who rule, cannot avoid being a witness to the rule of Christ.[5] Even the rejection of Christ's lordship cannot help but testify to him.

The church simply names those whom God has called to live faithfully according to the redemption wrought through Christ. The difference between church and world is not an ontological difference, but rather a difference of agency. The world, by being the world, is not condemned to live violently, but rather the violence that grips it is the result of sin. This understanding of

2. Oliver O'Donovan, *The Desire of the Nations: Rediscovering the Roots of Political Theology* (Cambridge: Cambridge University Press, 1996), 211.

3. Ibid., 193.

4. Ibid., 212.

5. By calling attention to the ascension I am not suggesting that O'Donovan isolates the ascension from the crucifixion and resurrection. Rather he sees the crucifixion, resurrection, and ascension as bound together "in a knot of mutual intelligibility" (*Resurrection and Moral Order: An Outline for Evangelical Ethics*, 2nd ed. [Grand Rapids: Eerdmans, 1994], 14).

church and world is, therefore, a "duality without dualism" because Christians believe that the church is what the world can be.[6]

Because Christians believe we are what the world can be, we can act in the hope that the world can and will positively respond to a witness of peace.[7] That witness begins with Christians refusing to kill one another in the name of lesser loyalties and goods. Such a refusal creates the necessity for Christians to imagine what it might mean to live in a world in which war has been abolished. That is no easy task given the way war shapes our habits of speech, our fundamental explanatory accounts of the way things are, and the way we see the world. The challenge for those who would worship Christ, therefore, is to allow what we do in prayer to confront the habits that seem to make war inevitable.

John Howard Yoder observes that to imagine a world in which war has been abolished requires that we live in a community that celebrates and shares a language that helps us see an alternative world. According to Yoder, because the church is that kind of alternative community, Christians can see things that other people cannot see, we can notice what others fail to notice, and we can make connections that otherwise would be overlooked. Such a community, moreover, "enables perseverance, it motivates, it protects us from the erratic and the impulsive, because the stance we take is a shared and celebrated stance. We live with one another the maintenance of the language that gives meaning to our countercultural identity."[8]

The heart of this book is my attempt to imagine what it means for the church to be an alternative to war. Those concerned with the fragmented character of our lives might interpret my suggestion that the church is an alternative to war as a reactionary response. Many long for a universal ethic that promises the means to secure agreements between diverse people as an alternative to war.[9] To emphasize the church as an alternative to war will seem from such a perspective to introduce the kind of particularistic commitment that is the source of the problem. Too often, however, those who presume they are representatives of a

6. John Howard Yoder, *The Christian Witness to the State* (Newton, KS: Faith and Life, 1964), 31.

7. John Howard Yoder observes that "peace" is not an accurate description of what has happened to those who have identified with "Historic Peace Churches." Nor does Christian pacifism guarantee a warless world. Rather " 'peace' describes the pacifist's hope, the goal in the light of which he acts, the character of his action, the ultimate divine certainty which lets his position make sense; it does not describe the external appearance or the observable results of his behavior. This is what we mean by eschatology: a hope which, defying present frustration, defines a present position in terms of the yet unseen goal which gives it meaning" (*The Original Revolution: Essays on Christian Pacifism* [Scottdale, PA: Herald, 2003], 53).

8. John Howard Yoder, *For the Nations: Essays Public and Evangelical* (Grand Rapids: Eerdmans, 1997), 153. For an extremely important essay on Yoder's work that highlights this quotation, see Mark Thiessen Nation, "The Politics of Yoder Regarding *The Politics of Jesus*," in *Radical Ecumenicity: Pursuing Unity and Continuity after John Howard Yoder*, ed. John Nugent (Abilene, TX: Abilene Christian University Press, 2010), 37–56.

9. For an insightful account of the main characteristics of universal ethics as a "type," see Samuel Wells and Ben Quash, *Introducing Christian Ethics* (Oxford: Wiley-Blackwell, 2010), 115–45.

universal ethic find it difficult to place a limit on war. For example, if a war is fought "to be a war to end all wars" or "to make the world safe for democracy" or as "a war against terrorism," then war cannot come to an end.

By beginning with the church, and in particular with the liturgy, I have tried to develop a perspective on the character of war that helps us see why we find it so hard to imagine a world without war. By doing so I hope, as one committed to Christian nonviolence, to give an account of war that acknowledges the real sacrifices of those who have participated in war. One of the reasons I think it is difficult for many to think of themselves as pacifist is that such a position seems to dishonor those who have gone to war. Defenders of war may say that they respect those who are pacifist, but they continue to assume that there are times when war is a necessity. That assumption seems justified because if, as most rightly think, good people fought in past wars, then it may be necessary to fight in future wars so that those who fought in past wars are not forgotten or dishonored. From this perspective the pacifist disavowal of war seems to suggest that those who have fought in past wars are morally culpable.

If we hope to avoid the unhappy characterizations pacifists and nonpacifists make of one another, it is crucial that those of us committed to Christian nonviolence make clear that we do not understand our disavowal of war to be a position of "purity." A commitment to nonviolence rightly requires those who are so committed to recognize that we are as implicated in war as those who have gone to war or those who have supported war. The moral challenge of war is too important for us to play the game of who is and who is not guilty for past or future wars. We are all, pacifist and nonpacifist alike, guilty. Guilt, however, is not helpful. What can be helpful is a cooperative effort to make war less likely.

Many have assumed that the best way to begin that task is to develop increasingly sophisticated accounts of the classical moral alternatives of the crusade, pacifism, and just war.[10] I am deeply respectful of the work done by those who have tried to clarify these ways of thinking about war.[11] However,

10. John Howard Yoder rightly argues that these "types" can blind us to the fact that the dominant response of Christians to war has been what Yoder calls the "blank check." The blank check assumes that we should go kill whoever our leader says we should go kill. Though often associated with kings, this type is particularly powerful in alleged democracies because it is assumed that those who make the decision to go to war represent the interests of "the people." Yoder's account of the types is to be found in his *Christian Attitudes to War, Peace, and Revolution*, ed. Theodore Koontz and Andy Alexis-Baker (Grand Rapids: Brazos, 2009), 27–41.

11. I am particularly impressed by Daniel Bell's recent book *Just War as Christian Discipleship: Recentering the Tradition in the Church Rather Than the State* (Grand Rapids: Brazos, 2009). Bell provides an important argument to suggest that the just war tradition is best understood as a means for those who are to go or have been to war to test their conscience as followers of Christ. As Bell puts it, "with regard to just war, if in the last analysis just war is a compromise between Jesus's nonviolent ideal and the demands of a violent reality, if it is something other than following Jesus, then it cannot be a faithful form of discipleship" (36). Bell accordingly draws on Augustine to argue that just war as an act of love can be a form of discipleship.

I am not persuaded that attempts to gain clarity about the ethics of war do justice to the moral reality of war. I am not suggesting (though I am in some sympathy with the suggestion) that just war considerations have little effect on decisions to go to war or the actual conduct of war. I am rather suggesting that this way of approaching war as a moral reality fails to do justice to the morally compelling character of war.

For in spite of the horror of war, I think war, particularly in our times, is a sacrificial system that is crucial for the renewal of the moral commitments that constitute our lives.[12] That is why, as Jonathan Tran argues, memory is a crucial constituent of the moral reality that makes war seem unavoidable. We ask soldiers to kill and be killed, and in order to make sense of what they have done we identify them with those patriotic stories that enable us to remember the dead.[13]

Tran observes that most soldiers cannot "long live with the memory of killing if the nation does not provide both narratives and narratival enactments that circumscribe those memories within the national myth, engrafting killers into the lore of patriots."[14] That, of course, is what did not happen for those who fought in Vietnam. And lacking any culminating liturgies, the Vietnam war seems to have never ended—particularly for those who fought in it. This means, according to Tran, "for the first time in American history, soldiers came home killers" because they were not given the means to return to "normality."[15]

Ivan Strenski complements Tran's analysis of the liturgical character of war by suggesting that the sacrifices demanded of war cause certain effects in the society for which the war has been fought. The sacrifice of war, that is, that a society must receive the giving up of self by those who have fought and died, "authorizes conceptions of an ideal community, it energizes a society to flourish, it inspires it to resist extermination, it weaves the networks of obligation that make societies cohere."[16] Those who die in war make those for whom they have died feel obligated to accept the gift of their death and, more importantly, "be obliged to repay this gift of their heroic deaths in some appropriate way."[17]

The 2010 Supreme Court decision concerning the cross erected on public lands to remember the casualties of WWI reinforces Tran's and Strenski's account of war as a liturgical event. In defense of the cross, Justice Kennedy observed that "a Latin cross is not merely a reaffirmation of Christian beliefs.

12. I hesitate to use the phrase "particularly in our times" because I am convinced that war has always had a sacrificial character in diverse societies and times. I do think, however, that the language of sacrifice became particularly prominent in the American Civil War and WWI. I am also hesitant to generalize about the sacrificial character of war because I am hesitant to generalize about war.

13. Jonathan Tran, *The Vietnam War and Theologies of Memory* (Oxford: Wiley-Blackwell, 2010), 176–80.

14. Ibid., 198.

15. Ibid., 184.

16. Ivan Strenski, *Why Politics Can't Be Freed from Religion* (Oxford: Wiley-Blackwell, 2010), 176.

17. Ibid., 181.

It is a symbol often used to honor and respect those whose heroic acts, noble contributions, and patient striving help secure an honored place in history for this Nation and its people."[18] Kennedy continues by suggesting that the meaning of this cross cannot be limited to the cross of Christ. In Kennedy's words, "Here, one Latin cross in the desert evokes far more than religion. It evokes thousands of small crosses in foreign fields marking the graves of Americans who fell in battles, battles whose tragedies are compounded if the fallen are forgotten."[19]

Interestingly, in dissent, Justice Stevens gave voice to what I think Christians should say in response to Kennedy's decision. Justice Stevens said he could not agree that this bare cross was nonsectarian simply because crosses are often used to commemorate heroic acts of fallen soldiers. Stevens contended that "the cross is not a universal symbol of sacrifice. It is the symbol of one particular sacrifice, and that sacrifice carries deeply significant meaning for those who adhere to the Christian faith."[20] Justice Stevens acknowledges that the cross has sometimes been used to represent the sacrifice of an individual, but even then the cross carries a religious meaning. Stevens observes, "the use of the cross in such circumstances is linked to, and shows respect for, the individual honoree's faith and beliefs. I too would consider it tragic if the Nation's fallen veterans were forgotten. But there are countless different ways, consistent with the Constitution, that such an outcome can be averted."[21]

Justice Kennedy's decision makes clear what I mean by "the American difference." I am not suggesting that the sacrificial character of war is unique to America. For as I make clear in chapter 5, "Sacrificing the Sacrifices of War," the Germans, French, and English often understood WWI in similar terms. Yet war has a role in the American story that is quite unique. For even if it is true (and I think it is), as Michael Howard contends, that the state as we know it is the creature of war, America is a society and a state that cannot live without war.[22] Though a particular war may be divisive, war is the glue that gives Americans a common story.

My focus on the liturgical character of war has shaped the organization of this book. I begin with chapters on the American difference. As is true of all the chapters in the book, these essays touch on matters that are not strictly about war. Yet, as is my wont, I think everything is related to everything else. In the first part I try to show that war as a moral and liturgical enterprise is shaped by a death-denying politics that is an affront to the Christian passion for life. War is a theological challenge to the very intelligibility of Christian

18. Salazar, Secretary of the Interior, et al. v. Buono, 599 U.S. 08–472 (2010), available at http://www.supremecourt.gov/opinions/09pdf/08-472.pdf.

19. Ibid.

20. Ibid.

21. Ibid.

22. Sir Michael Howard, foreword to Bobbitt, *Shield of Achilles*, xvi.

practice. That many insist on the incoherence of Christianity, I believe, has its roots in the Christian legitimization of war.

The essays in part two, "The Liturgy of War," are meant to sharpen the focus on violence and war. I would not pretend that these essays do all the work that needs to be done, or say all that needs to be said about war. Indeed I would not pretend that the book as a whole adequately defends the suggestions I am trying to make for how we might understand the church as an alternative to war. I am well aware that this book is "suggestive." I hope, however, that the reader will find the suggestiveness of the book rewarding enough to follow up on some of its suggestions.

C. S. Lewis was obviously not an American, but I have included the essay on Lewis because Lewis, as was his habit, gave voice to the assumptions many have about the problematic character of a pacifist stance. By including this essay on Lewis I hope to address some of the worries many have about the viability of Christian nonviolence. The chapter on King is my attempt to challenge the assumption that those committed to Christian nonviolence are not or cannot be politically relevant.

The chapters that make up the last part, entitled "The Ecclesial Difference," are my attempt to develop an account of church as an alternative to war. In these essays I try to avoid the dualism that many assume is a given, that is, that between the universal and the particular.[23] The Christian word for universal is "catholic," but "catholic" does not name a proposition that can be recognized by just anyone to be true. Rather, "catholic" names a people whose worship of God means they must recognize others who may well worship God in strikingly different ways. I do not pretend that process is easy. In fact, it is because of this immense difficulty that the commitment not to kill is constitutive of those who claim to follow Christ.

I have written often on the ethics of war and peace, but this is the first book that has those motifs as its primary focus. I have avoided focusing on war and peace because to do so might give some the impression that nonviolence is all that Christianity is about. If nonviolence becomes an abstraction, an ideal Christians pursue that can be separated from our convictions about the cross and resurrection, nonviolence threatens to become another manipulative form of human behavior. I hope, therefore, that my attempt to (re)describe war as an alternative to the sacrifice of the cross at once illumines why war is so morally compelling and why the church is an alternative to war.

23. For a fascinating analysis of the issues in relation to Pauline literature in contemporary political theology, see Derek Woodard-Lehman's "One in Christ Who Lives Within: Dispersive Universality and Pnuema-Somatics of Identity," in *The Bible and Critical Theory* 3, no. 3 (2007): 39.1–7.

Part 1

America and War

1

War and the American Difference

A Theological Assessment

America is assumed to be different, because Christianity is still thought to thrive in the United States. Whereas Christianity is allegedly dying in Europe, it seems alive and well here, which confirms for many the contention that there is an inherent link between Christianity and democracy. For it is assumed not only that America is a Christian nation, but also that it is the paradigmatic exemplification of democracy.

In *A Secular Age* Charles Taylor tries to explain this presumed difference between America and Europe. At least one of the reasons that may account for the difference, Taylor suggests, is that America never had an *ancien régime* in which the church legitimized a hierarchical social order. Also at work may be the different role that elites play in determining general attitudes toward belief and unbelief. For example, the skepticism of academic elites in British society had more effect in England because elites have more prestige in British society than elites in America.

The primary reason for the American difference, according to Taylor, is the development of a common civil religion that allowed Americans, as well as immigrants in America, to understand their faiths as contributing to a consensus summed up by the motto "E pluribus unum." This is in marked contrast to Europe, where religious identities have been the source of division either between dissenters and the national church, or between church and lay forces. In America, religious difference, which is even more varied than in Europe, is subordinated to "one nation under God." Religious people may find they are in deep disagreement about abortion or gay marriage, but those disagreements are subordinated to their common loyalty to America.[1] Their subordination also includes their faith in God; that is, whatever kind of Christian (or non-Christian) they may or may not be, their faith should be in harmony with what it means to be an American.

Taylor observes that this difference also accounts for the respective attitudes Europeans and Americans have toward national identities. Europeans generally are quite reticent about national identity, which Taylor attributes to the European memory of the First and Second World Wars. He observes that war, even wars that seem "righteous," now make most Europeans uneasy. Yet that is not the case with Americans. Americans' lack of unease with war may stem from their (incorrect) belief that there are fewer skeletons in the American closet than in the European closet. But Taylor thinks the reason for the American support of war is simpler. "It is easier," Taylor observes, "to be unreservedly confident in your own righteousness when you are the hegemonic power."[2]

Taylor is right to recognize that America's unrivaled power in the world gives Americans a sense of confidence about our role as the "world's policeman," but he does not *articulate*—to use one of his favorite words—how American civil religion (our assumption that we are a "religious nation") relates to the fact that war for most Americans is unproblematic.[3] War is a moral necessity for America because it provides the experience of the "unum" that makes the "pluribus" possible. War is America's central liturgical act necessary to renew our sense that we are a nation unlike other nations.[4] World War I was the decisive moment because it was that war that finally healed the wounds caused by the American Civil War.

This is well documented by Richard Gamble in his book *The War for Righteousness: Progressive Christianity, the Great War, and the Rise of the Messianic Nation*. Gamble provides ample evidence to show how liberal Protestants justified the First World War as redemptive for the nation and church. For example, Lyman Abbott, a well known progressive Protestant who had sought to reconcile Christianity with evolution, argued that America as a Christian nation must be willing to be self-sacrificial in service to other nations. Therefore America rightly opposed "pagan" Germany because Germany

1. Charles Taylor, *A Secular Age* (Cambridge, MA: Belknap, 2007), 522–27.

2. Ibid., 528.

3. For Taylor's emphasis on the significance of being articulate for locating our lives morally, see *Sources of the Self: The Making of Modern Identity* (Cambridge, MA: Harvard University Press, 1989), 92–107.

4. I develop this account of war in my essay "Sacrificing the Sacrifices of War," first published in the *Criswell Theological Review* 4, no. 2 (2007): 77–96, but also included in part 2 of the present volume. The significance of the American Civil War is crucial in order to understand the liturgical significance of war in American life.

is a society in which "the poor serve the rich, the weak serve the strong, the ignorant serve the wise." By contrast, America is a society of "organized Christianity" in which the "rich serve the poor, the strong serve the weak, the wise serve the ignorant."[5]

Harry Emerson Fosdick, the exemplar of Protestant liberalism, even suggested that returning troops would present a special challenge to the nation and the churches since the soldiers would have learned the meaning of self-sacrifice through the experience of the war.[6] They also would have experienced the potential of cooperative action through the regenerative power of devotion to a higher cause. Accordingly, the returning soldiers would challenge reactionary views of society and the church because they would expect to remake their world in accordance with the lessons they learned from the war.[7] War, in short, was seen as the laboratory for the more egalitarian social policies that advocates of the Protestant social gospel so desperately desired.

Christianity and democracy in America were and continue to be, through the experience of war, inextricably linked. Arthur McGiffert, the president of Union Theological Seminary, argued that religion was necessary "to promote and sustain democracy." Religion, according to McGiffert, had to dispose of its "egoistic and other-worldly character" by becoming socially responsible. "The religion of democracy," he warned, "must cease to minister to selfishness by promising personal salvation, and must cease to impede human progress by turning the attention of religious men from the conditions here to rewards elsewhere."[8] Such was the lesson to be learned from war.

I call attention to how Americans understood the theological and moral significance of World War I because I think we fail to appreciate what Taylor identifies as the American civil religion if we do not take the American understanding of war into account. For example, Taylor observes that the traditional American synthesis of "civil religion," associated with a nondenominational Christianity with a strong connection to civilized order, is still, unlike its British counterpart, in its "hot" phase. That it is so, however, has everything to do with the American experience of war as constitutive of the substance of our civil religion.

Even political theorists as insightful as C. B. Macpherson can miss the significance of war for American civil religion. Macpherson identified two versions of liberal democracy, which he argues shape American democracy but are in conflict with one another. In the first, a capitalist market society is assumed to be compatible with democratic processes. This form of democracy,

5. Richard Gamble quoting Abbott in *The War for Righteousness: Progressive Christianity, the Great War, and the Rise of the Messianic Nation* (Wilmington, DE: Intercollegiate Studies Institute, 2003), 155.

6. Harry Emerson Fosdick, "The Trenches and the Church at Home," *Atlantic Monthly*, 1919.

7. Gamble, *War for Righteousness*, 211.

8. Quoted in ibid., 214.

no matter how much the rise of the welfare state modifies it, remains dominant—particularly in America, and various balance-of-power models from American political science have given renewed theoretical legitimacy to it.

Macpherson associates the other version of liberal democracy with John Stuart Mill's attempt to moralize liberalism by arguing that a liberal society must be one in which all the members of the social order are equally free to realize their capabilities. From Macpherson's perspective liberal democracy, particularly the democracy of the United States, has tried to combine both forms of liberalism.[9] Thus at times "liberal" means *the stronger can dominate the weak as long as they follow market rules*, while at other times it means *the attempt, usually through state agency, to achieve freedom for all to develop their capacity*. As a result, American politics cannot help but appear incoherent, as different and contradictory policy alternatives are put forward in the name of "freedom."[10]

For example, one defense for abortion is the right of an individual to have control over her body, but it is still assumed that laws against suicide make sense in the name of preventing harm. While some portions of the American society think it legitimate to appeal to their religious convictions to address such issues, others see this as a threat to the consensus that makes America work. Thus Taylor's observation that, even though the Protestant character of the original American civil religion has been broadened to include "all faiths" or "no faiths," there is still a strong "religious" character to American public life. That such is the case is confirmed by the very existence of secularist and liberal believers who seek a more secular America.[11]

I agree with Macpherson that both forms of liberalism shape American life, but the tension between them can go unnoticed exactly because America is so wealthy and has the common moral experience of war. Of course wealth, as it turns out, makes war necessary; yet Americans assume that we never go to war to sustain our wealth, because they understand war as a moral enterprise commensurate with our being a democracy. From such a perspective, the military adventures prompted by September 11, 2001, were absolutely necessary for the moral health of the republic. That America must fight an unending war against terrorism means Americans have a common enemy that unites us.

If I am right about the place of war for sustaining the American difference, as a Christian I wish America as a nation was more "secular" and the Christianity of America was less American. Put differently, I wish America was more like Europe, for I fear that the American version of Christianity cannot

9. C. B. Macpherson, *The Life and Times of Liberal Democracy* (Oxford: Oxford University Press, 1977), 1.

10. Thus Alasdair MacIntyre's now classic description in *After Virtue: A Study in Moral Theory*, 3rd ed. (Notre Dame: University of Notre Dame Press, 2007) of the inability in liberal societies to know what might count as an argument.

11. Taylor, *Secular Age*, 528.

provide a political challenge to what is done in the name of the American difference. In short, the great difficulty is how to keep America, in the proper sense, secular.

In order to elaborate this observation I think it helpful to call attention to Mark Lilla's important book *The Stillborn God: Religion, Politics, and the Modern West*. Lilla begins his book by giving voice to a sentiment raised after September 11, 2001, and occasioned by the Bush presidency. He (and many on the Left) had assumed that battles over revelation and reason, dogmatic purity and toleration, divine duty and common decency, had been relegated to the scrap heap of history. So people like Lilla "find it incomprehensible that theological ideas still inflame the minds of men, stirring up messianic passions that leave societies in ruin. We had assumed that this was no longer possible, that human beings had learned to separate religious questions from political ones, that fanaticism was dead. We were wrong."[12]

Lilla seeks, therefore, to defend "the great separation," that is, "to develop habits of thinking and talking about politics exclusively in human terms without appeals to divine revelation or cosmological speculation."[13] Lilla understands this separation to be an extraordinary achievement because political theology is a "primordial form of thought" that for millennia provided the well of ideas and symbols for organizing society and shaping moral lives. In the West, Christianity was the source of political theology even though the political theology Christianity represented could not help but create political societies that were and are inherently unstable. The instability results from the Christian presumption that believers are in the world but not of it. For example, Christians have always had trouble making sense of an empire they accidentally acquired.[14]

12. Mark Lilla, *The Stillborn God: Religion, Politics, and the Modern West* (New York: Knopf, 2007), 3.

13. Ibid., 5. Charles Taylor, in a very interesting review of Lilla's book, argues that Lilla's understanding of political theology fails to do justice to the natural law justifications of early modern thought that did not appeal directly to revelation or to premises drawn from revelation. According to Taylor, Lilla's argument depends on his view of political theology (suggested later in his book) that a genuine secular politics presumes a mechanistic understanding of the cosmos. Taylor thus challenges Lilla's presumption that "the great separation" has ever been quite the achievement Lilla assumes. Taylor's review of *The Stillborn God* is available at http://blogs.ssrc.org/tif/2008/01/24/two-books-oddly-yoked-together/.

14. Lilla, *Stillborn God*, 42–45. Lilla observes that although Christianity "is inescapably political, it proved incapable of integrating this fact into Christian theology. The political organization of medieval Europe, tottering on that theological ambivalence, could not have been more perfectly arranged to exacerbate the conflict inherent in all political life. . . . Perhaps if Christianity had seen itself as the political religion it really was, presenting the pope as an earthly sovereign with full authority over secular matters, some bloodshed could have been avoided. But living as a Christian means being in the world, including the political world, while somehow not being of it. It means living with a false consciousness" (86). Lilla associates this instability in Christian political theology with the dialectic between transcendence and immanence at the heart of the

Lilla argues it was Hobbes who found the way, after a millennium of Christian political theology, to discuss religion and the common good without making reference to the nexus between God, man, and the world. Hobbes was able to do so because he, anticipating Feuerbach, had the wisdom to turn questions about God into questions about human behavior; to reduce that behavior to psychological states; and then to portray those states as artifacts of desire, ignorance, and the material environment.[15]

For Hobbes the gods are born out of fear of death, poverty, and calamity; but Hobbes knew better than to try to deny such fear. Rather he focused fear on one figure alone, the sovereign. Such a sovereign—Hobbes called him an "earthly God"—could ensure that his subjects should fear no other sovereigns but him. No longer would there be a tension between church and crown because now the sovereign would make clear that salvation depended on obedience to himself.

Lilla thinks Hobbes's great achievement, this great separation that is crucial for the art of living in a liberal democratic order, is secured by three developments. The first is the intellectual separation made possible by the scientific revolution, in which a now mute natural world is separated from its Creator. As a result, investigations into nature can be separated from thoughts about God. Second, the crucial distinction between the public and the private was developed, relegating religious convictions and practices to the latter. To be sure, Lilla acknowledges, Hobbes made the sovereign responsible for public worship, but not for actually mounting an inquisition to determine if citizens really believed "Jesus is the Christ." Third, perhaps less obviously but equally consequential, is Hobbes's argument for separating academic inquiry from ecclesiastical control. One of the achievements of Hobbes's project can be seen in theology's becoming, as it has in modernity, but another academic discipline relegated to divinity schools.[16]

Though Hobbes is often thought to legitimate a violent understanding of politics, that is, human existence as a war of all against all, Lilla argues that Hobbes is actually trying to limit the violence that is unleashed by political theology. For when war is undertaken in the name of God, there can be no limit to killing, because so much is allegedly at stake. That is why human beings who believe in God commit acts in war that no animal would even commit. Animals kill only to eat and reproduce, but humans fight to get into heaven.[17] Hobbes, on Lilla's reading, is the first great realist in international affairs. After Hobbes, war at least has the potential to be humanely limited because it can be fought for selfish reasons.

---

incarnation. For such an astute reader of Barth, it is surprising that Lilla fails to understand that what is meant by such a dialectic must be Christologically determined.

15. Ibid., 88.

16. Ibid., 89–91.

17. Ibid., 84–85.

According to Lilla's argument, Locke and Hume provided softer accounts of Hobbes's Leviathan but nonetheless remained fundamentally Hobbesian. Like Hobbes, they wanted to protect modern man from the superstition and violence associated with political theology by developing liberal habits of mind. In particular Locke thought it possible and necessary to liberalize Christianity itself, which Lilla suggests bore fruit in the work of Rousseau, Kant, and Protestant liberals such as Schleiermacher and Troeltsch. Yet Lilla judges the attempt of Protestant liberals to ground religion in human experience to be a failure because

> It failed to inspire conviction about the Christian faith among nominal Christians, or attachment to Jewish destiny among nominal Jews. Once liberal theologians succeeded, as they did, in portraying biblical faith as the highest expression of moral consciousness and the precondition of modern life, they were unable to explain why modern men and women should still consider themselves to be Christians and Jews rather than simply modern men and women.[18]

Such is the dilemma of Christians in America. To the extent that Christians try to be "political" by playing by the rules set down by "the great separation," they cannot help but become unintelligible not only to their neighbors but, more importantly, to themselves. I think this helps account for the strident rhetoric of the Religious Right in America. Though claiming to represent a conservative form of Christianity, the Religious Right is politically a form of Protestant liberalism. The Religious Right makes a fetish of this or that belief (e.g., the substitutionary account of the atonement they take to be the hallmark of Christianity), but by doing so they play the game determined by the great separation—that is, Christianity becomes primarily a matter of "belief."

Yet secular people in America fear the Religious Right, because they think that the rise of the Religious Right and Islam threatens the "great separation." Thus Lilla ends his book by reminding those who, like him, are committed to Hobbes's great achievement that they are the exception. They cannot expect other civilizations to follow the path of the West. But according to Lilla, the West has made the choice to protect individuals from the harm they can inflict on one another in the name of religion. It has done so by securing fundamental liberties and by leaving the spiritual destinies of each person in their own hands. In short, Americans have chosen to keep our "politics unilluminated by the light of revelation. If our experiment is to work, we must rely on our own lucidity."[19]

But Lilla's account of the great separation does not explain how a country allegedly shaped by Hobbes and Locke is, particularly in reference to war,

18. Ibid., 248.
19. Ibid., 308–9.

nevertheless a nation that understands itself in religious terms.[20] Americans are said to be the beacon of hope for all people. They must be ready, therefore, to make sacrifices, for example, to go to war for the good of the world. In short, Lilla does not explain why it is very hard to keep the secular "secular" in America. Even though the church has been relegated to the "private" realm, the nation is still conceived and legitimated in salvific terms. It is not Christians and Muslims that challenge the great separation, but rather it is "America."

Lilla's sense that Hobbes's achievement may be threatened is widely shared by others in America. For example, in his book *Education's End: Why Our Colleges and Universities Have Given Up On the Meaning of Life*, Anthony Kronman sounds themes very similar to Lilla's. The university, as Lilla suggested, is the key agent for sustaining the great separation. Kronman acknowledges that Protestant piety had shaped the early universities in America, but he argues that after the Civil War, universities were organized to sustain a secular and humanistic account of life. Students would be initiated into secular humanism by reading the great texts of the Western tradition, and through such reading they would learn "that it is possible to explore the meaning of life in a deliberate and organized way even after its religious foundations have been called into doubt."[21]

As a result of this humanistic emphasis in the universities, those in the humanities came to believe they had the competence and the authority to lead students in a disciplined study of the human condition, in order that students might pursue their own personal search for meaning. Their pedagogy assumed that no fixed conception of the end of human life or of a single right way to live could be sustained. For, according to Kronman, there simply is no "vantage point we can ever occupy from which our lives can be seen as a whole."[22] Secular humanism does not require that God be rejected or even thought to be irrelevant to life, as long as such judgments are left to the individual.

Kronman acknowledges that death is the most determinative challenge that confronts the secular humanist. "We all die, and know we will, and must adjust ourselves to the shadow which the foreknowledge of death casts over the whole of our lives."[23] Yet death also forces us to recognize that whatever meaning life may have depends on us. Accordingly, for Kronman, life for the secular humanist is self-contradictory. The secular humanist seeks to abolish the limits that give their longings meaning; that is, they seek to be in control. Yet in the attempt to seize control, they come to recognize that without the limits they seek to overcome, the ends they seek could not exist.[24]

20. See, for example, Michael Northcott, *An Angel Directs the Storm: Apocalyptic Religion and American Empire* (London: I. B. Tauris, 2004).

21. Anthony Kronman, *Education's End: Why Our Colleges and Universities Have Given Up on the Meaning of Life* (New Haven: Yale University Press, 2007), 74.

22. Ibid., 34.

23. Ibid., 76.

24. Ibid., 232.

Sounding very much like Lilla in his account of Hobbes, Kronman argues that religion, drawing on our fears, encourages us to revalue the limits of life by accepting those limits as an occasion for gratitude rather than rebellion. The smug cosmopolitan observers of this religious revival think this development to be shallow and mindless. Kronman thinks such an attitude fails to recognize that the problem is not the death of God but the death of man. The university's task is to preach the rebirth of a humanism that is more honest and honorable than anything religion can offer.[25]

Kronman's understanding of secular humanism assumes what Lilla calls "the great separation," thus confirming Lilla's contention that the university is the crucial institution to sustain liberal social orders. Yet Kronman fears that the secular university has lost its way by becoming a research university beset by the demands of the politically correct. I certainly think the humanities have lost their centrality in the modern university, but I think that loss is due much more to the humanism Kronman advocates. For once the "great separation" is accepted, a Hobbesian world cannot be avoided—that is, a death-determined world committed to the defeat of death. In such a world, the university cannot help but become the home of technologies designed to increase our power over fate. In the process, we are fated by our creations.

Such a world, and the universities that serve it, must go to war in an effort to defeat those forces that threaten our security. Americans are determined to live in a world of safety even if we have to go to war to make the world safe. That project is often justified, according to Kronman, in the name of individual freedom and toleration; democratic government; respect for the rights of minorities and for human rights generally; a reliance on markets as a mechanism for the organization of economic life; and the acceptance of the truths of modern science and the ubiquitous employment of its technological products as aspirational goals all should want. According to Kronman, "To be openly opposed to any of these things is to be a reactionary, a zealot, an obscurantist who refuses to recognize the moral and intellectual authority of this ensemble of modern ideas and institutions."[26] I have little doubt that Kronman believes this, but that he does so means he simply cannot see what the rest of the world sees, namely, that this is an ideology for a culture of death.

Kronman and Lilla are to be commended for their willingness to advocate secular humanism as a moral, educational, and political project. They seem

25. Ibid., 243. Kronman is more than ready to declare that any "religion" at some point must demand a sacrifice of the intellect because a religion finally insists that at some point thinking is not adequate to questions of life's meaning. So every religion in a basic sense must be fundamentalist because the answers it is prepared to give to life's questions are anchored in its own convictions (198–99). Kronman does not supply the necessary philosophical defense of his understanding of rationality.

26. Ibid., 172–73.

to assume, however, that the secular humanist will be more peace loving, and I find it hard to locate any evidence that would support such a conclusion.

By calling attention to Lilla and Kronman I hope to have helped us see that if we as Christians are to reclaim the political theology required by the truthfulness of Christian convictions, we will need to begin by doing theology unapologetically. In particular that means Christians must reclaim theology as a knowledge central for the work of any university worthy of the name "university." That will require, at least in America, a recovery of the church as a polity capable of challenging the presumption that the state is the agency of peace. In short, if my analysis concerning the American difference is close to being right, it should make clear that a commitment to Christian nonviolence is the presumption necessary for the church to reassert its political significance.

In *Veritatis Splendor* John Paul II claimed that there is an inseparable connection between truth and freedom, which, if broken, results in totalitarianism.[27] America is a society built on the assumption that freedom must precede truth. Therefore America is presumed to be the alternative to totalitarianism. However, if my account of the American difference is correct, I think this presumption needs to be reexamined, particularly in light of the way war sustains American political life.

27. John Paul II, *Veritatis Splendor* 3.99, available at http://www.vatican.va/edocs/ENG0222/_INDEX.HTM.

2

America's God

I am going to make some quite critical remarks about Protestantism and America, but I do not want to be misunderstood. Of course, to make critical remarks about America is a very American thing to do. To be an American often means you want the approval of people you assume are more sophisticated than you are, and Americans assume that Europeans are more sophisticated because they have all that "history."[1]

An American in Europe is rather like a Catholic in America. Catholics in America know they do not belong, but they are determined to show that they are more American than the Americans. Thus my observation that all you need to know to understand America is that the FBI is made up of Catholics and Southerners—because Catholics and Southerners have to show they are more loyal than most Americans, since Southerners have a history of disloyalty and Americans fear that Catholics may owe their allegiance to some guy in Rome. That is why the FBI is given the task of examining graduates of Harvard and Yale, that is, high-culture Protestants who of course no longer believe in God, to see if they are loyal enough to be operatives for the CIA.

1. I borrow this title of this chapter from Mark Noll who titled his book on the history of Christian theology in America from 1730 to 1860 *America's God: From Jonathan Edwards to Abraham Lincoln* (New York: Oxford University Press, 2002). This chapter is a revised version of a paper presented at the meeting of Communio et Liberatio in Rimini, Italy, in 2007.

There is also the phenomenon of what I call the *New York Times* Catholics. These are the Catholics, usually clergy, that a *New York Times* reporter has learned to call after the Pope has issued an encyclical or given a speech that seems offensive to American sensibilities. They call a Catholic whom they have previously identified as a critic of the church to confirm that whatever the Pope has said, Catholics in America are not required to obey, or even if they are so required, will not take seriously. From the perspective of the *New York Times*, therefore, a good Catholic is one who would be regarded by the Vatican as a bad Catholic. In a similar fashion, it is quite tempting for an American in Europe to be a good American for Europeans by being a bad (i.e., disloyal) American.

The challenges facing Christians who are determined to reclaim the significance of the church in modernity are serious, and my hope in this chapter is to go beyond simply confirming European prejudices against America. I think America and Americans often deserve the prejudices of Europeans, but the problem with those prejudices is that too often, particularly when it comes to religion, they fail to appreciate the complexity of the place of religion in American life. For example, Europeans often think that the American people are, particularly in contrast to Europeans, deeply religious because they go to church. It will be the burden of my remarks, however, to suggest that American culture is more determinedly secular than most Europeans can imagine.

I will address the character of American Protestantism as well as the religious awareness of the American people and the impact that awareness has on society and politics—no small topic. But I think it first important to identify the perspective from which I speak. I am a Protestant, and I am a communicant at the Church of the Holy Family, an Episcopal church in Chapel Hill, North Carolina. I teach in the Divinity School at Duke University, a very secular university. But before Duke I taught for fourteen years at the University of Notre Dame. I relate this history in order to inform you that I come from the Catholic side of Protestantism.

At the very least, to say I come from the Catholic side of Protestantism means that I do not think Christianity began with the Reformation. When I was interviewed for possible appointment to the faculty at Notre Dame I was asked what Protestant courses I would teach, and I responded that I did not teach Protestant theology because I thought the very notion was a mistake. Rather I would teach Thomas Aquinas, because his work was crucial for my attempt to recover the virtues for understanding the Christian life. I saw no reason that Aquinas should be assumed to be only a thinker for Roman Catholics.

But my presumption that I could claim Aquinas as a theologian in my tradition betrays a Protestant consciousness that may be distinctly American. It is an indication of the complexity I mentioned above, for even those of us who would like to be identified as representing the Catholic side of Protestantism do so as a matter of *choice.*

This dilemma, I believe, is crucial for understanding the character of religious life in America. America is the first great experiment in Protestant social formation. Protestantism in Europe always assumed and depended on the cultural habits that had been created by Catholic Christianity. America is the first place Protestantism did not have to define itself over against a previous Catholic culture. So America is the exemplification of a constructive Protestant social imagination.

Again, these are very complex matters, but I believe—as Mark Noll rightly suggests in his magisterial book *America's God*—America is a synthesis of evangelical Protestantism, republican political ideology, and commonsense moral reasoning.[2] Americans were able to synthesize these antithetical traditions by making their faith in God indistinguishable from their loyalty to a country that ensured them that they had the right to choose which god they would or would not believe in. That is why Bonhoeffer accurately characterized American Protestantism as "Protestantism without Reformation."[3]

American Protestants do not have to believe in God because they believe in belief. That is why we have never been able to produce interesting atheists in America. The god most Americans say they believe in is just not interesting enough to deny. Thus the only kind of atheism that counts in America is to call into question the proposition that everyone has a right to life, liberty, and happiness.[4]

So constituted, America did not need to have an established church because it was assumed that the church was virtually established by the everyday habits

2. Noll, *America's God*, 9.

3. Dietrich Bonhoeffer, *No Rusty Swords: Letters, Lectures, and Notes, 1928–1936*, trans. Edwin Robertson and John Bowden (New York: Harper & Row, 1965), 92–93.

4. John Haught rightly calls attention to the superficial character of that new atheism represented by Richard Dawkins, Samuel Harris, and Christopher Hitchens. But he suggests that their appeal to science to guarantee truth is a "faith" stance that like religious faith cannot be proved. He quotes the Hitchens contention that "if one must have faith in order to believe in something, then the likelihood of that something having any truth is considerably diminished." He argues such a statement cannot be invalidated by science and, therefore, it "arises out of faith in things unseen." I think Haught's attempt to defend religious faith unfortunately replicates the strategy of liberal Protestants to "protect" Christian convictions by showing all belief is based on an irrational starting point. As a result, Christian convictions appear as superficial as the convictions of new atheists. Haught's strategy has the unfortunate effect of making "faith" an epistemological strategy rather than naming the faithfulness constitutive of being a disciple of Jesus. The new atheists are quite right to protest against Haught-like strategies in the name of "reason," but it is by no means clear they have developed an adequate account of rationality. From my perspective the claims of the Christian faith are rational just to the extent that they rightly claim this is the way things are. See John Haught, "Amateur Atheists," *Christian Century*, February 26, 2008, 22–29. For the best available response to the new atheists see David Bentley Hart, *Atheist Delusions: The Christian Revolution and Its Fashionable Enemies* (New Haven: Yale University Press, 2009).

of public life. For example, Noll calls attention to the 1833 amendment to the Massachusetts Constitution that did away with church establishment but nonetheless affirmed "the public worship of God, and the instructions in piety, religion, and morality," and promoted "the happiness and prosperity of a people, and the security of republican government." Noll points out that these words were written at the same time that Alexis de Tocqueville had just returned to France from his tour of North America. Tocqueville descriptively confirmed the normative point made in the Massachusetts Constitution, observing, "I do not know if all Americans have faith in their religion—for who can read to the bottom of hearts?—but I am sure that they believe it necessary to the maintenance of republican institutions. This opinion does not belong only to one class of citizens or to one party, but to the entire nation; one finds it in all ranks."[5]

Protestantism came to the land we now call American to make America Protestant. It was assumed that being American and Protestant meant having faith in the reasonableness of the common man and the establishment of a democratic republic. But in the process, the church in America became American; or, as Noll puts it, "because the churches had done so much to make America, they could not escape living with what they had made."[6] As a result, Americans continue to maintain a stubborn belief in a god, but the god they believe in turns out to be the American god. To know or worship that god does not require that a church exist, because that god is known through the providential establishment of a free people. Religious people on both the Right and the Left share the presumption that America is the church.

Noll ends his account of these developments with the end of the Civil War, but the fundamental habits he identifies as decisive in the formation of the American religious and political consciousness continue to shape the way Christians, and in particular Protestant Christians, understand their place in America. Yet I think we are beginning to see a loss of confidence by Protestants in their ability to sustain themselves in America, just to the extent that the inevitable conflict between the church, republicanism, and common-sense morality has now worked its way out. America is the great experiment in Protestant social thought, but the world Protestants created now threatens to make Protestantism unintelligible to itself. It is to this subject that I now turn.

I believe we may be living at a time when we are watching Protestantism, at least the kind of Protestantism we have in America, come to an end. It is dying of its own success. Protestantism became identified with the republican presumption in liberty as an end reinforced by belief in the common

5. Noll, *America's God*, 10.

6. Ibid., 194.

sense of the individual. As a result Protestant churches in America lost the ability to maintain the disciplines necessary to sustain a people capable of being an alternative to the world. Ironically, the feverish fervency of the Religious Right in America to sustain faith as a necessary condition for supporting democracy cannot help but ensure that the faith sustained is not the Christian faith.

More Americans may go to church than their counterparts in Europe, but the churches to which they go do little to challenge the secular presumptions that form their personal and communal lives. The church is expected to reinforce the presumption that those who come to church have done so freely. Its primary function, therefore, is to legitimate and sustain the assumption that America represents what all people would want to be if they had the benefit of American education and money.

Let me try to put this in a different register. America exemplifies what I call the project of modernity—the attempt to produce a people who believe that they should have no story except the story that they chose when they had no story. That is what Americans mean by freedom. The institutions that constitute the disciplinary forms of that project are liberal democracy and capitalism. Americans presume that they have exercised their freedom when they get to choose between a Sony or Panasonic television. The same presumption works for choosing a president, and once you have made your choice you have to learn to live with it. So freedom requires a kind of resignation.

I try to help Americans see that this narrative—that they should have no story except the story that they chose when they had no story—is their story by asking them this question: "Do you think you ought to be held accountable for decisions you made when you did not know what you were doing?" They answer negatively; that is, they do not think they should be held accountable for decisions they made when they did not know what they were doing, because it is assumed that you should only be held accountable when you acted *freely*. And to act freely, you had to know what you were doing.

One of the difficulties with such an account of responsibility, for example, is that it makes marriage unintelligible. How could you ever know what you were doing when you promised lifelong, monogamous fidelity? Since no one can fully know what this commitment will entail, the church insists that your vows be witnessed by the church and believes it has the duty to hold you responsible to promises you made when you did not know what you were doing. This narrative—that you should have no story but the story you chose when you had no story—also makes it unintelligible to try having children. You never get the ones you want. Of course Americans try to get the ones they want by only having children when they are "ready," but this is a utopian desire that wreaks havoc on children so born, just to the extent they come to believe they can only be loved if they fulfill their parents' desires.

Of course another problem with this narrative is that the narrative itself (that you should have no story except the story you chose when you had no story) is a story you have not chosen. But Americans do not have the ability to acknowledge that they have not chosen it. As a result they must learn to live with decisions they made when they thought they knew what they were doing, even if they later realized they did not know what they were doing. (Of course they have a remedy when it comes to marriage. It is called divorce. They also have a remedy regarding children. It is called abortion.)

The narrative that you should have no story except the story you chose when you had no story obviously has implications for how faith is understood. It produces people who say things such as, "I believe Jesus is Lord—but that is just my personal opinion." The grammar of this kind of avowal obviously reveals a superficial person. But such people are the kind many think crucial for sustaining democracy. For in order to sustain a society that shares no goods in common other than the belief that there are no goods in common other than avoiding death, there must be people who will avoid any conflicts that might undermine the order, which is confused with peace. So an allegedly democratic society that styles itself as one made up of people of strong conviction in fact becomes the most conformist of social orders, because of the necessity to avoid conflicts that cannot be resolved.

Such a view has devastating effects on the church. For the church does not believe that you should have no story except the story you chose when you had no story. Rather the church believes that we are creatures of a good God who has storied us by engrafting us to the people of Israel through the life, death, and resurrection of Jesus of Nazareth. Christians do not believe we get to choose our story, but rather we discover that God has called us to participate in a story not of our own making. That is why we are called into the church and why we are called "Christian." A church so formed cannot help but challenge a social order built on the contrary presumption that I get to write my own life story

But forming a church that is capable of challenging the reigning ethos that sustains America is no easy achievement. You may well think that the Catholic Church surely would be up to that task, but you need to remember that, as Archbishop George of Chicago often remarks, Catholicism in America has largely become a form of Protestant Christianity. Catholics in America, like their Protestant sisters and brothers, are likely to assume that there is no essential tension between being a Christian and being an American. As a result, Catholics in America think the distinction between the public and the private (and their "faith" clearly falls into the latter) is a given that cannot be questioned.

If I am right about the story that shapes the American self-understanding, I think we are in a position to better understand why since September 11, 2001, the self-proclaimed "most powerful nation in the world" runs on fear. It does so because the fear of death is necessary to ensure a level of cooperation between people who otherwise share nothing in common. That is, they share nothing in common other than the presumption that death is to be avoided at all costs. That is why in America hospitals have become our cathedrals and physicians our priests. Medical schools are much more serious about the moral formation of their students than divinity schools. Americans do not believe that an inadequately trained priest may damage their salvation, but they do believe an inadequately trained doctor can hurt them.

The American desire to use medicine in an attempt to get out of life alive is but the domestic form of American foreign policy. September 11, 2001, gave America exactly what it so desperately needed after the end of the Cold War, for it is unclear if America can live without a war. Otherwise, what would give us a moral compass? So we got a "war against terrorism," which is a war without end. That Americans are willing to die for America is indicative of their most basic conviction. As Carolyn Marvin and David Ingle observe in their book *Blood Sacrifice and the Nation*:

> In an era of Western ascendancy, the triumph of Christianity clearly meant the triumph of the states of Christianity, among them the most powerful of modern states, the United States. Though religions have survived and flourished in persecution and powerlessness, supplicants nevertheless take manifestations of power as blessed evidence of the truth of faith. Still, in the religiously plural society of the United States, sectarian faith is optional for citizens, as everyone knows. Americans have rarely bled, sacrificed or died for Christianity or any other sectarian faith. Americans have often bled, sacrificed and died for their country. This fact is an important clue to its religious power. Though denominations are permitted to exist in the United States, they are not permitted to kill, for their beliefs are not officially true. What is really true in any society is what is worth killing for, and what citizens may be compelled to sacrifice their lives for.[7]

America is a culture of death because Americans cannot conceive of how life is possible in the face of death. "Freedom," as understood in American culture, names the attempt to live as though we will not die, and lives lived as though death is only a theoretical possibility can only be sustained by a wealth otherwise unimaginable. But America is an extraordinarily wealthy society determined to remain so even if it requires our domination of the rest of the world. We are told that others hate us because they despise our freedoms, but it may be that others sense that what Americans call freedom is bought at the expense of the lives of others.

I love America and I love being an American.[8] The energy of Americans—their ability to hew out their lives, often in unforgiving land, and their natural

7. Carolyn Marvin and David Ingle, *Blood Sacrifice and the Nation: Totem Rituals and the American Flag* (Cambridge: Cambridge University Press, 1999), 9.

8. In his lovely book *A Gathering of Memories: Family, Nation, and Church in a Forgetful World* (Grand Rapids: Brazos, 2006), Charlie Pinches notes he is happy enough to call himself

generosity—I cherish. But I am a Christian. I cannot avoid the reality that American Christianity has been less than it should have been just to the extent that the church has failed to distinguish America's god from the God we worship as Christians. If I am right that we are now facing the end of Protestantism, hopefully that will leave the church in America in a position with nothing to lose. When you have nothing to lose, all you have left is the truth. God may yet make the church faithful—even in America.

---

an American patriot, but he does not think that is a name tag "Stanley Hauerwas will ever wear around his shoulders" (12). I suspect Charlie is right about that, though I am more than ready to support his understanding of memory and its relation to the land we call America.

3

Why War Is a Moral Necessity for America

Or, How Realistic Is Realism?

The Idealism of Realism

Pacifists always bear the burden of proof for their ideology, because as attractive as nonviolence may be, most people assume pacifism just will not work. You may want to keep a few pacifists around for reminding those burdened with running the world that what they sometimes have to do is a lesser evil, but pacifism simply cannot and should not be, even for Christians, a normative stance. To call for the abolition of war, as Enda McDonagh and I have, is then viewed as an unrealistic proposal made possible by our isolation (as academics) from the real world. Nonviolence is unworkable, or to the extent that it works, it does so only because it is parasitic on more determinative forms of order secured by violence. Those committed to nonviolence, in short, are not realistic.

In the first part of this chapter I will explore the evidence for "just war" theory. In contrast to pacifism it is often assumed that just war reflection is "realistic." It is by no means clear, however, whether advocates of just war have provided an adequate account of what kind of conditions would be necessary for just war to be a realistic alternative for the military policy of a nation. In the second part I will explore the American understanding of war as sacrifice in order to raise questions about how realistic it is to think war can be limited. The understanding of war as sacrifice, I believe, was forged in the American Civil War and continues to shape how Americans morally comprehend war. War is necessary for America's moral well being, which means it is by no means clear what it would mean for Americans to have a realistic understanding of war.[1]

1. WWI is equally important for the American sacralization of war as sacrifice. Jonathan Ebel has recovered how the American soldiers understood their participation in the war as redemptive in his *Faith in the Fight: Religion and the American Solider in the Great War* (Princeton: Princeton

In Christian tradition, realism is often thought to have begun with Augustine's account of the two cities, hardened into doctrine with Luther's two kingdoms, and given its most distinctive formulation in the thought of Reinhold Niebuhr. Thus Augustine is often identified as the Christian theologian who set the stage for the development of just war reflection, which enables Christians to use violence in a limited way in order to secure tolerable order.[2] It is assumed, therefore, that just war is set within the larger framework of a realist view of the world.

With his customary rhetorical brilliance, Luther gave expression to the realist perspective, asking:

> If anyone attempted to rule the world by the gospel and to abolish all temporal law and the sword on the plea that all are baptized and Christian, and that, according to the gospel, there shall be among them no law or sword—or the need for either—pray tell me friend, what would he be doing? He would be loosing the ropes and chains of the savage wild beasts and letting them bite and mangle everyone, meanwhile insisting that they were harmless, tame, and gentle creatures; but I would have the proof in my wounds. Just so would the wicked under the name of Christian abuse evangelical freedom, carry on their rascality, and insist that they were Christians subject neither to law nor sword as some are already raving and ranting.[3]

Luther is under no illusions. War is a plague, but it prevents a greater one. Of course slaying and robbing do not seem the work of love, but "in truth even

---

University Press, 2010). Drawing on letters and poetry written by those who fought in the war, he documents that participants "believed that by involving themselves in the war, assenting to its demands, and achieving victory, they would attain at least this more general redemption of the world and of America. By exposing themselves to the mysterious and powerful forces of combat, many believed they would achieve a personal redemption of great metaphysical consequence" (27). The significance of WWI for underwriting the sacrificial character of war cannot be overestimated. See, for example, Richard Koenigsberg's *Nations Have the Right to Kill: Hitler, Holocaust, and War* (New York: Library of Social Science, 2009) for the effect WWI had on Hitler's understanding of the sacrificial character of war. Koenigsberg argues that Hitler understood war as a sacrifice necessary for the renewal of the German people. "The Aryan" was therefore understood as someone willing to sacrifice himself or herself for the nation. The Jew, in contrast, was individualistic and selfish. Accordingly, the Jew could be sacrificed for the good of the nation (7). The destructive character of war is crucial for the moral purpose war should serve, from Hitler's perspective. For war is a form of sacrifice "whereby human beings give over their bodies and possessions to the objects of worship with names like France, Germany, Japan, America, etc." (xv). War, in short, is the human activity in which "human bodies are sacrificed in the name of perpetuating a magical entity, the body politic" (42).

2. Needless to say, I think Niebuhr's use of Augustine to justify war in the name of "realism" to be a simplification of Augustine. Robert Dodaro provides a much more complex understanding of the two cities in his *Christ and the Just Society in the Thought of Augustine* (Cambridge: Cambridge University Press, 2004).

3. Martin Luther, "On Temporal Authority: To What Extent It Should Be Obeyed," in *Luther: Selected Political Writings*, ed. J. M. Porter (Philadelphia: Fortress, 1974), 56.

this is the work of love."[4] Christians do not fight for themselves, but for their neighbor. So if they see that there is a lack of hangmen, constables, judges, lords, or princes, and find they are qualified, they should offer their services and assume these positions.[5] That "small lack of peace called war," according to Luther, "must set a limit to this universal, worldwide lack of peace which would destroy everyone."[6]

Reinhold Niebuhr understood himself to stand in this "realist" tradition. In 1940 in his "Open Letter (to Richard Roberts)," Niebuhr explains why he left the Fellowship of Reconciliation: he did not believe that "war is merely an 'incident' in history" but rather that it "is a final revelation of the very character of human history."[7] According to Niebuhr the incarnation is not "redemption" from history as conflict because sinful egoism continues to express itself at every level of human life, making it impossible to overcome the contradictions of human history. Niebuhr, therefore, accuses pacifists of failing to understand the Reformation doctrine of "justification by faith." From Niebuhr's perspective, pacifists are captured by a perfectionism that is more "deeply engulfed in illusion about human nature than the Catholic pretensions, against which the Reformation was a protest."[8]

"Just war" proponents argue that war is justified because our task as Christians and as citizens is first and foremost to seek justice. Paul Ramsey understood his attempt to recover just war as a theory of statecraft to be "an extension within the Christian realism of Reinhold Niebuhr."[9] Ramsey saw, however, that there was more to be said about "justice in war than was articulated in Niebuhr's sense of the ambiguities of politics and his greater/lesser evil doctrine of the use of force."[10] That "something more," Ramsey asserted, is the principle of discrimination, which requires that war be subject to political purpose through which war might be limited and conducted justly, that is, that noncombatants be protected.

Yet it is by no means clear if just war reflection can be yoked consistently to a Niebuhrian realism. Augustine's and Luther's "realism" presupposed there was another city that at least could call into question state powers. For Niebuhr,

4. Luther, "Whether Soldiers, Too, Can Be Saved," in Porter, *Luther*, 103.

5. Luther, "Temporal Authority," 58.

6. Luther, "Whether Soldiers," 103. For a fuller account of Luther on the ethics of war, see Joel Lehenbauer, "The Christological and Ecclesial Pacifism of Stanley Hauerwas: A Lutheran Analysis and Appraisal" (PhD diss., Concordia Seminary, St. Louis, 2004). Lehenbauer's dissertation is an extremely fair account of my (and Yoder's) work in comparison to Luther's thought on war.

7. Reinhold Niebuhr, "An Open Letter (to Richard Roberts)," in *Love and Justice: Selections from the Shorter Writings of Reinhold Niebuhr*, ed. D. B. Robertson (Louisville: Westminster John Knox, 1957), 268.

8. Ibid., 269.

9. Paul Ramsey, *The Just War: Force and Political Responsibility* (New York: Rowman & Littlefield, 2002), 260.

10. Ramsey, *Just War*, 260.

realism names the development of states and an international nation-state system that cannot be challenged. Niebuhrian realism assumes that war is a permanent reality for the relation between states because no overriding authority exists that might make war analogous to the police function of the state.[11] Therefore each political society has the right to wage war because it is assumed that doing so is part of its divinely ordained work of preservation. "Realism," therefore, names the reality that at the end of the day in the world of international relations, the nations with the largest army get to determine what counts for "justice." To use Augustine or Luther to justify this understanding of "realism" is in effect to turn a description into a recommendation.

In an article entitled "Just War Theory and the Problem of International Politics," David Baer and Joseph Capizzi admirably try to show how just war requirements, as developed by Ramsey, can be reconciled with a realistic understanding of international relations. They argue that even though a certain pessimism surrounds a realistic account of international politics, that does not mean such a view of the world is necessarily amoral. To be sure, governments have the right to wage war because of their responsibility to a particular group of neighbors, but that does not mean that governments have a carte blanche to pursue every kind of interest. "The same conception that permits government to wage war also restricts the conditions of legitimate war making. . . . Because each government is responsible for only a limited set of political goods, it must respect the legitimate jurisdiction of other governments."[12]

Yet who is going to enforce the presumption that a government "must respect the legitimate jurisdiction of other governments"? Baer and Capizzi argue

11. For the best defense of this view, see Philip Bobbitt's *The Shield of Achilles: War, Peace, and the Course of History* (New York: Anchor, 2003). Bobbitt puts it starkly by observing, "War is not a pathology that with proper hygiene and treatment can be wholly prevented. War is a natural condition of the State, which was organized in order to be an effective instrument of violence on behalf of society. Wars are like death, which, while they can be postponed, will come when they will come and cannot finally be avoided" (819). I admire Bobbitt's analysis of the development of constitutional orders that war makes possible, as well as his account of the transition from nation-states to market states. I do not think, however, that he shows how the latter can sustain the ethos necessary to produce people capable of sustaining the kind of military he admires. Why should consumers care about honor?

12. Helmut David Baer and Joseph E. Capizzi, "Just War Theory and the Problem of International Politics: On the Central Role of Just Intention," *Journal of the Society of Christian Ethics* 26, no. 1 (2006): 167–68. George Weigel argues in a similar fashion in his article "World Order: What Catholics Forgot," *First Things* 143 (May 2004): 31–38. Weigel argues the Catholic tradition insists that "politics is an arena of rationality and moral responsibility. Unlike those theories of international relations which insisted that world politics is amoral or immoral, classic Catholic thinking about international relations taught that every human activity, including politics, takes place within the horizon of moral judgment, precisely because politics is a human activity and moral judgment is a defining characteristic of the human person. That is true of politics among nations, the Catholic tradition insisted, even if there are distinctive aspects to the moral dimension of world politics" (31). I could not agree more, but it is one thing to make such a claim and quite another to suggest that is the way the world works.

that Ramsey's understanding of just war as the expression of Christian love by a third party in defense of the innocent requires that advocates of just war favor the establishment of international law and institutions to better regulate the conduct of states in pursuit of their self-interest.[13] Yet Baer and Capizzi recognize that international agencies cannot be relied on because there is no way that such an agency can judge an individual government's understanding of just cause. As they put it, "absent effective international institutions, warring governments are like Augustine's individual pondering self-defense, moved by the temptation of inordinate self-love."[14]

Baer and Capizzi argue that a more adequate understanding of just war will combine a realist understanding of international politics with a commitment to international order by emphasizing the importance of just intention.[15] This means that a war can be undertaken only if peace, which is understood as a concept for a more "embracing and stable order," be the reason a state gives for going to war. The requirement that the intention for going to war be so understood is an expression of love for the enemy just to the extent that the lasting order be one that encompasses the interests of the enemy.[16]

And pacifists are said to be unrealistic? The idealism of such realist justifications of just war is nowhere better seen than in these attempts to fit just war considerations into the realist presuppositions that shape the behavior of state actors.[17] Ramsey, Baer and Capizzi, and Oliver O'Donovan are to

13. Baer and Capizzi, "Just War Theory," 164–66.

14. Ibid., 168.

15. Baer and Capizzi argue that this means going to war requires increasing reliance on international agencies. Weigel, in the article mentioned above, argues exactly the opposite. Indeed, Weigel wrote his article in response to the Vatican's deferral to the United Nations concerning the legitimacy of the war against Iraq. Weigel defends the preemptive war strategy of the Bush administration in the name of preserving a more nearly just world order.

Martha Nussbaum argues that the very idea of a world state is not desirable because it is very unlikely that such a state could be held accountable. Moreover, such a state would be dangerous. "If a nation becomes unjust, pressure from other nations may prevent it from committing heinous crimes (whether against its citizens or against other nations). If the world state should become unjust, there would be no corresponding recourse; the only hope would be for rebellion from within" (Martha Nussbaum, *Frontiers of Justice: Disability, Nationality, Species Membership* [Cambridge, MA: Belknap, 2006], 313).

16. Baer and Capizzi, "Just War Theory," 170–71. One wonders what empirical tests might exist to test this requirement of enemy love. Would the "enemy" need to say after being defeated that they were glad to lose the war?

17. It would be quite interesting, for example, for Baer and Capizzi to address Bobbitt's claim that the deepest immorality is to be found in those who attempt to avoid war. To make going to war "a last resort" would only make the world more dangerous. Bobbitt argues the issue is never whether we ought to avoid war, but rather "we must choose what sort of war we will fight, regardless of what are its causes, to set the terms of the peace we want." The avoidance of war, therefore, cannot and should not be an objective because such a policy "counsels against the preparations for war that might avert massive, carefully planned, large-scale attacks by one state on another." Such a view rightly rejects those who assume war is a pathology of the state.

be commended for trying to recover just war as a theory of statecraft rather than as a checklist to judge whether a particular war satisfies enough of the criteria to be judged just.[18] Yet by doing so they have made apparent the tensions between the institutions necessary for just war to be a reality and the presumptions that shape international affairs.

For example, what would an American foreign policy determined by just war principles look like? What would a just war Pentagon look like? What kind of virtues would the people of America have to have to sustain a just war foreign policy and Pentagon? What kind of training do those in the military have to undergo in order to be willing to take casualties rather than conduct the war unjustly?[19] How would those with the patience necessary to ensure that a war be a last resort be elected to office? Those are the kind of questions that advocates of just war must address before they accuse pacifists of being "unrealistic."

To put the challenge more concretely, we could ask, why was it possible for the United States to conduct the second war against Iraq? The answer is very simple. America had a military left over from the Cold War, a war that was fought according to an amoral realism, and therefore America could go to war in Iraq because nothing prevented America from going to war in Iraq—a war that is, moreover, justified as part of a "war against terrorism." Yet, in spite of the title of Jean Bethke Elshtain's book, *Just War against Terror*, it is by no means clear that you can fight a just war against terrorism.[20] If one of the crucial conditions of a just war is for the war to have an end, then the war against terrorism clearly cannot be just because it is a war without end.

I think the lack of realism about realism by American just war advocates has everything to do with their being American. In particular, American advocates of just war seem to presume that democratic societies place an inherent

---

Rather war is understood as that which gives birth to the state and is necessary for sustaining the state's existence (Bobbitt, *Shield of Achilles*, 780).

18. O'Donovan's account of just war can be found in his *The Just War Revisited* (Cambridge: Cambridge University Press, 2003).

19. There is a complex relation between the public reasons given for war and the reasons that actually shape those who fight the war. This is explored in fine detail by Nancy Sherman in her book *The Untold War: Inside the Hearts, Minds, and Souls of Our Soldiers* (New York: W. W. Norton, 2010). She begins the book with an observation from Anthony Miller, who warned, as he was preparing to write a Hollywood movie in 1940 about G. I. Joe, that soldiers abhor an ideological vacuum. Miller accordingly argued that "unless the American people can explain and justify this war, they are going to injure and sometimes destroy the minds of a host of their returning veterans" (39). There are no doubt many reasons for post-traumatic stress disorder (PTSD) but one cannot help but think part of the problem for many who return from combat so affected is due to the failure of American soldiers' ability to match the reality of war with the reasons for which the war is being fought. One cannot help but wonder, moreover, if the tension is not endemic to a just war position.

20. Jean Bethke Elshtain, *Just War against Terror: The Burden of American Power in a Violent World* (New York: Basic Books, 2003). The subtitle of Elshtain's book is revealing just to the extent the subtitle suggests that America's role in the world, a role shaped by a realistic foreign policy shaped by American self-interest, is the necessary condition for fighting a just war.

limit on war that more authoritarian societies are unable to do. While such a view is quite understandable, I want to suggest that democratic societies, or at least the American version of democracy, are unable to set limits on war because they are democratic.[21] Put even more strongly, for Americans, war is necessary to sustain our belief that we are worthy to be recipients of the sacrifices made on our behalf in past wars. Americans are a people born of and in war, particularly the Civil War, and only war can sustain our belief that we are a people set apart.

Upon the Altar of the Nation[22]

In his extraordinary book *Upon the Altar of the Nation: A Moral History of the Civil War*, Harry Stout tells the story of how the Civil War began as a limited war but ended as total war. He is well aware that the language of total war did not exist at the time of the Civil War, but he argues that by 1864 the *spirit* of total war emerged and "prepared Americans for the even more devastating total wars they would pursue in the twentieth century" (xv). Stout's story of the transformation of the Civil War from limited to total war is also the story of how America became the nation we call America. According to Stout,

> Neither Puritans' talk of a "city upon a hill" or Thomas Jefferson's invocation of "inalienable rights" is adequate to create a religious loyalty sufficiently powerful to claim the lives of its adherents. In 1860 no coherent nation commanded the

21. In his article "Authority, Lies, and War: Democracy and the Development of Just War Theory" (*Theological Studies* 67 [2006]: 378–94), David DeCosse argues that Catholic deference to political authority has inadequately integrated democratic ideas into just war theory as is evident by the lying that justified the Iraq war. Though I am sympathetic with DeCosse's claim that lying is analogous to the use of physical force, I am not at all convinced that paying more attention "to the rights, responsibilities, and virtues of democratic citizens in time of war" (393) means we will ensure more truthful speech about war.

22. The following account is dependent on Harry S. Stout's *Upon the Altar of the Nation: A Moral History of the Civil War* (New York: Viking, 2006). (Page references will appear in the text.) Stout is to be commended for his courage as a historian to make candid that he is writing a "moral history" of the Civil War. He does not elaborate in this book what it means methodologically for him to assume a moral stance other than to accept just war as normative for the story he tells. One can only hope in the future he might tell us more about what it means for a historian to acknowledge that history is a moral endeavor. Though he ends his book making clear that he does not regard the Civil War to justify pacifism, he nonetheless remains deeply ambiguous about the reality of war. It remains true for him that "at its most elemental, war is evil. War is killing. War is destroying. War may be a necessary evil, and in that sense 'right,' but it is nevertheless lethally destructive" (xii). Stout dedicates his book to his father, who he says fought in a "just war," but if that was WWII, there are very real questions if in fact WWII was fought justly. Of course it does not mean that those who fought in that war were unjust. I am hesitant to call attention to Stout's regard for his father's military service, but I think his ambiguity about war reflects the tendency we all have to justify war because of our love of those who fought in past wars.

> sacred allegiance of all Americans over and against their states and regions. For the citizenry to embrace the idea of a nation-state that *must* have a messianic destiny and command one's highest loyalty would require a massive sacrifice—a blood sacrifice. . . . As the war descended into a killing horror, the grounds of justification underwent a transformation from a just defensive war fought out of sheer necessity to preserve home and nation to a moral crusade for "freedom" that would involve nothing less than a national "rebirth," a spiritual "revival." And in that blood and transformation a national religion was born. Only as casualties rose to unimaginable levels did it dawn on some people that something mystically religious was taking place, a sort of massive sacrifice on the national altar. The Civil War taught Americans that they were a Union, and it absolutely required a baptism of blood to unveil transcendent dimensions of that union. (xxi)[23]

The generals on both sides of the Civil War had not only been trained at West Point to embody American might and power; they were also taught to be gentlemen. The title of "gentlemen" not only carried with it expectations that the bearers of the title would be honorable, but that they would also pursue their profession justly. They "imbibed" the code of limited war, which demanded that they protect innocent lives and minimize destructive aspects of war. According to Stout they were even taught by Dennis Mahan, a professor of civil engineering, to use position and to maneuver interior lines of operations against armies rather than engaging in crushing overland campaigns that would involve civilian populations (21).

Stout argues that Lincoln, as early as 1862, and prior to his generals, realized that the West Point Code of War would have to be abandoned. After Bull Run,

23. Stout documents how during the Civil War the flag became the central symbol of American patriotism. Prior to 1860 the flag was barely visible, flying primarily on ships, but after 1861 the flag was flown on churches, storefronts, homes, and government buildings to signify loyalty and support (28). The title of Stout's book, as well as his understanding of the flag as a totem, is supported by Carolyn Marvin and David Ingle in their book *Blood Sacrifice and the Nation: Totem Rituals and the American Flag* (Cambridge: Cambridge University Press, 1999). They argue "that violent blood sacrifice makes enduring groups cohere, even though such a claim challenges our most deeply held notions of civilized behavior. The sacrificial system that binds American citizens has a sacred flag at its center. Patriotic rituals revere it as the embodiment of a bloodthirsty totem god who organizes killing energy" (1).

In *Redeemer Nation: The Idea of America's Millennial Role* (Chicago: University of Chicago Press, 1968), Ernest Tuveson traces the background of millennial theological categories for shaping American national identity. Accordingly he observes "that the apocalyptic vision of the Civil War was far more than a spontaneous response to a great crisis by a nation of Bible-readers, who naturally saw it as a moral conflict. It seemed to fit exactly into a pattern long established, and seemed to confirm the validity of that pattern. Thus it was more than just another war about a moral issue, even if a great one; it was *the* crisis of mankind, even if only one nation was involved" (196). Tuveson's book is essential reading if we are to understand the rhetoric that shapes American foreign policy after September 11, 2001. For an astute and informative analysis of that rhetoric, see Michael Northcott, *An Angel Directs the Storm: Apocalyptic Religion and American Empire* (London: I. B. Tauris, 2004).

and frustrated by McClellan's timidity, Lincoln understood that if the Union was to be preserved, the war would need to escalate into a war against both citizens and soldiers. In response to Unionists in New Orleans who protested Lincoln's war policy, Lincoln replied,

> What would you do in my position? Would you drop the war where it is? Or would you prosecute it in future with elder-stalk squirts charged with rose water? Would you deal lighter blows than heavier ones? I am in no boastful mood. I shall not do more than I can, and I shall do all I can, to save the government, which is my sworn duty as well as my personal inclination. I shall do nothing in malice. (139)[24]

Crucial to Lincoln's strategy for the prosecution of the war against the population of the South was the Emancipation Proclamation, which Lincoln signed on September 22, 1862. Lincoln's primary concern was always the preservation of the Union, but the Emancipation Proclamation made clear to both sides that a way of life was at issue, requiring a total war on all fronts.[25] Emancipation blocked any attempt to reconcile the North and South, because now the war by necessity stood for moral aims that could not be compromised. Stout quotes Massachusetts's abolitionist senator Charles Sumner, who supported the Emancipation Proclamation as a "war measure" in these terms:

> But, fellow-citizens, the war which we wage is not merely for ourselves; it is for all mankind. . . . In ending slavery here we open its gates all over the world, and let the oppressed go free. Nor is this all. In saving the republic we shall save civilization. . . . In such a cause no effort can be too great, no faith can be

24. Grant and Sherman are, of course, those who are most associated with pursuing a brutal strategy in the war, but Stout makes clear each was in quite different ways doing Lincoln's bidding. In a letter to General Halleck about his destruction of Atlanta, Sherman concluded, "If the people raise a howl against my barbarity and cruelty, I will answer that war is war, and not popularity-seeking. If they want peace, they and their relatives must stop the war" (369). Stout provides a very illuminating account of how the generals, and in particular Stonewall Jackson, in the Civil War were seen as "saviors." Indeed he notes that Jackson became a "messianic figure" who could "never die" because he incarnated the Confederate civil religion through a violent atonement (229). For a depiction of the complex character of Sherman, see E. L. Doctorow's *The March* (New York: Random House, 2006). *The March* is a novel, but it may give us a better sense of the anarchy of Sherman's march across the South than many of the histories on the same subject.

25. On August 22, 1862, Lincoln sent a letter to Horace Greeley that was printed in the *New York Tribune* in which he made clear his primary purpose in pursuing the war:

> My paramount object in this struggle is to save the Union, and is *not* either to save or to destroy slavery. If I could save the Union without freeing *any* slave I would do it, and if I could save it by freeing *all* slaves I would do it, and if I could save it by freeing some and leaving others alone I would also do that. What I do about slavery, and the colored race, I do because I believe it helps to save the Union; and what I forbear, I forbear because I do *not* believe it would help to save the Union. . . . I have here stated my purpose according to my view of *official* duty; and I intend no modification of my oft-expressed *personal* wish that all men every where could be free. (184)

> too determined. To die for country is pleasant and honorable. But all who die for country now die also for humanity. Wherever they lie, in bloody fields, they will be remembered as the heroes through whom the republic was saved and civilization established forever. (174–75)[26]

Stout's book is distinguished from other books on the Civil War by his close attention to what religious figures on both sides were saying about the war. It was ministers of the gospel who supplied the rhetoric necessary for the war to achieve its mythic status. To be sure, the South represented a more conservative form of Christianity than the North, as Christianity was recognized as the established religion in the Confederacy's Constitution, but for both sides "Christianity offered the only terms out of which national identity could be constructed and a violent war pursued" (43).

Stout provides plenty of examples of how Christians narrated the bloody sacrifice of the war, but Horace Bushnell's contribution is particularly noteworthy for no other reason than that his Christianity was liberal. Early in the war Bushnell suggested that morally and religiously a nation was being created by the bloodshed required by the war. According to Bushnell, through the shed blood of soldiers, soldiers of both sides, a vicarious atonement was being made for the developing Christian nation.[27] Such an atonement was not simply a metaphor, "but quite literally a blood sacrifice required by God for sinners North and South if they were to inherit their providential destiny" (249).[28] Shortly after Gettysburg, Bushnell identified those who gave their lives in the war with the martyrs, writing,

26. Tuveson calls attention to the significance of Julia Ward Howe's "Battle Hymn of the Republic" for giving the war its apocalyptic cast. What makes Howe's hymn so significant is her identification with such liberal thinkers as Theodore Parker, Ralph Waldo Emerson, and Oliver Wendell Holmes. Tuveson observes that though Howe had no use for faith in a special revelation, she could still write lines such as the following:

> I have seen Him in the watch-fires of a hundred circling camps;
> They have builded Him an altar in the evening dews and damps;
> I can read His righteous sentence by the dim and flaring lamps:
> His day is marching on. (Tuveson, *Redeemer Nation*, 197–98)

27. Lincoln shared Bushnell-like sentiments most clearly articulated in the Second Inaugural. Yet as early as 1862 Stout quotes Lincoln reflecting on the imponderable purpose of God in relation to the war. Lincoln says, "In the present civil war it is quite possible that God's purpose is something different from the purpose of either party—and yet the human instrumentalities, working just as they do, are of the best adaptation to effect this purpose. I am almost ready to say this is probably true—that God wills this contest, and wills that it shall not end yet." Stout observes that Lincoln's sense of destiny "provided for Lincoln a Christlike compassion for his foes; in death, it would render him a Christlike messiah for the reconstituted American nation" (146).

28. Stout quotes from a sermon concerning the flag, preached after Lincoln's assassination by N. H. Chamberlain. Chamberlain said:

> Henceforth that flag is the legend which we bequeath to future generations, of the severe and solemn struggle for the nation's life. . . . Henceforth the red on it is deeper, for the crimson

> How far the loyal sentiment reaches and how much it carries with it, or after it, must also be noted. It yields up willingly husbands, fathers, brothers, and sons, consenting to the fearful chance of a home always desolate. It offers body and blood, and life on the altar of devotion. It is a fact, a political worship, offering to seal itself by martyrdom in the field. (251)[29]

As the toll of the war mounted, the most strident voices calling for blood revenge came from the clergy. Thus Robert Dabney, at the funeral of his friend Lieutenant Carrington, CSA, told his listeners that Carrington's blood "seals upon you the obligation to fill their places in your country's host, and 'play the men for your people and the cities of your God,' to complete the vindication of their rights" (201). One Confederate chaplain even prayed, "We should add to the prayer for peace, let this war continue, if we are not yet so humbled and disciplined by its trials, as to be prepared for those glorious moral and spiritual gifts, which Thou deignest it should confer upon us as a people" (197). Such a prayer makes clear that the war had become for both sides a ritual they had come to need in order to make sense of their lives.

Stout's account of the religious character of the Civil War, perhaps, is best illustrated by the most celebrated speech ever given by an American: the Gettysburg Address. Stout observes that something "emerged from Gettysburg that would become forever etched in the American imagination. A sacralization of this particular battlefield would mark it forever after as the preeminent sacred ground of the Civil War—and American wars thereafter" (269). Stout is surely right, making these words all the more chilling:

> It is for us the living, rather, to be dedicated here to the unfinished work which they who fought here have thus far so nobly advanced. It is rather for us to be here dedicated to the great task remaining before us—that from these honored

---

with which the blood of countless martyrs has colored it; the white on it is purer, for the pure sacrifice and self-surrender of those who went up to their graves bearing it; the blue on it is heavenlier, for the great constancy of those dead heroes, whose memory becomes henceforth as the immutable upper skies that canopy our land, gleaming with stars wherein we read their glory and our duty. (454–55)

29. The language of laying lives on the altar is repeated often in sentiments expressed by wives on hearing of their husbands' deaths (200) as well as soldiers reflecting on the deaths of their friends (340). Stout quotes a pastor at a funeral for two soldiers crying out: "We must be ready to give up our sons, brothers, friends—if we cannot go ourselves—to hardships, sufferings, dangers and death if need be, for the preservation of our government and the freedom of the nation. We should lay them, willing sacrifices, upon the altar" (341). Drew Gilpin Faust observes that the way of death in the Civil War transformed not only the individuals directly affected by the loss, but the entire American nation. The war created, in the words of Frederick Law Olmstead, a veritable "republic of suffering." As a result, "sacrifice and the state became inextricably intertwined. . . . Death created the modern American union—not just by ensuring national survival, but by shaping enduring national structures and commitments" (*The Republic of Suffering: Death and the American Civil War* [New York: Alfred A. Knopf, 2008], xiii–xiv).

> dead we take increased devotion to that cause for which they gave the last full measure of devotion—that we here highly resolve that these dead shall not have died in vain—that this nation, under God, shall have a new birth of freedom—and that government of the people, by the people, for the people, shall not perish from the earth.

A nation determined by such words, such elegant and powerful words, simply does not have the capacity to keep war limited.[30] A just war that can only be fought for limited political purposes cannot and should not be understood in terms shaped by the Gettysburg Address.[31] Yet after the Civil War, Americans think they must go to war to ensure that those who died in our past wars did not die in vain.[32] Thus American wars are justified as a "war to end all wars" or "to make the world safe for democracy" or for "unconditional surrender" or "freedom." Whatever may be the realist presuppositions of those who lead America to war, those presuppositions cannot be used as the reasons given to justify the war. To do so would betray the tradition of war established in the Civil War. Wars, American wars, must be wars in which the sacrifices of those doing the dying and the killing have redemptive purpose and justification.

30. Charlie Pinches rightly argues that the Lincoln Memorial is the proper place for the Gettysburg Address to be read, because there it is complemented and qualified by Lincoln's Second Inaugural Address. The rousing end of Gettysburg, according to Pinches, is enabled by the appeal that we "cherish a just, and a lasting peace, among ourselves, and with all nations" (*A Gathering of Memories: Family, Nation, and America in a Forgetful World* [Grand Rapids: Brazos, 2006], 103–4).

31. In essay after essay, Paul Ramsey insists that at the heart of the just war is the requirement that a war have a recognizable political purpose. Indeed, from Ramsey's perspective, a failed nation is one unable to fight a "good war," that is, "a war in which force begins and ends in subordination to national purpose and policy, even the purpose of the arbitrament of a civil war waged to determine what a national purpose shall be" (*Just War*, 15). Accordingly, Ramsey thought a nation's "self-interest" should be constitutive of any reason given for going to war, and therefore he argued that the goal of American foreign policy should be the creation of a system of free and independent nations (8). Yet in a "democracy" it proves quite difficult to convince civilians they should go to war to maintain a reasonable balance of power in Asia.

32. Ramsey recognizes that war has a sacral quality. On the same page he argues that war can only be fought by nations capable of disciplining war to a national purpose; "but who can deny that there is a strong feeling for the sacred in the temporal person at work delaying and weakening political resolve until a more inclusive entity is vitally challenged—the nation which is felt to be immortal and transcendent over the individual in value and in the perdurance of its life? Thus the nation affords a provisional solution of the ambiguity of finite sacrifice, and only if this is the case does the nation or any other political entity become the 'subject' of political agency capable of legitimating finite sacrifice" (*Just War*, 15). But Ramsey does not tell us what keeps finite sacrifice finite. Interestingly enough I suspect you can only keep the sacrifice of war finite if you have a church strong enough to discipline a nation's ambition, which presents an interesting challenge to just war thinkers; that is, do they think the church in America has the strength to keep the finite finite? Critical though I may be of Constantinianism, at least the Constantinian churches at one time had the power to keep the finite finite by reminding those who ruled that they were destined to die. Once "the people" are said to rule themselves, the church, at least the church in America, seems to have lost that ability.

War is America's altar. Confronted by such a tradition of war, the attempts to justify war using just war considerations, no matter how sincerely done, cannot help but be ideological mystifications.[33]

In his book, *The Civil War as a Theological Crisis*, Mark Noll asks why the Civil War, in contrast to past wars, produced no "deep theological insights from either elites or the masses."[34] At least one of the reasons may be, as Noll amply documents, that religious thinkers in America assumed the people of America had a covenantal relationship with God.[35] America was identified with the tribes of Israel in which it was assumed that the federal union "created a higher bond than the bond constituted by the unity of all Christian believers in the church."[36] This was combined with the confidence of the Enlightenment that the common man was capable of reading Scripture without guidance from any other authority, which meant that it was a simple matter to read God's providential will for political events.[37] The war did not force American Christians to deeper theological insights because the war was, for America, our church.[38]

33. In an essay on Martin Luther King, Timothy Jackson distances himself from King's pacifism, observing that "in a fallen world, at any rate, I believe that protecting the innocent may move some Christians, properly, to take up the sword against evil, as in the American Civil War" ("Martin Luther King," in *The Teaching of Modern Christianity on Law, Politics, and Human Nature: Volume 1*, ed. John Witte and Frank Alexander [New York: Columbia University Press, 2006], 456). One would like to know what "evil" Jackson assumes the sword was taken up against in the Civil War. Was it the "evil" of secession? Was it the "evil" of slavery? Does the reality of the "cause" of the war matter for Jackson-like appeals to the Civil War to justify the use of the sword? I think Jackson's appeal to the Civil War to justify Christian participation in war exemplifies the presumption that finally "pacifism" just will not do. Yet show me how, in the light of Stout's history of the Civil War, the Civil War can be used as a justification for just war reasoning. Of course I think slavery should have been brought to an end. I think, moreover, pacifists should have been more prominent in that struggle. We can point to the example of John Woolman and other Friends who tirelessly worked to convince slaveholders of the evil of slavery, but obviously slavery was and is a judgment on Christians. But to say war is the alternative form of faithfulness is surely a mistake.

34. Mark Noll, *The Civil War as a Theological Crisis* (Chapel Hill: University of North Carolina Press, 2006), 15.

35. Ibid., 18.

36. Ibid., 61.

37. Ibid., 19. I argued a similar case in *Unleashing the Scripture: Freeing the Bible from Captivity to America* (Nashville: Abingdon, 1993).

38. One of the great virtues of Noll's study is his chapter on Catholic viewpoints on the Civil War and, in particular, French and Italian Catholic responses to the war. Noll thinks conservative Catholics rightly assessed American inability to disentangle race from slavery or to free the Bible from the certainties of "common sense" because they saw that American culture was characterized by a set of elective affinities: "fundamental principles of the Protestant Reformation linked to a liberal economic order linked to unfettered access to the Bible linked to liberal democracy linked to practical materialism linked to a bloated and dangerous republican government linked to theological confusion" (Noll, *Civil War*, 157).

Pacifism as Realism

Where has all this gotten us? I think it helps us recognize that we live in the worst of all worlds. Realism is used to dismiss pacifism and to underwrite some version of just war. But it is not at all clear that the conditions for the possibility of just war are compatible with realism. At least it is not clear that just war considerations can be constitutive of the decision-making processes of governments that must assume that might makes right. Attempts to justify wars begun and fought on realist grounds in the name of just war only serve to hide the reality of war.

Yet war remains a reality. War not only remains a reality, but if Stout's account of the ongoing significance of the Civil War is even close to being right, war remains for Americans our most determinative moral reality. How do you get people who are taught they are free to follow their own interest to sacrifice themselves and their children in war? Democracies by their very nature seem to require that wars be fought in the name of ideals, which makes war self-justifying. Realists in the State Department and Pentagon may have no illusions about why American self-interest requires that a war be fought, but Americans cannot fight a war as cynics. It may be that those who actually have to fight a war will have no illusions about the reality of war, but the rest of the nation justifies war, using categories that necessitate a "next war."

Pacifists are realists. We have no reason to deny that the "realism" associated with Augustine, Luther, and Niebuhr has much to teach us about how the world works, but that is why we do not trust those who would have us make sacrifices in the name of preserving a world at war. We believe a sacrifice has been made that has brought an end to the sacrifice of war. Augustine and Luther thought Christians might go to war because they assumed a church existed that provided an alternative to the sacrificial system war always threatens to become. If the Civil War teaches us anything, it is that when Christians no longer believe that Christ's sacrifice is sufficient for the salvation of the world, we will find other forms of sacrificial behaviors that are as compelling as they are idolatrous. In the process, Christians confuse the sacrifice of war with the sacrifice of Christ.

If a people does not exist that continually makes Christ present in the world, war will always threaten to become a sacrificial system. War is a counter church. It is the most determinative moral experience many people have. That is why Christian realism requires the disavowal of war. Christians do not renounce war because it is often so horrible, but because war, in spite of its horror, or perhaps because it is so horrible, can be so morally compelling. That is why the church does not have an alternative to war. The church *is* the alternative to war. When Christians no longer see the reality of the church as an alternative to the world's reality, we abandon the world to war.

Part 2

THE LITURGY OF WAR

4

Reflections on the "Appeal to Abolish War"

Or, What Being a Friend of Enda's Got Me Into

A Visit with Enda

Paula and I were coming to the end of our vacation in Ireland. We had arranged to see Enda McDonagh on our way to Dublin, where we were to leave for home. It is always good to see Enda. We had become good friends during Enda's stay at Notre Dame, and when Paula and I had come to Ireland for our honeymoon, Enda had arranged a luncheon at Maynooth that we will never forget. I thought our trip to Maynooth would primarily be an opportunity to catch up, but in a phone conversation arranging our meeting, Enda had suggested there was a project that he wanted to talk with me about.[1]

Arriving at Maynooth, we were as usual welcomed by Enda's wonderful hospitality. Paula and I always enjoy finding out about the many projects with which he seems to be involved. I have always thought that if Catholicism names anything, it names the life of Enda McDonagh. Or put even more strongly, if the Catholic Church *is* the church, the best evidence that it is so is Enda McDonagh. For surely the catholicity of the church is to be found in his life. His is a life at once so deeply at home in Ireland, but equally at home in Africa; a life dedicated to those who suffer from AIDS and sustained by the work of artists who help us see beauty without denying such suffering.

1. Originally published in *Between Poetry and Politics: Essays in Honour of Enda McDonagh*, ed. Linda Hogan and Barbara FitzGerald (Dublin: Columba, 2003), 135–47.

So I am usually not surprised by Enda's wonderfully creative mind.[2] However, I have to confess I was not prepared when he laid out the project for which he wanted my help. He thought he had three to five years of active life left, and said this with no hint of regret, but rather as a realistic report about his life.[3] He then said that in the time he had left he wanted to devote himself to the elimination of war. He explained that even though he had more or less always assumed a position of just war, he was really more of a pacifist. So, he thought the two of us ought to draft an "Appeal to Abolish War."

Enda went on to explain that two hundred years ago slavery not only existed, but many people also thought it was morally unproblematic. Slavery, he observed, still exists; but no one now thinks slavery can be morally justified. The attempt to draft an "Appeal to Abolish War" would only be a beginning, but by writing the appeal we might start a discussion about war that would make war as morally problematic as slavery. Enda observed that war might still exist two hundred years into the future, but at least we could begin the process in the hope that no one in the future would think war to be a good idea. I confess I was stunned by the simple brilliance of Enda's proposal. I blurted out, "That is a terrific idea" and happily agreed to work with Enda to write the appeal.

I do think the appeal is a "terrific idea," but it is an idea that presents some difficulty for those who, like myself, are advocates of Christian nonviolence. I realize that may seem strange, for what does it mean to be a pacifist if you do not want to abolish war? Those of us committed to Christian nonviolence clearly want to work for a world in which war does not exist. But we also believe, at least those of us whose pacifism has been learned from the work of John Howard Yoder, that we are pacifist not because pacifism is a strategy for ending war, but because that is the way we must live if we are to be faithful followers of Jesus. I often try to make this point by noting that Christians are not called to nonviolence because we believe nonviolence is a way to rid the world of war; but rather in a world of war, as faithful followers of Jesus, we cannot imagine being anything other than nonviolent.

An appeal to abolish war might give the impression that the nonviolence it presupposes is shaped by humanistic assumptions rather than the Christological pacifism I represent. A call to abolish war could be interpreted as a denial of the eschatological presumptions that should shape Christian pacifism. As John Howard Yoder pointed out in his extraordinary essay "Peace without Eschatology,"

> "Peace" is not an accurate description of what has generally happened to nonresistant Christians throughout history, nor of the way the conscientious objector

2. For example, I think Enda's book *Gift and Call: Towards a Christian Theology* (St. Meinrad, IN: Abbey, 1975) remains one of the most interesting early attempts to rethink what moral theology might look like after Vatican II. In *Gift and Call* Enda reminds us that every gift is also a threat, which is as relevant today as it was then.

3. I am happy to report that Enda is well beyond his estimated "active" years.

> is treated in most countries today. Nor does Christian pacifism guarantee a warless world. "Peace" describes the pacifist hope, the goal in the light of which he acts, the character of his action, the ultimate divine certainty which lets his position make sense; it does not describe the external appearance or the observable results of his behavior. This is what we mean by eschatology: a hope which, defying present frustration, defines a present position in terms of the yet unseen goal which gives it meaning.[4]

If Yoder is right, and I certainly think he is, had I made a decisive mistake in my response to Enda's initial proposal that we develop an "Appeal to Abolish War"? Was I letting a Roman Catholic moral theologian tempt me to forget my Anabaptist convictions? Put differently, is not a call to abolish war exactly the kind of Constantinianism that any serious pacifist position must disavow? Do I really think that the world—that is, all of God's creation that refuses to acknowledge that Christ is truly Lord—is capable of choosing against war?

I obviously do not think my signing on to Enda's "terrific idea" has these implications, but I think it important to say why. The reason is quite simple. The assumption that Christological pacifists could not work to abolish war only underwrites the oft made claim that pacifists may be morally admirable, but that they must disavow political relevance.[5] Yoder spent his whole life trying to challenge that assumption. The eschatological convictions that shape Christian nonviolence assume this is God's world. Accordingly, we do not believe that the boundary between church and world is a barrier that cannot be breached. Indeed we believe that the division between church and world is permeable. Therefore I see no reason that an "Appeal to Abolish War" necessarily betrays the eschatological convictions that shape the Christian witness of nonviolence; however, *who* such an appeal addresses and the reasons given for it obviously make a difference—and these were both issues that Enda and I discussed.

Enda wrote the first draft to which I only made a few changes. We addressed it to fellow Christians, hoping in particular to elicit response from theologians and ethicists in the Christian tradition.[6] The appeal makes clear that the call for an end to war is not restricted to Christians, but the reason we believe we

4. John Howard Yoder, *The Original Revolution: Essays on Christian Pacifism* (Scottdale, PA: Herald, 1971), 56. The original title of this essay was changed to "If Christ Is Truly Lord" in *The Original Revolution.*

5. Reinhold Niebuhr is, of course, the most powerful proponent of this account of Christian nonviolence. See, for example, his essays on pacifism and war in *Love and Justice: Selections from the Shorter Writings of Reinhold Niebuhr*, ed. D. B. Robertson (Louisville: Westminster John Knox, 1957), 241–301.

6. It is not our presumption that theologians will want to sign on to our "Appeal," but we hope the very decision not to sign it will challenge those who do not sign to think through why it is they cannot. For at the very least we hope the appeal will occasion reflection about war that too often does not take place until an actual war occurs.

can call for an end to war is our conviction that God has in fact abolished war through the cross and resurrection of Christ. Of course, many of the reasons for calling for an end to war are not based on apocalyptic presumptions, but we are convinced that the strongest case for the elimination of war entails the Christological commitments at the center of the appeal.

While we were working on the draft, I began to think that a good place to launch the appeal might be the annual "Culture of Life" conference sponsored by the Center for Ethics and Culture at the University of Notre Dame.[7] These conferences were dedicated to exploring the themes of the cultures of life and death at the heart of John Paul II's papacy. The center's director, Professor David Solomon, graciously invited Enda and me to present our appeal during the conference held at Notre Dame on October 28, 2002. I shall never forget Enda's eloquent remarks as he introduced the appeal. He began by noting that he was neither a pacifist nor an advocate of just war, but simply a disciple of Jesus. John Howard Yoder could not have stated it better.

Theologian Mike Baxter and I also made presentations in defense of the appeal, but neither of us could match Enda's wonderful account of how his experiences with war in Ireland and Africa had convinced him of the importance of such an appeal.

I wish I could reproduce Enda's remarks here because I have seldom heard a more eloquent defense of nonviolence,[8] but my memory and the limitations of space preclude this. Instead I will reproduce the text of the "Appeal," followed by my defense of our text. At this point very little has resulted from our efforts, but we recognize that, as in the work of peace, we must be patient. I wrote this just days before the United States attack on Iraq (in 2003)—a sobering reminder that our imaginations remain possessed by the assumption that war is a noble human undertaking. That we can think of no alternatives to war, I believe, makes the work of the appeal all the more important.

The Text of the "Appeal"

An Appeal to Abolish War

To Christian Leaders and Theologians

As Christians called out to serve the church in differing Christian traditions, we appeal to our Christian sisters and brothers to join in a campaign to abolish

7. This conference series concluded in 2002, but video footage can still be found on the Notre Dame website for the Center for Ethics and Culture: https://sites.google.com/a/nd.edu/the-notre-dame-center-for-ethics-and-culture/video/fall-conference-videos/from-death-to-life-videos.

8. For video footage of Enda's remarks and the full panel discussion go to https://sites.google.com/a/nd.edu/the-notre-dame-center-for-ethics-and-culture/video/fall-conference-videos/from-death-to-life-videos.

war as a legitimate means of resolving political conflict between states. Though our Appeal is addressed to the Christian community, we fervently believe that if our witness is true, many not part of that community may want to join our appeal to abolish war. God has, after all, created us all to desire the Kingdom of Peace.

To many theologians this call for the abolition of war will appear presumptuous on our part (who are these people anyhow?). To others it may seem theologically flawed and practically futile. Yet with John Paul II's phrase from *Centesimus Annus*, "War never again," ringing in our ears, and Tertullian's succinct summary of early church teaching before our eyes, "The Lord in disarming Peter henceforth disarms every soldier," we are driven back to that basic conviction that in the death, resurrection, and ascension of Jesus Christ, the destructive powers of this world, prominent among them *War*, were radically overcome. It is loyalty to the example and teaching of Jesus Christ which first and foremost summons Christians to renounce war and to seek with the wider religious and human communities to develop alternatives in protecting the innocent, restraining aggressors, and overcoming injustice. Let us study war no more. Let us study peace.

From their fourth-century origins, Christian attempts at justifying war have always been intellectually and spiritually vulnerable as well as practically inadequate. It is very doubtful if any actual war during that period fulfilled the traditional criteria of *jus ad bellum* and *jus in bello*. In more recent times Christian leaders and thinkers who still endorse some theory of just war are finding it increasingly difficult to see how criteria such as having exhausted all nonviolent means ("last resort"), noncombatant immunity, and proportionality could be observed. In official documents and theological analyses alike there is a discernible unease with the applicability of "just war theory" but even greater unease with its Christian authenticity.

This Appeal, based primarily on the behalf of the incompatibility of war with the teaching and example of Jesus Christ, wishes to draw all Christians into a serious conversation about the Christian and moral acceptability of war and indeed to draw all concerned humans into the examination and development of alternatives to war. Only in such a comprehensive enterprise can this Appeal's final goal of actually abolishing war hope to have any chance of success. We hope those committed to just war reflection will join us in calling for the abolition of war. For it surely must be the case that advocates of just war have as we do a stake in making war a doubtful enterprise.

Why now? We do not think so much that the peculiar horror of modern war is the primary reason or that people are so much more enlightened today that they will more readily respond to such an appeal or that alternatives are already in the making, although these may be auxiliary or indeed persuasive reasons for many. Rather, we call for the end of war now because all time is under God's judgment. So there is no time like the present (or the past) to say again in John Paul II's words what has already been said by God in Christ: "War never again." Such a call seems all the more important, however, in a world where the uses of communication and its manipulation make war not only a greater possibility but more hidden.

We have no illusions that our call for the abolition of war will bring an immediate or even quick end to the massacres called war. So we are phrasing it in terms for interrogation and dialogue, seeking as we have said to promote serious conversation and analysis among Christian leaders and thinkers on the Christian roots and possibilities of the project. We hope to enlist university faculties in the theological and secular sciences as well as research institutes in the search for the peaceful alternatives that would be more easily convincing of the immorality of war for a wider and (non-) Christian public by revealing it as also unnecessary.

This, of course, calls for an energetic and lengthy campaign of conversation and perhaps better than conversation the conversion of Christians to the true anti-war dimension of their own faith and the conversion of all to the enriching potential of their fellow humans. Our call for the abolition of war will hopefully put us on the long hard road towards the hope of developing peaceful witness as well as developing attitudes and structures for resolving conflicts nonviolently. We believe the serious study of the process of peace will only begin once the necessity of war is denied.

There are encouraging precedents for the larger hope. It was once assumed that slavery was simply part of "the natural order." Those calling for slavery's abolition were thought to be foolish utopian dreamers. We are well aware that slavery still exists in multiple disguises, but no one thinks aloud that slavery can be justified or that a public profit can be made from it. We know that what we call war will continue in various guises, but we trust that in the near future at least no Christian will be tempted to think that when they say "war" they are affirming the necessity of wars or giving them justification. Let the twenty-first century be for war what the nineteenth was for slavery, the era of its abolition, and let Christians give the leadership necessary in achieving that.

September 6, 2002

In Defense of the "Appeal"

To call for the end of war can reproduce a problem that bedevils all attempts to think about war in a morally serious manner. The problem quite simply is whether we know what we are talking about when we call for an end to "war." The problem can be illumined by asking questions like: why do we continue to call a war a war if it is not a just war? or, is the kind of war created by the modern nation-state system the same kind of killing that often occurred between peoples and/or tribes? Supporters of war seem quite confident they know what they are talking about when they defend the necessity of war.[9] We

9. John Howard Yoder notes that there is a historiography of violence just to the extent that historians of violence choose to observe those matters dealing with the fate of nations determined by their armies. Yet there could also be (and there is already a beginning of) a historiography "of the community structures of ordinary people which, by looking for other facts, find other facts. This historiography teaches us that most of the human community's quality is necessarily dependent upon

are less confident we know what we are talking about when we call for the abolition of war, but it is exactly that kind of confidence characteristic of the normal discourse about war we hope our appeal calls into question.[10]

The question whether we know what we are talking about when we talk about war can be illustrated by asking whether it is possible to write a history of war. Such a question may appear to be as odd as whether one believes in the church. One is tempted to say, "Believe in it? Hell, I've seen it!" So, of course you can write a history of war because it has been done. John Keegan wrote a book entitled *A History of Warfare*, so we know it can be done.[11] Yet Keegan's history of warfare only confirms the difficulty of knowing what is meant by "war."

For example, Keegan criticizes Clausewitz for advancing "a universal theory of what war *ought* to be, rather than what it actually was and has been."[12] Accordingly Keegan argues that "war is *not* the continuation of policy by other means," because "war antedates the state, diplomacy and strategy by many millennia." From Keegan's perspective, war comes close to naming the human condition. He observes:

> Warfare is almost as old as man himself, and reaches into the most secret places of the human heart, places where self dissolves rational purpose, where pride reigns, where emotion is paramount, where instinct is king. "Man is a political animal," said Aristotle. Clausewitz, a child of Aristotle, went no further than to say that a political animal is a war making animal. Neither dared confront the thought that man is a thinking animal in whom the intellect directs the urge to hunt and the ability to kill.[13]

Yet it is the same John Keegan who observes in a recent book, *War and Our World*, that war is a protean activity that unpredictably changes form. War, he observes, is like a disease that exhibits a capacity to mutate and mutates fastest in the face of efforts to control or eliminate it. Therefore Keegan offers no more determinative description of war than "war is collective killing for some collective purpose."[14]

Keegan obviously intended his description of war to offer a morally neutral account of war, but even a description as bland as his is not successful in avoiding moral implications. For example, his description seems to make any attempts

avoiding violence and that truly foundational values are seldom served by those who claim to do it with the sword" (*Nonviolence—A Brief History: The Warsaw Lectures*, ed. Paul Martens, Matthew Porter, and Myles Werntz [Waco: Baylor University Press, 2010], 68).

10. I use "we" in this response to indicate that this is a joint project, not only for Enda and myself but for all Christians.

11. John Keegan, *A History of Warfare* (New York: Vintage, 1993).

12. Ibid., 6.

13. Ibid., 3.

14. John Keegan, *War and Our World* (New York: Vintage, 1998), 72.

to distinguish between war and terrorism problematic.[15] Moreover, his claim that warfare is as old as mankind surely is overstated. Why does he not say that violence, rather than warfare, is the mark of our nature? Keegan is trying to provide an account of war that avoids questions of whether war is a good or bad thing. For Keegan, war just "is." But he fails to see that even the claim that "war just is" gives a moral status to violence that must be defended.[16]

Keegan's reticence to describe or "define" war is interesting because it helps make clear that "war" comes freighted in our speech with normative commitments. Even when we think we are doing no more than "describing war," the notion of "war" carries with it (to revert to terms made famous by C. L. Stevenson) a "pro" or "con" attitude. But "attitude" only names the habits in which our speech is embedded that make descriptions seem inevitable and undeniable. Understanding war as a habit leads us to assume that even if a war is not a just war, though regrettable, it remains a moral necessity. In other words, we continue to think that killing in war is somehow morally different than other forms of killing. Yet it is by no means clear why we think war can be so distinguished from unjustified forms of violence.

At the very least, our "Appeal to Abolish War" is meant to challenge the assumption that war can be easily distinguished from other forms of unjustified killing. We therefore challenge those habits of speech that make war a normalizing discourse. We want to call into question the assumption made by many that, although war is horrible, we simply have no alternatives in the world as we know it. Too many think that as destructive as war may be, it is a necessary practice that we cannot live without.

15. The assumption that a clear line can be drawn between war and terrorism often has the result of legitimating war. For example, Wendell Berry observes, "Supposedly, if a nation perpetuates violence officially—whether to bomb an enemy airfield or a hospital—that nation is not guilty of 'terrorism.' But there is no need to hesitate over the difference between 'terrorism' and any violence or threat of violence that is terrifying. The National Security Strategy wishes to cause 'terrorism' to be seen 'in the same light as slavery, piracy, or genocide'—but not in the same light as war. The Strategy accepts and affirms the legitimacy of war." Berry is commenting on the National Security Strategy published by the Bush White House in September 2002. Berry notes the most significant statement in the document is this: "While the United States will constantly strive to enlist the support of the international community, we will not hesitate to act alone, if necessary, to exercise our right of self-defense by acting preemptively against such terrorists." Furthermore, the Bush statement claims that the United States is justified in attacking any state that even thinks about developing weapons that may threaten us (Wendell Berry, "A Citizen's Response to the National Security Strategy," *Orion Magazine*, March/April 2003, http://www.orionmagazine.org/index.php/articles/article/20).

16. I think the position that assumes that war is neither good nor bad but just "is" is quite interesting. It helps us see that we continue to have war, because we had war. War turns out to be a habit constitutive of human history that cannot be broken. I argued something like this in my essay "Should War Be Eliminated?" in my book *Against the Nations: War and Survival in a Liberal Society* (Notre Dame: University of Notre Dame Press, 1992), 169–208. What the church offers the world is not, therefore, simply a people committed to peace, but a counter-history to that which can only tell the story of how we got to where we are at in terms of war.

In short, we seek nothing less than to have our everyday use of the word "war" disciplined by how we must learn to speak as Christians. Christians pray for peace. We often say, "Christ is our peace." We hear read from Scripture Sunday after Sunday that Christians are recipients of the peace only God can give. We celebrate peace in our hymns, which not only call for peace but may be one of the gifts God has given to help us share peace with one another. For we do not sing hymns alone; we sing them together in a manner that anticipates our unity.[17] Such unity is what we Christians have learned to call "peace."

For example, consider this stanza from the hymn "O God of Every Nation":

> Keep bright in us the vision of days when war shall cease,
> when hatred and division give way to love and peace,
> till dawns the morning glorious when truth and justice reign,
> and Christ shall rule victorious o'er all the world's domain.[18]

Nothing is exceptional about this hymn. I assume that you can find numerous hymns in every denominational hymnal that would express quite similar views. But if war is assumed by Christians to be morally unproblematic, or even the lesser of two evils, then how can we sing such hymns? To do so while assuming that war may be a good is to make the Christian desire for peace nothing more than pious sentiment that does not work; it is to make "peace" some distant ideal rather than an eschatological reality. Our "Appeal for the Abolition of War" is a call for our theology and ethics to catch up with the church's songs and poetry.

However, it may well be asked if all the appeal amounts to is a language-transforming proposal. We certainly hope it is more than that, but it is at least a call for us to discipline our speech. After all, to call Christians to reexamine how our speech about war may betray the gospel is no small thing. If the appeal could help Christians speak about war in a manner that does not reproduce the assumption that war is a necessary evil, then a great thing will have been done—the result being, at the very least, that the burden of proof will shift to those who support war as the only way that nations and peoples can relate to one another.

Finally, some may be hesitant to support the appeal because they assume that signing it would commit them to a pacifist position. But we have carefully worded the appeal to avoid that conclusion. It is our hope that many who have struggled to make the just war tradition relevant in our world will find

17. Dennis O'Brien makes this point in his lovely book *God and the New Haven Railroad (and Why Neither One Is Doing Very Well)* (Boston: Beacon, 1986). O'Brien observes, "Religion is about singing—praying, talking, gesturing—about the humanly unfixable. That is why religious ceremonies have clustered about the celebration of our chains—the places where we are stuck" (133).

18. *The United Methodist Hymnal* (Nashville: United Methodist Publishing House, 1989), 435.

themselves able to sign. We understand that many assume war is necessary to achieve justice. We have no reason to challenge the justice that just war accounts remind us to pursue. But we hope the appeal provides the context for exploring how such an understanding of justice is, as Aquinas maintained, also the subject of charity.[19]

The appeal is first and foremost addressed to Christian theologians and leaders, but we assume and hope that non-Christians may have reasons to support it too. We believe that Christians, when they are thinking like Christians, will discover that they cannot underwrite the assumption that war is one of the necessities of life. For as Christians we believe war is but a name for the powers defeated by the death and resurrection of Jesus. So let us no longer serve such "elemental spirits," but rather be what we are: the church of Jesus Christ. We are bold to call for the abolition of war because we believe war has been abolished through the triumph of the resurrection of Jesus Christ.

A Final Word to Enda

Such is the story of how Enda got me involved in the project to write an appeal to abolish war. I remain extremely grateful that he did so. God knows what effect the appeal may have, but we cannot pretend that what we are doing is being done for effect—unless the effect is a sustained peace among peoples. I think we have written the appeal because we are friends, which is a reminder to me of how grateful I am to Enda for claiming me as a friend. Such friendship is surely the gift God has given us so that we, that is, the church, might be God's alternative to war.

19. I have probably loaded more into this paragraph than any paragraph can stand, but the point is extremely important. Many just war advocates suggest that just war is an attempt to provide a series of exceptions from the general stance of Christian nonviolence. In contrast, Paul Ramsey argues that advocates of just war should not think the object of just war is first of all peace, but rather justice. Accordingly, it is a mistake to assume that just war is a strategy to achieve peace, because in this time between times peace cannot and should not exist. I think this is the strongest defense that can be given of just war, but I also think that just war proponents are seldom candid about whether such an account of just war can be theologically justified. For a discussion of Ramsey's views on this matter, see my foreword to Paul Ramsey's *Just War* (1983; repr., Lanham, MD: Rowman and Littlefield, 2002), ix–xiii. For a recent defense of just war as the pursuit of justice, see George Weigel, "Moral Clarity in a Time of War," *First Things*, January 2003, 20–27. Weigel argues that just war, understood as a pursuit of justice, means that *jus ad bellum* considerations require a nation to go to war before any analysis of *jus in bello* concerns is raised. He notes, for example, that many after September 11, 2001, have raised questions about avoiding indiscriminate noncombatant casualties in the war against terrorism, "while little attention was paid to the prior question of the moral obligation of government to pursue national security *and world order*, both of which were directly threatened by the terrorist networks" (23). I have italicized the phrase *and world order* to indicate how just war can quickly become an ideological tool for those who assume that their country knows what is good for "world order." What could it mean for such an understanding of "justice" to be shaped by Christian charity?

Appendix

To call for the abolition of war will strike most in the "field" of Christian ethics as at best naive, or worse, just downright silly. That the appeal will elicit such a response is but an indication of why it is so badly needed. War possesses our imaginations, our everyday habits, and our scholarly assumptions. Thinking about what it might mean to abolish war inevitably calls into question some of our most cherished convictions: convictions whose importance may not be recognized because they so seldom need to be articulated. I suspect that among our deepest moral intuitions is the presumption that war is necessary if we are to live "worthy" lives.

As I said above, one of the difficulties in calling for the abolition of war is whether anyone knows what it is you are calling to be abolished. War may be ubiquitous, but that there always seems to be a war taking place somewhere does not mean we know what we mean when we say war.

Clearly war is a contested concept that requires analogical display. For example, is the violence, often highly ritualized, between some people the same as the kind of conflict exemplified by World War I? I cannot pretend to have answered this question; I can only note that defining what makes war war is an ongoing problem. It is, moreover, a problem not just for pacifists but also for those representing the just war tradition. Just war is perhaps best understood not as an attempt to test whether a war meets the criteria of justice but rather an attempt to control the description "war." In other words, only if a war is just does it deserve the description "war."

One of the most determinative intellectual challenges facing those who would call for the abolition of war surely involves how we understand history, including how history is written. As might be expected, no one has made this clearer than Michel Foucault. In his lectures at the Collège de France in 1975 through 1976, entitled *Society Must Be Defended*, Foucault argues that Clausewitz's famous proposition "War is the continuation of politics by other means" should be inverted. Foucault observes, "The role of political power is perpetually to use a sort of silent war to reinscribe that relationship of force, and to reinscribe it in institutions, economic inequalities, language, and even the bodies of individuals. This is the initial meaning of our inversion of Clausewitz's aphorism—politics is the continuation of war by other means. Politics, in other words, sanctions and reproduces the disequilibrium of forces manifested in war."[20]

According to Foucault, the inversion of Clausewitz's proposition helps us see that a crucial transition in the practices and institutions of war, which were initially concentrated in the hands of a central power, became associated both in *de facto* and *de jure* terms with emerging state power. "The State acquired

20. Michel Foucault, *"Society Must Be Defended": Lectures at the Collège de France, 1975–1976*, ed. Mauro Bertani and Alessandro Fontana, trans. David Macey (New York: Picador, 2003), 15–16.

a monopoly on war," which had the effect of making war seem to exist only on the outer limits of the great state units. War became the technical and professional prerogative of a carefully defined and controlled military apparatus. The army became an institution.[21] This means, Foucault argues, that we cannot assume that society, the law, and the state are like armistices that put an end to wars. Beneath the law, war continues to rage. "War is the motor behind institutions and order. In the smallest of its cogs, peace is waging a secret war. To put it another way, we have to interpret the war that is going on beneath peace; peace itself is a coded war. We are all inevitably someone's adversary."[22] Contrary to Hobbes, sovereignty is not the result of the war of all against all. Rather, what we should learn from Hobbes is that it is not war that gives birth to states, but rather sovereignty is always shaped from below by those who are afraid.[23]

According to Foucault, history has always been a form of discourse related to rituals of power. From the first Roman annalists to the late Middle Ages (and perhaps even the seventeenth century and later), history had two roles: (1) to recount the history of kings and their victories, and (2) to use the continuity of the law to establish a juridical link between the king and power.[24] But in the eighteenth century there emerged a specifically modern dimension of politics in which historical knowledge became an element of the struggle. "History gave us the idea that we are at war; and we wage war through history."[25]

Foucault suggests that this is why philosophers, scientists, and political thinkers have tried to ward off historicism. They do so because historicism makes the link between war and history and shows how history participates in war. No matter how far one goes back, history discovers only unending war. Thus we have the "Western organization of knowledge" according to the dictum that truth must belong to the register of order and peace, that is, that truth can never be found on the side of violence, disorder, and war becomes

21. Ibid., 48–49.

22. Ibid., 50–51.

23. Ibid., 96. Foucault has an extended discussion of Hobbes that is as interesting as it is counterintuitive. For example, Foucault suggests that rather than being the theorist of the relationship between war and political power, Hobbes wanted to eliminate the genesis of sovereignty. "A large part of the discourse of *Leviathan* consists in saying: It doesn't matter whether you fought or did not fight, whether you were beaten or not; in any case, the mechanism that applies to you who have been defeated is the same mechanism that we find in the state of nature, in the constitution of a State, and we also find, quite naturally, in the most tender and natural relationship of all: that between parents and children. . . . It is not really war that gives birth to States, and it is not really war that is transcribed in relations of sovereignty or that reproduces within the civil power—and its inequalities—the earlier dissymmetries in the relationship of force that were revealed by the very fact of the battle itself" (ibid., 97). Foucault argues that the main purpose of Hobbes was to render invisible the conquest of England by the Normans.

24. Ibid., 66.

25. Ibid., 172.

the way the modern state "has now reimplanted it in what we might call the eighteenth century's 'disciplinarization' of knowledges."[26] Historicism becomes unacceptable to us because of the unavoidable circularity between historical knowledge and the wars that historicism speaks about and that history itself is enacting. Foucault, therefore, takes his task as a historicist "to analyze this perpetual and unavoidable relationship between the war that is recounted by history and that is traversed by the war it is recounting."[27]

Foucault's argument involves ontological claims that require a historical display. Accordingly he provides a fascinating account of how war as a contest between kings, or a revolt against kings, has been replaced by what he calls "race wars." One no longer kills because of loyalty to this or that monarch, but because one is a Frank or Gaul. This creates a new form of historical discourse in which sovereignty is no longer the central problem; now the story is about "race struggles that go on within nations and within laws."[28]

The complex challenge Foucault presents to our call for the abolition of war cannot be done justice here. However, I think that Foucault is right to direct attention to history as the crucial category. Indeed his understanding of the relation of history and war is extremely important for the case I want to make, as he shows that any call for the abolition of war entails a different historical imaginary. Such a call would inevitably challenge the disciplines of knowledge that are now enshrined in the modern university.[29] Moreover, given the power of those disciplines to make war seem a necessity, it is quite understandable that our call for the abolition of war seems naive.

Foucault rightly helps us see that the call for the abolition of war requires that we challenge our most basic explanatory modes of knowledge. Nothing less than an alternative history is required. In his book *The Unconquerable World: Power, Nonviolence, and the Will of the People*, Jonathan Schell begins to offer the kind of history I think is so desperately needed. Schell begins his book by describing the "war system," that is, the view of the world that assumes that the normal relation between states is one of war. The war system, he argues, forces all reality to submit to its power: "The democratic revolution brought the Rights of Man *and* millions of willing recruits for war; the scientific revolution offered pure knowledge *and* better artillery and explosives; the industrial revolutions created consumer goods *and* provided

26. Ibid., 173. Foucault observes that "knowledge is never anything more than a weapon in a war, or a tactile deployment within that war. War is waged throughout history, and through the history that tells the history of war. And history, for its part, can never do anything more than interpret the war it is waging or that is being waged through it" (173).

27. Ibid., 173–74. Foucault acknowledges that this argument owes much to Nietzsche.

28. Ibid., 69.

29. Foucault has several pages in these lectures dedicated to the university as the state apparatus to centralize knowledge through organization into disciplines. The university becomes the way knowledge is domesticated in the name of "science" (ibid., 182–83).

more material for larger and longer wars; imperial possession won trade and spoils *and* strategic global position."[30]

Schell does not deny the descriptive power of the history that has been created by the war system, but he argues that there is a "less-noticed, parallel history of nonviolent power. The chronicle has been a hopeful one of violence disrupted or in retreat—of great-power war immobilized by the nuclear stalemate, of brutal empires defeated by local peoples fighting for their self-determination, of revolutions succeeding without violence, of democracy supplanting authoritarian or totalitarian repression, of national sovereignty yielding to systems of mixed and balanced powers."[31]

For example, Schell has an extensive account of that extraordinary figure Gandhi, in which he argues quite persuasively that Gandhi's ability to combine nonviolence with political reality has not been appropriately appreciated. Schell rightly praises Gandhi's campaigns of noncooperation, *satyagraha*, but points out that Gandhi's most persistent efforts were in support of constructive programs. His "fasts unto death" were launched in the name of bringing justice to workers of Ahmedabad, of no longer having an "untouchable" caste, of making peace between Hindus and Muslims.[32] Schell is well aware that Gandhi is "strange," but he argues that Gandhi is a resource for a way of telling the story of our time that makes war less likely.

Schell argues that revolutions first occur nonviolently simply by people discovering forms of cooperation that make it possible to say "no" to the established powers. For example, he observes that the Bolsheviks did not need to use violence to win power, but they used it to keep power.[33] When violence is used to keep power, the revolution is lost. Thus the extraordinary events of 1989 in which Eastern Europe was freed from totalitarian control remain a testimony to the power of nonviolence. Schell suggests the secret to that continuing revolution was that Michnik and Havel saw it would be a mistake to think they should overthrow the system, and instead they directed their attention to achieving modest and concrete goals that affected everyday life on the local level.[34]

Schell, drawing on the work of Hannah Arendt, argues that politics is nonviolent action. He uses Arendt's argument that power is not the result of some people coercing others, but rather is common action in support of common purposes, to suggest that liberal democracy can be understood to be a peace movement.[35] Yet Schell also rightly sees that the very character of

30. Jonathan Schell, *The Unconquerable World: Power, Nonviolence, and the Will of the People* (New York: Henry Holt, 2003), 31.

31. Ibid., 305.

32. Ibid., 139.

33. Ibid., 179.

34. Ibid., 193.

35. Ibid., 217–19, 240.

liberalism can lead to imperialism just to the extent that liberalism assumes an international character shaped by universalistic pretensions.[36] In fact the great challenge before America is the possession of a massive military with no enemy to fight.[37] Possession of such a military is very dangerous for a country like America, which fails to understand Arendt's point that a country's violence can destroy its power.[38] Schell concludes, "The days when humanity can hope to save itself from force with force are over. None of the structures of violence—not the balance of power, not the balance of terror, not empire—can any longer rescue the world from the use of violence, now grown apocalyptic. Force can lead only to more force, not to peace. Only a turn to structures of cooperative power can offer hope."[39]

This is not to suggest that Schell provides a sufficient response to Foucault's challenge. What the juxtaposition of Foucault and Schell suggests, however, is that if we are to untangle ourselves from the logic of war and the imperatives of the war system, then an alternative imaginary needs to be constructed. Schell's alternative history is crucial to the construction of that new imaginary because it helps us to see that nonviolence is deeper than the violence that possesses our speech and our imagination. As such, Schell's work is precisely the kind of investigation needed if a call for the abolition of war is to be persuasive.

36. Ibid., 269–70.
37. Ibid., 322.
38. Ibid., 344.
39. Ibid., 345.

5

Sacrificing the Sacrifices of War

The Moral Practice Called War

War is a moral practice. By calling war a moral practice I am not suggesting that I believe war to be "a good thing." James McClendon, drawing appreciatively on Alasdair MacIntyre's understanding of practices, rightly argues that powerful practices can be narrated through the New Testament notion of "principalities and powers." McClendon, moreover, is surely right to suggest that such powers are all the more dangerous because they can be perversions of God's good creation.[1]

I use the phrase "the practice of war" to enable us to think through the ethics of war in a different manner than beginning with positions such as pacifism and/or just war. I do not want to be misunderstood: I think the kind of work done to clarify pacifism or just war is necessary and invaluable if it helps us understand better how Christians should respond to war.[2] But I am also impressed that no matter how hard we work to understand either the moral limits or the form war should take, it makes very little difference for the actual practice of war.

1. James McClendon, *Systematic Theology*, vol. 1, *Ethics* (Nashville: Abingdon, 1986), 170–77.

2. In his fine book *Arguing about War* (New Haven: Yale University Press, 2004), Michael Walzer characterizes pacifists as those who deny that war is sometimes justifiable because they believe war is a criminal act (ix). I should like to think this chapter suggests that the pacifist position can appreciate the complex moral character of war.

That pacifism or just war reflection have little effect, I think, is not because some people perversely think war is a good thing. Neither is it the result of some conspiracy of the military-industrial complex. I certainly do not need to suggest, as the current war in Iraq and Afghanistan amply demonstrates, that for many war turns out to be a great economic boon. But surely something deeper is going on. Everyone confesses "war is horrible," yet we continue to have war. Sentimental appeals to peace too often turn out to be the grounds to justify the judgment that even if war is horrible and terrifying, sometimes we must be willing to go to war.

In the past I have argued that war continues to seem necessary because we have found no way to tell the stories of our lives without war playing a role.[3] We cannot get rid of war because war has captured the habits of our imaginations. We quite simply cannot comprehend a world without war. This is as true of the pacifist as it is for the just war advocate. What would the pacifists do if they actually got the world they say they want? In an odd way pacifists can be as dependent on the existence of war to make their world intelligible as those who think war must be tragically accepted. That is why I have argued that pacifism and nonviolence are inadequate descriptions for the disavowal of violence required by being a disciple of Jesus. Peace is a deeper reality than violence[4]—but to recognize the truth of this statement, we need to locate the peaceful practices that constitute our lives, which too often fail to be named as such.

Yet to say that war is a habit of our imaginations does not tell us enough. Enda McDonagh and I have called for the abolition of war, but in order to appreciate why war is such a stubborn reality, I think we need to better understand why war remains so morally compelling.[5] War is, in fact, not only

3. See "Should War Be Eliminated?" in my book *Against the Nations: War and Survival in a Liberal Society* (Notre Dame: University of Notre Dame Press, 1992), 169–208, and "Can a Pacifist Think about War?" in my book *Dispatches from the Front: Theological Engagements with the Secular* (Durham, NC: Duke University Press, 1994), 116–35.

4. This was, of course, at the heart of Yoder's account of the peace made possible by Christ. For my explicit reflections on the issue, see my *Performing the Faith: Bonhoeffer and the Practice of Nonviolence* (Grand Rapids: Brazos, 2004), 169–83.

5. See chapter 4 in the present book, "Reflections on the 'Appeal to Abolish War': Or, What Being a Friend of Enda's Got Me Into." I recently discovered a remarkable passage in Keegan's *History of Warfare*. Keegan says, "War is now avoidable; war is no longer *necessary*. The poor may fight, but the right rule. It is with their weapons that the mad ideologies of peasant countries tread the path of blood. . . . We can stop now if we only choose, by a simple economic decision of the governments of the rich states not to make more arms than they need for their own purposes, and not to supply any surplus that remains to the poor, the have-nots. . . . The time has come to end war" (8). I discovered this quote in Jeremy Black's book, *War: Past, Present, and Future* (New York: St. Martin's, 2000). Professor Black used the quote to exemplify what he took to be a great silliness. I believe debates among military historians concerning how the history of war can or should be written to be quite important for those wanting to write about the morality of war.

morally compelling; it is also quite fascinating, if not beautiful.[6] I want to therefore offer some suggestions about the very character of war as a practice, the loss of which would make the lives of many less full.

My strategy is not unlike that of William James in his famous essay "The Moral Equivalent of War."[7] James argued, in spite of his pacifism, that if war is to be abolished, we must find a moral equivalent to war.[8] According to James, war was the institution that "is the great preserver of our ideals of hardihood, and human life with no use for hardihood would be contemptible. Without risks or prizes for the darer, history would be insipid indeed; and there is a type of military character which everyone feels that the race should never cease to breed, for everyone is sensitive to its superiority."[9] Therefore "war is a permanent human *obligation*" we abolish to our detriment.[10]

James thought that war could not be eliminated unless some alternative were found to preserve the virtues war requires. He thought this particularly important in developing bourgeois social orders and what he quite wonderfully called "the pleasure economies" of such societies. James proposed,

6. J. Glen Gray, in *The Warriors: Reflections on Men in Battle* (New York: Harper, 1967), 28–29, 30–31, observes,

> What are these secret attractions of war, the ones that have persisted in the West despite revolutionary changes in methods of warfare? I believe that they are: the delight in seeing, the delight in comradeship, the delight in destruction. . . . That war is a spectacle, as something to see, ought never to be underestimated. . . . There is a popular conviction that war and battle are the sphere of ugliness, and, since aesthetic delight is associated with the beautiful, it may be concluded that war is the natural enemy of the aesthetic. I fear that this is in large part an illusion. It is first of all wrong to believe that only beauty can give us aesthetic delight; the ugly can please us too, as every artist knows. And furthermore, beauty in various guises is hardly foreign to scenes of battle. . . . If we think of beauty and ugliness without their usual moral overtones, there is often a weird but genuine beauty in the sight of massed men and weapons in combat. Reputedly, it was the sight of advancing columns of men under fire that impelled General Robert E. Lee to remark to one of his staff: "It is well that war is so terrible—we would grow too fond of it."

7. William James, "The Moral Equivalent of War," in *The Moral Equivalent of War and Other Essays*, ed. John Roth (New York: Harper, 1971), 3–16.

8. The war to which James sought to find an equivalent was surely the Civil War. One of James's brothers had been wounded in that war and in many ways never recovered. In *The Metaphysical Club: A Story of Ideas in America* (New York: Farrar, Straus & Giroux, 2001), Louis Menand discusses the effects of the war on Oliver Wendell Holmes. Menand wonderfully observes that Holmes had gone off to fight because of his moral beliefs, but the experience of the war "did more than make him lose those beliefs. It made him lose his belief in beliefs" (4). According to Menand, Holmes concluded from his experience of the war that certitude leads to violence. He was determined to avoid certitude about anything. Holmes assumed, of course, that we could not live if there were not some things we are certain about. Truth, therefore, is just the "name for what it is impossible for a person to doubt" (63). Though not a philosopher, I think Menand rightly presents Holmes as the embodiment of the spirit that led to American pragmatism. James did not lose his belief in belief, but then neither did James experience the combat that shaped Holmes's life.

9. James, "Moral Equivalent," 7.

10. Ibid., 8.

> If now there were instead of military conscription a conscription of the whole youthful population to form for a certain number of years a part of the army enlisted against *Nature*, the injustice would tend to be evened out, and numerous other goods to the commonwealth would follow. The military ideals of hardihood and discipline would be wrought into the growing fibre of people; no one would remain blind as the luxurious classes now are blind to man's relations to the globe he lives on, and to the permanently sour and hard foundations of his higher life.[11]

The line of reflection I take in this paper is analogous to James's suggestion, but I hope it will become obvious that I think James's understanding of war is inadequate. He failed to see that war is a sacrificial system and any alternative to war must be one that sacrifices the sacrifices of war. Indeed, I will argue that the greatest sacrifice of war is not the sacrifice of life, great as such a sacrifice may be, but rather the sacrifice of our unwillingness to kill. That sacrifice of our unwillingness to kill is why war is at once so morally compelling and morally perverse.

By calling attention to the sacrificial character of war, I hope to show that the Christian "dis-ease" with war is liturgical. The sacrifices of war are a counter-liturgy to the sacrifice at the altar made possible by Christ. Christians believe that Christ is the end of sacrifice—that is, any sacrifice that is not determined by the sacrifice of the cross—and therefore that we are free of the necessity to secure our existence through sacrificing our and others' lives on the world's altars. However, the sacrifice that war requires seems to mirror our lives as Christians, making war at once attractive and repelling to Christians.[12]

11. Ibid., 13. James's was the epitome of the ethos of the Victorian male. Every life should be the strenuous life; so testing oneself in "nature" was essential to being "manly." That "nature" was to be "tamed" was, therefore, a given. The significance of the "Moral Equivalent of War" for understanding James's position has seldom been developed. In his book *William James: On Radical Empiricism and Religion* (Toronto: University of Toronto Press, 2000), Hunter Brown, rightly, I think, sees the continuity between this essay and James's *The Varieties of Religious Experience*. Brown notes, "Material self-abdication through the voluntary adoption of poverty is the strenuous life, James says; it is the 'moral equivalent of war' which transforms the ideal of selfless heroism, traditionally associated with military risk and self-sacrifice, into a strenuous heroism of ascetic identification with the disenfranchised through the personal abdication of one's material privileges" (98).

12. The grammar of this sentence gives the impression that war is a constant running through history, but I think that presumption is problematic. The kind of war constitutive of the modern nation-state system is quite different than the wars fought between "kingdoms." "War" is a contested concept that requires analogical display. I continue to wonder, however, if a history of war can be written that does justice to the disanalogies between different kinds of conflicts. Moreover I continue to think that just war theorists owe us an answer to the question, "If a war is unjust, is it still a war?" That people continue to describe an unjust war as war still seems to suggest that war can be distinguished from systematic killing and therefore in some sense be "legitimate." Thus the assumption: "I had to kill *x* or *y*, but that I had to do so is legitimate because it was war." That is the assumption that I think must be challenged. The need to describe unjust war as nonetheless

The Moral Logic of the Sacrifice of War

In his extraordinary book *War Is a Force That Gives Us Meaning*, Chris Hedges, a war correspondent, tries to explain why he became so addicted to war that he could not live without being in a war. War had quite simply captured his imagination, making it impossible for him to live "normally." Hedges observes:

> I learned early on that war forms its own culture. The rush of battle is a potent and often lethal addiction, for war is a drug, one I ingested for many years. It is peddled by myth makers—historians, war correspondents, film makers, novelists, and the state—all of whom endow it with qualities it often does possess: excitement, exoticism, power, chances to rise above our small stations in life and a bizarre and fantastic universe that has a grotesque and dark beauty. It dominates culture, distorts memory, corrupts language, and infects everything around it, even humor, which becomes preoccupied with the grim perversities of smut and death. Fundamental questions about the meaning, or meaninglessness, of our place on the planet are laid bare when we watch those around us sink to the lowest depths. War exposes the capacity for evil that lurks not far below the surface within all of us. And this is why for many war is so hard to discuss once it is over.
>
> The enduring attraction of war is this: Even with its destruction and carnage it can give us what we long for in life. It can give us purpose, meaning, a reason for living. Only when we are in the midst of conflict does the shallowness and vapidness of much of our lives become apparent. Trivia dominates our conversations and increasingly our airways. And war is an enticing elixir. It gives us resolve, a cause. It allows us to be noble.[13]

According to Hedges, war makes the world coherent, understandable, because in war the world is construed as black and white, them and us. Moreover, echoing J. Glen Grey's account in *The Warriors*, Hedges notes that war creates a bond between combatants found almost nowhere else in our lives. War unites soldiers because in war they are bound by suffering for the pursuit of a higher good. Through war we discover that though we may seek happiness, meaning is far more important.[14] "And tragically war is sometimes the most powerful way in human society to achieve meaning."[15]

---

war instead of state-sponsored murder seems analogous to the need to describe the American treatment of prisoners as "abuse" rather than torture. I owe this observation to Charlie Collier.

13. Chris Hedges, *War Is a Force That Gives Us Meaning* (New York: Public Affairs, 2002), 3. Hedges argues that war correspondents are crucial for the legitimization of war. The story of a war, a story that often belies the anarchy of battle, becomes the way war is legitimated. So newspapers and magazines are essential parts of the war machine.

14. Interestingly enough, often the anti-war efforts function in a similar way for participants; that is, the anti-war movement needs an enemy if it is to have some common purpose.

15. Hedges, *War Is a Force*, 10. Hedges's book has been rightly celebrated as an honest and insightful account of war, but in many ways Grey's book remains the classical description of the moral power war has over our imaginations.

The meaning that participation in war presumably gives, particularly in the West, draws on the close identification of the sacrifice required by war and the sacrifice of Christ. Allen Frantzen calls attention to the influence of the ideal of chivalry for how English and German soldiers in World War I understood their roles. He notes that development of chivalry depended on the sacralization of violence so that the apparent conflict between piety and predatoriness simply disappeared. The great manuals of chivalry "closed the gap between piety—which required self-abnegation and self-sacrifice—and violence rooted in revenge. The most important presupposition of chivalry became the belief that one bloody death—Christ's—must be compensated by others like it."[16] Drawing on pictorial evidence, Frantzen helps us see that the connection between Christ's death and those who die in war is at the heart of how the sacrifice of the English, Germans, and Americans who died in World War I was understood.

Moreover, the language of sacrifice continues to play a central role in how war is understood, not only in WWII but in the current Iraq war. I think the language of sacrifice is particularly important for societies like the United States, in which war remains our most determinative common experience,[17] because such nations depend on the story of our wars to narrate our history as a unified story.[18] World War I was particularly important just to the extent

16. Allen Frantzen, *Bloody Good: Chivalry, Sacrifice, and the Great War* (Chicago: University of Chicago Press, 2004), 24. Frantzen's use of pictorial evidence to sustain his argument is overwhelming. After reading his book, we see that war monuments are much less innocent than we normally assume.

It was only after I finished this essay that I discovered Ivan Strenski's extraordinary book, *Contesting Sacrifice: Religion, Nationalism, and Social Thought in France* (Chicago: University of Chicago Press, 2002). Strenski argues that Catholic Eucharistic theology of sacrifice, a theology in reaction to Protestant denial of the centrality of the Eucharist, provided the discourse for the French understanding of sacrifice for the nation and, in particular, for war. Strenski's story is a fascinating account of how the language of sacrifice worked for the way WWI and the Dreyfus affair were understood. His book is as good a documentation as I could want for the argument of this essay.

17. In his article "How to Get Out of Iraq," Peter Galbraith quotes the historian J. W. Chambers, who maintains that war has been "central to the way the United States has developed as a nation and a society" from the very beginning. Galbraith continues, "The conquest of Indian lands, the expulsion of first the French and then the British Empires, western expansion, the preservation of the Union, and America's accession to global power status after 1914 were all accompanied by, and in part accomplished through military exertion" (*New York Review of Books*, May 13, 2004, 41). But what has changed is American spending on the military. Before 1939 American spending was comparable to the standards of other great powers, but because of American wealth, we can budget for guns on a vast scale while still allowing most citizens to enjoy a high standard of living (I have to say, this may be changing).

18. Recent American war-fighting strategy—that is, the use of massive force to eliminate the need for American soldiers to be killed—has created a moral crisis in the American military and society. Michael Walzer critiques American war strategy in Kosovo by reminding us of Camus's dictum: "You can't kill unless you are prepared to die." This at the very least requires that American generals be prepared to risk the lives of their soldiers (Walzer, *Arguing about War*, 101–2).

I suspect the American unwillingness to sacrifice our troops has everything to do with the ethos that currently grips the American people. Russell Baker, for example, observes that a kind of sterility

that it represented the reintegration of the American South into the union called the United States.[19]

Whatever one may think of Carl Schmitt's argument that all the legitimating concepts of the modern state—a state according to Schmitt that gains its moral intelligibility from war—are secularized theological concepts, I certainly think his analysis helps us understand much about America.[20] For example, Carolyn Marvin and David Ingle begin their book *Blood Sacrifice and the Nation: Totem Rituals and the American Flag* by asking,

> What binds the nation together? How vulnerable to ethnic and religious antagonism is our sense of nationhood? What is the source of the malaise we have felt for so much of the post-World War II period? Above all, what moves citizens to put group interests ahead of their own, even to surrendering their lives? No strictly economic explanations, no great-man theory of history, no imminent group threat fully accounts for why members of enduring groups such as nations consent to sacrifice their immediate well being and that of their children to the group. Whatever does, tells us a great deal about what makes nation-states enduring and viable. This book argues that violent blood sacrifice makes enduring groups cohere, even though such a claim challenges our most deeply held notions of civilized behavior. The sacrificial system that binds American citizens has a sacred flag at its center. Patriotic rituals revere it as the embodiment of a bloodthirsty totem god who organizes killing energy.[21]

---

has crept into American politics. He continues, "In this atmosphere history has a dreamlike quality. A war is said to be in progress, and the President describes himself as a 'war president,' but, except for military professionals, no one is asked to fight or sacrifice or even, as in World War II, to save waste fats and grease. We are asked only to shop with a generous hand, to accept a tax cut, and to be scared" ("In Bush's Washington," *New York Review of Books*, May 13, 2004, 25). One of the great divides in America is the increasing gulf between the moral commitments constitutive of the armed services and the general ethos of American society.

19. In *Women and War* (New York: Basic Books, 1987), Jean Bethke Elshtain observes that nation-states can exist on paper before they exist in fact. Accordingly she argues that the United States was a historical construction that visibly came into being as a cause and consequence of the "Great War." Prior to that war, America was a federation of strong local and regional identities in which the centralized federal government was fairly limited. The First World War reintegrated not only the South into the Union, but also the immigrants who had flooded into America in the nineteenth century (106–20).

20. Carl Schmitt, *Roman Catholicism and Political Form*, trans. G. L. Ulmen (Westport, CT: Greenwood, 1996).

21. Carolyn Marvin and David Ingle, *Blood Sacrifice and the Nation: Totem Rituals and the American Flag* (Cambridge: Cambridge University Press, 1999), 1. Marvin and Ingle's argument draws heavily on Emile Durkheim, whose general account of religion I find quite unpersuasive, but it works well for their purposes.

I think Marvin and Ingle's book lends some support to my contention that one of the reasons war has become a habit is that future generations feel the need to sacrifice their young to show they are worthy to represent those that sacrificed their youth to give them their life. It does not matter what the past war was about or what the present war concerns. What is important is that the sacrifice be repeated to show we are rightful heirs of the sacrifices that we believe have been

Marvin and Ingle argue that self-sacrifice is the central theme of the American civil religion of patriotism and that nowhere is that better exemplified than in the American fetish of the flag. They provide extraordinarily rich and diverse iconographic and textual evidence to sustain their argument. For example, they call attention to a quote from Dwight D. Eisenhower's published account of his induction into West Point. Eisenhower begins by describing the rough first day of initiation into West Point, at the end of which he confesses to being weary and resentful. Eisenhower writes, however, that "toward evening we assembled outdoors and, with the American flag floating majestically above us, were sworn in as cadets of the United States Military Academy. It was an impressive ceremony. As I looked up at our national colors and swore my allegiance, I realized humbly that *now I belonged to the flag*. It is a moment I have never forgotten."[22]

We should not dismiss sentiments like that expressed by Eisenhower simply because of the crudity that often accompanies the identification of the flag with the sacrifice of war. I think there is something profoundly right about the flag embodying the moral logic of the sacrifice of war.

The battle for Pork Chop Hill in the Korean War nicely illustrates the moral logic at the heart of war. Pork Chop Hill was a strategic point that controlled access to the Inchon valley, and in the course of the war it had changed hands many times. Late in the war the hill had been retaken by American troops, but at a terrible cost. By the end of the battle fewer than a dozen Americans were left on the top of the hill. This was in the last stages of the peace talks, and the Americans were afraid that if they withdrew the dozen men left on Pork Chop Hill, the retreat could be interpreted as a loss of the will to fight and could therefore prolong the war. They were sure the enemy would counterattack and the dozen left would be killed. Yet if the Americans reinforced the men left at the top of the hill, more than the twelve would be killed. There was a debate at division headquarters with the result that the twelve were reinforced, and the justification given for the decision was that if they had not done so it would have dishonored the memory of all the men who had died on Pork Chop Hill. The more sacrificed to honor past sacrifices, the more the moral stakes of the war (or battle) must be raised.[23]

---

made on our behalf. Think of the oft-made sentiment about those who have died in past wars: "We cannot allow them to have died in vain."

22. Ibid., 135. Marvin and Ingle quite rightly focus on the importance of the flag, but their case could have been made stronger if they had attended to the confusion in American churches between the cross and the flag. It is not uncommon for the flag to appear on church bulletins, particularly on the Fourth of July. There is even an anthem entitled the "Statue of Liberty,"which includes the lyrics, "I will honor our flag and trust in God, and the Statue of Liberty. . . . Oh, the Cross is my Statue of Liberty. It was there that my soul was set free. Unashamed I'll proclaim that a rugged cross is my Statue of Liberty, my liberty" (Kansas City, MO: Lillenas, 1974).

23. The necessity to raise the stakes for which a war is fought in order to do justice to the sacrifices made in the war is a troubling phenomenon for those committed to just war reflection. How do

In *He Came Preaching Peace*, John Howard Yoder wonders why it is so hard for political leaders to admit mistakes, to confess they were wrong. He asks, for instance, if it was necessary to withdraw American soldiers from Vietnam in 1975, or from Beirut in 1983, "Why can it not be admitted that it was wrong to send them there in the first place? Why can the statesman not afford to advocate peace without saying it must be 'with honor'? Why must the willingness to end the war be dulled or perhaps even denied by the demand that we must still seem to have won it?"[24] I think the answer to Yoder's perfectly sensible questions is quite simple: it is thought that to acknowledge a policy or a strategy was mistaken is to betray the sacrifices made by those who as a result of the policy died.

It is often observed that the first casualty of war is truth, but how do you tell the truth without betraying the sacrifice of those who accepted the terms of battle? War is a sacrificial system that creates its own justification. Hedges is right that war creates its own culture, but that it does so indicates the moral power of war. No doubt war creates a comradeship seldom found in other forms of life, but it does so because war subjects lives to sacrifices otherwise unavailable. That is the moral practice and power war *is*.

The Sacrifice of the Refusal to Kill

I think it is a mistake, however, to focus only on the sacrifice of life that war requires. War also requires that we sacrifice our normal unwillingness to kill. It may seem odd to call the sacrifice of our unwillingness to kill a "sacrifice," but I want to show that this sacrifice often renders the lives of those who make it unintelligible. The sacrifice of our unwillingness to kill is but the dark side of the willingness in war to be killed. Of course I am not suggesting that every

---

you keep war limited when it seems necessary to justify war using moral descriptions that can only make the war unlimited? This strikes me as particularly troubling for democratic societies in which the "real" reasons for going to war must be put in terms to justify citizen soldiers going to war.

In his extraordinary memoir of the war in the Pacific, William Manchester observes, "The longer the casualty lists—the vaster the investment in blood—the greater the need to justify the slain" (*Goodbye, Darkness: A Memoir of the Pacific War* [Boston: Little, Brown, 2002], 242). For a poignant, novelistic account of the need to prevent civilian populations from knowing of the horror of war in order to guard the sacrifice of the ordinary soldier, see Anne Perry, *Shoulder the Sky* (New York: Ballantine, 2004).

There has been insufficient investigation of the relation between democratic societies and just war requirements. George Weigel has recently called for the development of a "Catholic international relations theory" that is surely a step in the right direction. Weigel argues that such a theory must accept the "enduring reality of the nation-state system" and argues that the acceptance of such a system will not necessarily commit Catholics, and he also says American foreign policy, to a "realist" account of international relationships. And Weigel calls pacifists "naive" ("World Order: What Catholics Forgot," *First Things*, May 2004, 31–38).

24. John Howard Yoder, *He Came Preaching Peace* (Eugene, OR: Wipf and Stock, 1998), 138.

person who has killed in war suffers from having killed.[25] But I do believe that those who have killed without the killing troubling their lives should not have been in the business of killing in the first place.

In *On Killing: The Psychological Cost of Learning to Kill in War and Society*, Lt. Col. Dave Grossman reports on General S. L. A. Marshall's study of men in battle in the Second World War. Marshall discovered that of every hundred men along a line of fire during a battle, only fifteen to twenty would take part by firing their weapons. This led Marshall to conclude that the average or healthy individual, that is, the person who could endure combat, "still has such an inner and usually unrealized resistance toward killing a fellow man that he will not of his own volition take life if it is possible to turn away from that responsibility."[26]

Lt. Col. Grossman observes that to study killing in combat is very much like the study of sex. "Killing is a private, intimate occurrence of tremendous intensity, in which the destructive act becomes psychologically very much like the procreative act."[27] What, therefore, leads men to kill? Grossman suggests

25. It is equally true that those who return from war who have not killed may be deeply wounded both literally and figuratively. See, for example, Sara Corbett, "The Permanent Scars of Iraq," *New York Times Magazine*, February 15, 2004, 34–66.

26. Quoted in Lt. Col. Dave Grossman, *On Killing: The Psychological Cost of Learning to Kill in War and Society* (Boston: Little, Brown, 1995), 1. Grossman has a chapter that deals with those who are "natural soldiers," that is, they have the predisposition of a killer. He estimates that "those who like to kill" comprise no more than 2 percent of the military. He concludes: "Whether called sociopaths, sheepdogs, warriors, or heroes, they are there, they are a distinct minority, and in times of danger a nation needs them desperately" (185). Marshall's data has been challenged, but the crucial issue for my case is the "necessity" of training people to kill.

27. Ibid., 2. Reflecting on his returning to battle on Okinawa even though he had been wounded, William Manchester observes that his irrational act "was an act of love. Those men on the line were my family, my home. They were closer to me than I can say, closer than any friends had been or would be. They had never let me down. And I couldn't do it to them. I had to be with them, rather than let them die and me live with the knowledge that I might have saved them. Men, I now know, do not fight for flag or country, for the Marine Corps or glory or any other abstraction. They fight for one another. Any man in combat who lacks comrades who will die for him, or for whom he is willing to die is not a man at all. He is truly an animal" (*Goodbye, Darkness*, 391). In an extraordinary letter commenting on this chapter, my friend Fritz Oehlschlaeger observes,

> I suppose I wonder if it's as difficult for us to sacrifice our unwillingness to kill as you suggest. I found those quotes from General Marshall and Lt. Col. Grossman fascinating. If what they suggest is right, though, why, then, should war be so compelling? How does it square with the generally Darwinian image of ourselves we're almost inevitably disposed to adopt today—i.e., where we must, as successful survivors, view ourselves as the offspring of the apparently most efficient survivors (killers?) of the past? I notice all the accounts here of killing do stress its "private and intimate" quality (Grossman, Manchester, the powerful story of Harry Steward, etc.). But I wonder if that's the whole of the story; I wonder if the compelling quality of war resides precisely in the release from all that private inhibition. So that, in all the kinds of cases you cite, there is a tremendous psychological barrier to killing [it causes revulsion etc.], but it's the giving up of these internal restraints, the loss of oneself in the mass movement of force, the freedom to kill justifiably (or perhaps in

that what leads soldiers to kill is not the force of self-preservation but the power of another form of intimacy, that is, the accountability they feel with their comrades. Thus Richard Gabriel observes that "in military writings on unit cohesion, one consistently finds the assertion that the bonds combat soldiers form with one another are stronger than the bonds most men have with their wives."[28]

Because of the private nature of killing, Grossman found it was very difficult to get soldiers to talk about having killed. Many would take refuge in the impersonality of modern war, attributing most deaths to artillery or bombing. The same process seems to be at work in the attempt to depersonalize the enemy. Soldiers are often criticized for denying the enemy's humanity by calling the enemy names such as kraut, Jap, reb, gook, Yank, dink, slant, slope, or haji. Moreover, the enemy is not "killed" but knocked over, wasted, greased, taken out, mopped up, or lit up. But surely these attempts to depersonalize the enemy and rename the process of killing should be understood as a desperate effort to preserve the humanity of those who must kill. As Grossman observes, the dead take their misery with them, but the man who killed another must forever live and die with the one he killed. "The lesson becomes increasingly clear: Killing is what war is all about, and killing in combat, by its very nature, causes deep wounds of pain and guilt. The language of war helps us to deny what war is really about, and in doing so it makes war more palatable."[29]

Grossman's book reports conversations and interviews he has had with veterans who have killed. Often these reports include first a euphoria that they have survived followed by a overwhelming guilt that they have killed another human being. Often this guilt is so strong that the one who has killed is wracked by physical revulsion and vomiting.[30] For example, William Manchester, the historian, novelist, and WWII veteran, describes his assault on a sniper in a fishing shack who was picking off the Marines in his company one by one. Manchester was terrified, but he broke into the shack and found himself in an empty room. There was a door to another room he also broke down, momentarily fearing that in doing so the sniper would kill him. But it turned out the sniper was in a sniper harness, so he could not turn around fast enough. "He was entangled in the harness so I shot him with a .45 and I felt remorse and shame. I can remember whispering foolishly, 'I'm sorry'

some realm of war beyond good and evil where justifications no longer matter) that is the real source of the fascination and compelling quality of war.

28. Quoted in Grossman, *On Killing*, 149. The analogy between killing and sex invites the thought that mass killing in war is comparable to pornography. For if one of the conditions of pornography is its anonymous character, it is exactly the same kind of anonymity that characterizes much of the killing in modern war.

29. Ibid., 93.

30. Ibid., 115–16.

and then just throwing up . . . I threw up all over myself. It was a betrayal of what I'd been taught since a child."[31]

Particularly agonizing are the occasions when the enemy has been shot but does not instantly die. Harry Steward, a Ranger and U.S. Army master sergeant, tells of a remarkable incident during the Tet offensive in 1968, in which he and his men suddenly found themselves confronted by a "guy" firing right at them. Steward was wounded in the arm, but the men on each side of him were killed, so Steward charged with his M-16, mortally wounding the enemy. Steward reports that he can still see the man's eyes, as he was dying, looking at Steward with hate. Later as the flies began to swarm over the dying man, Steward covered him with a blanket and rubbed water onto his lips. The hard stare started to leave his eyes. He tried to talk, but he was too far gone. "I lit a cigarette, took a few puffs, and put it to his lips. He could barely puff. We each had a few drags and that hard look had left his eyes before he died."[32]

The pathos of such reports is how the very character of what is told isolates the teller. Killing creates a world of silence isolating those who have killed. One of the most poignant conversations Grossman reports took place in a VFW hall in Florida in 1989, where a Vietnam vet named Roger was talking about his experience in Vietnam. It was early in the afternoon, and down the bar an older woman began to attack him.

> "You got no right to snivel about your little piss-ant war. World War Two was a real war. Were you even alive then? *Huh*? I lost a brother in World War Two."
>
> We tried to ignore her; she was only a local character. But finally Roger had had enough. He looked at her and calmly, coldly said: "Have you ever had to kill anyone?"
>
> "Well no!" she answered belligerently.
>
> "Then what right have *you* got to tell *me* anything?"
>
> There was a long, painful silence throughout the VFW hall, as would occur in a home where a guest had just witnessed an embarrassing family argument.
>
> Then I asked quietly, "Roger, when you got pushed just now, you came back with the fact that you had to kill in Vietnam. Was that the worst of it for you?"
>
> "Yah," he said. "That's half of it."
>
> I waited for a very long time, but he didn't go on. He only stared into his beer. Finally I had to ask, "What was the other half?"
>
> "The other half was that when we got home, nobody understood."[33]

Grossman observes that if soldiers like Roger are to regain some sense of normality, they need to be reintegrated into society. Rituals of reentry, therefore,

31. In *Goodbye, Darkness*, Manchester describes why he had to write: "Abruptly the poker of memory stirs the ashes of recollection and uncovers a forgotten ember, still smoldering down there, still hot, still glowing, still red as red" (3–7).

32. Grossman, *On Killing*, 116–17.

33. Ibid., 249–50.

become extremely important to returning soldiers. Grossman suggests that those who have killed need to have constant praise and assurance from peers and superiors that they did the right thing. The awarding of medals becomes particularly important, because medals gesture to soldiers that what they did was right and that the community for which they fought is grateful. Medals indicate that their community of sane and normal people, people who do not normally kill, welcome them back into "normality."[34]

Grossman calls attention to Richard Gabriel's observation that "primitive societies" often require soldiers to perform purification rites before letting them rejoin the community.[35] Such rites often involve washing or other forms

34. Ibid., 272.

35. Of course one of those "primitive societies" was the church. Once even soldiers who had fought in "just wars" still had to confess and do penance before being allowed to partake of the Eucharist. See, for example, Bernard J. Verkamp, *The Moral Treatment of Returning Warriors in Early Medieval and Modern Times* (Scranton, PA: University of Scranton Press, 1993). In the same letter referred to above, Fritz Oehlschlaeger observes:

> Something you comment upon . . . reminds me of the (to me) most terrible moments of the Iliad. It concerns the observation by Richard Gabriel that primitive societies require soldiers to perform purification rites before rejoining the community. In Book X of the Iliad, Diomedes and Odysseus go on a mission in the night to discover what's going on in the Trojan camp and they run into a man, Dolon, who has been sent by Hektor to find out whether the Greek ships are guarded. Odysseus captures Dolon, who supplicates him; Odysseus, as I remember it, assures him he need not fear and then gets information from him about the camp, including some about splendid horses belonging to the Thracians who are sleeping nearby. Odysseus then kills Dolon, and he and Diomedes proceed to the Thracian camp, where Diomedes kills twelve of the men in their sleep, the resourceful Odysseus being careful to drag each out of the way as they're killed so that the horses do not step on the corpses after Diomedes and Odysseus take them. Diomedes kills the Thracian king and they leave just as the remaining Thracians are being aroused from sleep. After this particularly grisly and arguably not very honorable episode, Homer says of the two: 'And the men themselves waded into the sea and washed off the dense sweat from shin and shoulder and thigh. Afterwards when the surf of the sea had rinsed the dense-running sweat away from all their skin, and the inward heart had been cooled to refreshment, they stepped into the bathtubs smooth-polished, and bathed there, and after they had bathed and anointed themselves with olive oil they sat down to dine, and from the full mixing-bowl drawing the sweet-hearted wine poured out an offering to Athene' " (end of Book X, Lattimore's translation). I must say this always causes a visceral reaction in me. I've never actually vomited in response to it but that's distinctly the basic feeling I have. How are we to regard this? Is what's to be washed away merely sweat? What is the inward heart of Odysseus? What is it capable of? Does this ritual enable the killing they've just completed? How can they so easily be refreshed? How can they even consider eating? How can these apparently "civilized" practices (those "bathtubs smooth-polished") be related to, or integrated with, or dependent on, what has just occurred? What is a human being that he can resourcefully draw aside the dead as his companion kills them in their sleep and then sit down to dinner and wine?

I received Oehlschlaeger's letter before I read *Achilles in Vietnam: Combat Trauma and the Undoing of Character* (New York: Scribner's, 2003) by Jonathan Shay. Shay's book is an ongoing commentary on the experience of Vietnam through the interpretive lens of the *Iliad*. His account

of cleaning. Gabriel suggests the long voyage home on troop ships in WWII gave soldiers time to tell one another their stories and to receive support from one another. This process was reinforced by their being welcomed home by parades and other forms of celebration. Yet soldiers returning from Vietnam were flown home often within days and sometimes hours of their last combat. There were no fellow soldiers to greet them. There was no one to convince them of their own sanity. Unable to purge their guilt or to be assured they had acted rightly, they turned their emotions inward.[36]

I think it is a well attested fact that war veterans seldom want to talk about the experience of battle. The complex emotions of fear, the exhilaration danger produces, and the bonding between comrades make speaking of battle difficult. But how do you explain to another human being that you have killed? No doubt there are mechanisms that allow some to create an emotional distance between themselves and what they have done; but, at least if Grossman is right, men often remain haunted by their experience of having killed in a manner that can have—sometimes years later—destructive results.[37]

---

confirms many of the observations I make in this essay. In particular he stresses the importance of how "homecoming" is done for the continuing "health" of those who have killed.

36. Grossman, *On Killing*, 272–73. William Manchester notes that Navy nurses were rare in the Pacific, which resulted in the scuttlebutt that the Navy thought depraved Marines might rape them. He observed that the Marines "believed the story. We knew from our pony editions (small versions of American magazines) that there was some concern at home over how to handle trained killers like us when the war ended. One prominent New York clubwoman suggested that we be sent to a reorientation camp outside the States (she suggested the Panama Canal zone), and that when we were released there, we be required to wear an identification patch warning of our lethal instincts, like a yellow star" (*Goodbye, Darkness*, 273).

37. Grossman has a number of chapters in his book dealing with descriptions that allow the soldier to "explain" what they have had to do—e.g., "I was following orders," "He was killed by the group," "I was just doing my job." A recent letter reproduced by Deacon Stan Grenn in the *Jesus Journal* 88 (Spring 2004) makes for poignant reading.

> Dear Sir,
>
> For twenty-two years I have carried your picture in my wallet. I was only eighteen years old that day that we faced one another on that trail in Chu Lai, Vietnam. Why you did not take my life I'll never know. You stared at me for so long armed with your AK-47 and yet you did not fire. Forgive me for taking your life. I was reacting just the way I was trained, to kill V.C. or gooks, hell you weren't even considered a human, just a gook/target, one and the same.
>
> Since that day in 1967 I have grown a great deal and have a great deal of respect for life and other peoples of the world. So many times over the years I have stared at your picture and your daughter, I suspect. Each time my heart and guts would burn with the pain of guilt. I have two daughters myself now. One is twenty. The other one is twenty-two and has blessed me with two granddaughters, ages one and four.
>
> Today I visit the Vietnam Veterans Memorial in D. C. I have wanted to come here for several years now to say goodbye to many of my former comrades. Somehow I hope and believe they will know I'm here. I truly loved many of them, as I am sure you loved many of your former comrades.

To kill, in war or in any circumstance, creates a silence—and certainly it is right for silence to surround the taking of life. After all, the life taken is not ours to take. Those who kill, even when such killing is assumed to be legitimate, bear the burden that what they have done makes them "different." How do you tell the story of having killed? Killing shatters speech, ends communication, isolating us into different worlds whose difference we cannot even acknowledge. No sacrifice is more dramatic than the sacrifice asked of those sent to war, that is, the sacrifice of their unwillingness to kill. Even more cruelly, we expect those who have killed to simply return to "normality."[38]

The Sacrifice of Christ and the Sacrifices of War

Blood Sacrifice and the Nation, according to Marvin and Ingle, is a book about the religion of American patriotism. They acknowledge that nationalism is not usually considered a religion but claim that it shares with sectarian religions the worship of a killing authority, which they argue is central to religious practice and belief. According to Marvin and Ingle, that is why religions flourish when they are powerless and persecuted. As I noted in chapter 2, the authors then observe:

> As of today we are no longer enemies. I perceive you as a brave soldier defending his homeland. Above all else, I can now respect the importance that life held for you. I suppose that is why I am able to be here today.
>
> As I leave here today I leave your picture and this letter. It is time for me to continue the life process and release my pain and guilt. Forgive me Sir. I shall try to live my life to the fullest, an opportunity that you and many others were denied.
>
> I'll sign off now Sir, so until we chance to meet again in another time and place, rest in peace.

38. Manchester suffered a head wound, which means he was "never going to get the shattered pieces of remembrance just right. In addition [he] repressed what war memories [he did] have for so long that [he has] no way of knowing how distorted they are now" (*Goodbye, Darkness*, 194). Later Manchester says,

> It was somewhere on the slopes of that hill [Sugar Loaf on Okinawa] where I confronted the dark underside of battle, the passion died between me and the Marine Corps. The silver cord had been loosed, the golden bowl broken, the pitcher broken at the fountain, the wheel broken at the cistern. Half the evil in the world, I thought, is done in the name of honor. I now caught the jarring notes of the "Marine's Hymn"—which, after all, was a melody lifted from an obscure Offenbach operetta—and the tacky appeals to patriotism which lay behind the mass butchery on the islands. On Sugar Loaf, in short, I realized something within me, long ailing, had expired. Although I would continue to do the job, performing as the hired gun, I now knew that banners and words, ruffles and flourishes, bugles and drums, the whole rigmarole, eventually ended in squalor. (381–82)

This is why we so desperately need witnesses like William Manchester. We are just beginning to have those who have been in Iraq provide similar accounts. See, for example, Joseph Galloway's report as an officer of the actual experience of war in Iraq in his "Combat in Iraq: What's It Really Like?" *Durham Herald-Sun*, June 27, 2004, A13.

> In the religiously plural society of the United States, sectarian faith is optional for citizens, as everyone knows. Americans have rarely bled, sacrificed or died for Christianity or any other sectarian faith. Americans have often bled, sacrificed and died for their country. This fact is an important clue to its religious power. Though denominations are permitted to exist in the United States, they are not permitted to kill, for their beliefs are not officially true. What is really true in any society is what is worth killing for, and what citizens may be compelled to sacrifice their lives for.[39]

This is a sobering judgment, but one that cannot be ignored if Christians are to speak truthfully to ourselves and our neighbors about war. Contrary to Marvin and Ingle, however, I think Christians must insist that it is not what is worth killing for, but what is worth *dying* for that defines what a society really thinks is true. Indeed, I sometimes think that Christians became energetic killers because we were first willing to die rather than betray our faith. Yet Marvin and Ingle's claim that "what is worth killing for" points to "what is really true in any society" helps us see that the Christian alternative to war does not consist of having a more adequate "ethic" for conducting war.

No, the Christian alternative to war is worship. I am well known for the claim that the first task of the church is not to make the world more just, but to make the world the world. That claim is but a correlate of the assertion that the church does not *have* a social ethic, but *is* a social ethic. I am quite aware that such claims can lead to misunderstandings, but I think they are particularly useful in this context. The church does not so much have a plan or a policy to make war less horrible or to end war. Rather, the church is the alternative to the sacrifice of war in a war-weary world. The church is the end of war.

For example, consider these words from Augustine:

> It is we ourselves—we, his City—who are his best, his most glorious sacrifice. The mystic symbol of this sacrifice is celebrated in our oblations, familiar to the faithful. . . . It follows that justice is found where God, the one supreme God, rules an obedient City according to his grace, forbidding sacrifice to any being save himself alone; and where in consequence the soul rules the body in all men who belong to this City and obey God, and the reason faithfully rules the vices in a lawful system of subordination so that just as the individual righteous man lives on the basis of faith which is active in love, so the association, or people, of righteous men lives on the same basis of faith, active in love, the love with which a man loves God as God ought to be loved, and loves his neighbor as himself. But where this justice does not exist, there is certainly no "association of men united by a common sense of right and by a community of interest." Therefore there is no commonwealth; for where there is no "people," there is no "weal of the people."[40]

39. Marvin and Ingle, *Blood Sacrifice and the Nation*, 9.

40. Augustine, *City of God*, trans. Henry Bettenson (New York: Penguin, 1977), 889–90. Augustine's claims make clear that the aforementioned unity made possible by the spectacle of

The sacrifices of war are undeniable, but in the cross of Christ the Father has forever ended our attempts to sacrifice to God in terms set by the city of man. Christians have now been incorporated into Christ's sacrifice for the world so that the world no longer needs to make sacrifices for tribe or state, or even humanity. Constituted by the body and blood of Christ, we participate in God's kingdom so that the world may know that we, the church of Jesus Christ, are the end of sacrifice.[41] If Christians leave the Eucharistic table ready to kill one another, we not only eat and drink judgment on ourselves, but we rob the world of the witness it needs in order to know that there is an alternative to the sacrifices of war.

The silence that surrounds the taking of life in war is surely an indication, a judgment, that we were created to be at peace with one another and God. We were not created to kill one another, but to be in communion with one another. There is no more basic natural law than the prohibition against killing. When we kill, even when we kill in a just war, our bodies rebel. Yet that rebellion is a marker of hope. Christ has shattered the silence that surrounds those who have killed, because his sacrifice overwhelms our killing and restores us to a life of peace. Indeed we believe that it remains possible for those who have killed to be reconciled with those they have killed. This is no sentimental bonding represented by the comradeship of battle. This is the reconciliation made possible by the hard wood of the cross.

War is a mighty practice, a power, that destroys those ennobled by it.[42] We are fated to kill and be killed because we know no other way to live, but through the forgiveness made possible by the cross of Jesus we are no longer condemned to kill. A people have been created who refuse to resort to the sword, that they and those they love might not just survive, but live in the light of Christ's resurrection. The sacrifices of war are no longer necessary.

---

war (and anti-war) is really a false unity because it is founded on the injustice of established communities constituted by false sacrifices.

41. For those readers who may suspect I am underwriting a satisfaction theory of atonement, I need to say that is the last thing I want to do. Not only do I think there are deep difficulties with satisfaction theories (and it is disputable whether Anselm is appropriately associated with such theories), but even more importantly I think such "theories" wrongly separate the person and work of Christ. I am simply not convinced that Christians need an "atonement theory." For my reflection on these matters, see my *Cross-Shattered Christ* (Grand Rapids: Brazos, 2005). It is interesting that the view of Eucharistic sacrifice Strenski suggests intimates that after the Reformation, Catholic Eucharistic theology developed in ways that mirror Protestant sacrificial accounts of the atonement. See Strenski, *Contesting Sacrifice*, 12–51.

42. This sentence echoes Simone Weil's extraordinary essay, "The Iliad or the Poem of Force" (the whole essay can be found in *Revisions: Changing Perspectives in Moral Philosophy*, ed. Stanley Hauerwas and Alasdair MacIntyre [Notre Dame: University of Notre Dame Press, 1983], 222–48). Weil says, "Violence obliterates anybody who feels its touch. It comes to seem just as external to its employer as to its victim. And from this springs the idea of a destiny before which executioner and victim stand equally innocent, before which conquered and conqueror are brothers in the same distress. The conquered brings misfortune to the conqueror, and vice versa" (234).

We can now live free of the necessity of violence and killing. War and the sacrifices of war have come to an end. War has been abolished.[43]

43. In *He Came Preaching Peace*, Yoder observes that the gospel does not only imply an ethic of peacemaking, nor does it merely lead to a nonviolent lifestyle. Rather, the gospel proclaims a reconciled view of the world. Yoder calls attention to Phillips's translation of Ephesians 2:14–17, which reads: "Then he came and told both of you who were far from God (the outsiders, the Gentiles) and us who were near (the insiders, the Jews) that the war was over." Yoder comments: "That is the gospel—not that *war is sin*. That also is true, but alone it would not be the gospel. The gospel is that *the war is over*. Not merely that you *ought* to love your enemy. Not merely that if you have a 'born again experience,' some of your hateful feelings will go away and you maybe *can* love. Not merely that if you deal with your enemies lovingly enough, some of them will become friendly. All of that is true, but it is not the gospel. The gospel is that everyone being loved by God must be my beloved too, even if they consider me their enemy, even if their interests clash with mine" (54–55).

Alex Sider and Charlie Collier made invaluable criticisms and suggestions that have made this a better essay.

6

C. S. Lewis and Violence

Lewis and War

Many people are Christians because of the work of C. S. Lewis. By reading Lewis they discover, as he had, that what Christians believe is "it had really happened once."[1] With wit and wisdom Lewis imaginatively exploded the hollow pretensions of the secular. More, he helped many for the first time see the world in the light of "it had really happened once." Through wonderful, imaginative feats he created a magic that has encouraged many to trust God's kingdom of love.

Because he has such a devoted following, it is not easy to criticize Lewis. Yet I must write critically of his views concerning violence and war, since I am a pacifist and Lewis was anything but a pacifist.[2] I will try to demonstrate below that his arguments against pacifism are inadequate, but I also want to suggest that he provides creative resources that could help Christians to imagine a very different form of Christian nonviolence, a form unknown to Lewis, with which I hope he might have had some sympathy.

Before turning to Lewis's arguments against pacifism, I think it important to set the context for his more formal reflections on war by calling attention to Lewis's experience of war. Lewis fought in WWI and endured WWII. It never occurred to him that there was an alternative to war. War was simply a fact of

1. C. S. Lewis, *Surprised by Joy: The Shape of My Early Life* (London: Harcourt, 1955), 224.

2. He even wrote a famous essay explaining why he was not a pacifist: C. S. Lewis, "Why I Am Not a Pacifist," in *The Weight of Glory* (San Francisco: Harper, 1980), 64–90.

life—and this assertion was, for Lewis, not only an empirical generalization but a claim about the way things necessarily are. For Lewis war was a reality we must accept if we are to be rational.

Lewis, however, was anything but a war enthusiast. He tells us in *Surprised by Joy: The Shape of my Early Life* that as a student he began to realize he would probably have to go to war when he reached military age. Though he was Irish, and thus not subject to conscription, he decided when he reached military age he would allow himself to be drafted. Having made that fateful decision, he thought himself absolved from undertaking any further rational analysis of the war.

He knew some might consider such an attitude to be a flight from reality, but he thought of it as a "treaty with reality." It was as if, as he puts it, he was saying to his country, "You shall have me on a certain date, not before. I will die in your wars if need be, but till then I shall live my own life. You may have my body but not my mind. I will take part in battles but not read about them."[3] He acknowledged that the quality that allowed him to adopt such an attitude was "somewhat repellant," but he did not regret escaping the appalling waste of time and spirit involved in reading news of the war.

Lewis was conscripted and became a second lieutenant in the Somerset Light Infantry. In November 1917, around his nineteenth birthday, he found himself on the front in France, near the village of Arras. Since he was averse to being part of any "collective," Lewis was surprised to discover that he did not dislike the army as much as he thought he might. Not that he did not find life in the army detestable and war at best an "odious necessity"—but Lewis appreciated the honest recognition by all concerned that you were not supposed to like the army or war. War was a tribulation, but it was a tribulation that was bearable because it did not disguise itself as a pleasure.[4]

Lewis was, of course, lucky to have survived. Soon after arriving at the front he contracted "trench fever," which required hospitalization. He spent a delightful three weeks in a hospital in Le Treport, which gave him the opportunity to read a volume of G. K. Chesterton's essays, and then returned to the front only to be wounded by shrapnel in April 1918. Lewis's war had come to an end after he served for just three and a half months. However, he would not forget the eleven thousand British soldiers buried in a cemetery in Etaples not far from where he served.[5]

Like many who survived WWI, Lewis had no time for the glorification of war. He "came to know and pity and reverence" the ordinary men with whom he served, and had a particular fondness for his sergeant, a man named Ayres, who was killed by the same shell that wounded Lewis. Sergeant Ayers became

3. Lewis, *Surprised by Joy*, 158.

4. Ibid., 188.

5. Alan Jacobs, *The Narnian: The Life and Imagination of C. S. Lewis* (San Francisco: HarperSanFrancisco, 2006), 72.

"almost a father" to Lewis, and he credits Ayres with saving him from bad judgments and turning his ridiculous and painful position as a lieutenant into something beautiful.[6]

But the fact that war is capable of producing such close relationships does not mean that Lewis was ever tempted to think war a "good thing." In an extraordinarily moving passage, he reports that the horror of war—"the smashed men still moving like half-crushed beetles, the sitting or standing corpses, the landscape of sheer earth without a blade of grass, the boots worn day and night till they seemed to grow to your feet"—felt so cut off from the rest of experience that it seemed to be something happening to someone else. As a result, the horror of war could grow faint in memory.[7] Lewis, however, was able to remember the horror because of an "imaginative moment" that occurred early in his experience of war, a moment that seemed more real than all that followed. It was the first bullet he heard, which he said "whined"—as a journalist or poet might describe it. At that moment there was something not exactly like fear, even less like indifference, but rather a "little quavering signal that said, 'This is War. This is what Homer wrote about.' "[8]

As WWII neared, Lewis could be quite impatient with those who had forgotten the horror of war. In 1939 he heard a priest pray, "Prosper, O Lord, our righteous cause," and in a letter to his brother Lewis reports that as he left the church he reproved the priest for "the audacity of informing God that our cause was righteous . . . a point on which He may have his own view. . . . I hope it is quite like ours, of course: but you never know with him."[9]

Lewis often avoided exposing his "subjectivity," and he feared that *Surprised by Joy* may be "suffocatingly subjective." But in a letter occasioned by the approach of WWII, he confessed that his memories of the last war had haunted his dreams for years. War and military service, he observed, "includes the threat of every temporal evil, pain and death, which is what we fear from sickness; isolation from what we love, which is what we fear from exile; toil under arbitrary master, which is what we fear from slavery. . . . I am not a pacifist. If it has got to be it's got to be. But the flesh is weak and selfish, and I think death would be much better than to live through another war."[10]

6. Lewis, *Surprised by Joy*, 195.

7. Ibid., 196.

8. Ibid.

9. David Downing uses this quote from Lewis's letter to his brother (*Letters of C. S. Lewis*, ed. Walter Hooper [London: Harper Collins, 1988] 324–25) in his "Neither Patriot Nor Pacifist, but 'Patient': C. S. Lewis on War and Peace," C. S. Lewis Institute, 2006, available at http://www.cslewisinstitute.org/cslewis/downing_patient.htm. In his sermon "Learning in War-Time," Lewis explicitly says, "I believe our cause to be, as human causes go, very righteous, and I therefore believe it to be a duty to participate in this war. And every duty is a religious duty, and our obligation to perform every duty is therefore absolute" (*Weight of Glory*, 52–53).

10. Downing is quoting from Lewis's *Letters*, 320. There is a passage in "Why I Am Not a Pacifist" that is almost identical to this passage from his letters. The difference is that Lewis observes

The complexity of Lewis's attitude toward the war is made explicit in *The Screwtape Letters*. Lewis, for example, has Screwtape warn Wormwood against thinking that the European war is necessarily good for their cause. To be sure the war will involve a good deal of cruelty and unchastity, but the war will also lead many to have their attention diverted from themselves to values and causes higher than the self. Screwtape observes that "the Enemy" (that is, God) may disapprove of many of those values and causes, but war at least has the benefit from the Enemy's perspective of reminding humans that they are not going to live forever.[11]

Nor should Wormwood, Screwtape advises, rely too much on the generalized hatred the war engenders against Germans. The English, who at one moment say that torture is too good for their enemies, turn out to be more than willing to give tea and cigarettes to the first German pilot who turns up at their door after they have shot him down.[12] Far more promising is to encourage those faced with war to identify their patriotism or pacifism with their faith in God. Once Christians confuse their faith with their stance toward the war, Screwtape suggests, they will completely confuse the "cause" with faith in God. This is particularly useful when dealing with pacifists because they will be tempted to identify ending the war with Christianity, thereby forgetting we have another destiny.[13]

Lewis considered war to be horrible, but not the worst thing that could happen. He argues that to kill or to be killed in war is not murder. Rather, war is a species of punishment that may require our death or the death of the enemy, but we cannot hate those we kill or enjoy that which we must do in war. He even suggests that if in WWI some young German and he had simultaneously killed one another, the moment after their death neither of them "would have felt resentment or even any embarrassment. I think we might have laughed over it."[14]

During Lewis's time there was little discussion of the conditions necessary to make a war just. He was, however, a student of Thomas Aquinas and Richard Hooker and could not help, therefore, but have some understanding of what makes a war just. Throughout his discussions of war there are hints that he thought a just war should be a last resort, declared by a lawful authority, a defensive rather than an imperialistic endeavor, and that in a just war, the aims of the war are limited, there is some chance of success, and there is

in "Why I Am Not a Pacifist" that war "threatens *every* temporal evil—every evil except dishonour and final perdition, and those who bear it like it no better than you would like it" (89).

11. C. S. Lewis, *The Screwtape Letters*, rev. ed. (New York: Collier, 1961), 25–26. Lewis regarded cruelty as more evil than lust even though the world tends to concentrate on the latter (*Surprised by Joy*, 109).

12. Lewis, *Screwtape Letters*, 30.

13. Ibid., 35.

14. C. S. Lewis, *Mere Christianity* (San Francisco: Harper, 2001), 119.

a willingness of the combatants to take responsibility for their actions so that civilians are properly protected. But just as important for Lewis, as is clear from his description of the laugh he and the German soldier could share, was his hope that at the end of a war mercy and reconciliation would be possible.

Darrell Cole argues, therefore, that informing Lewis's understanding of war was an understanding of the kind of person necessary to make a war just. Too often, Cole observes, advocates of just war forget that those who would sustain a war that would be just must have a particular set of virtues.[15] Lewis rightly thought that only a just people would be capable of fighting a just war. His ideal was the knight—"the Christian in arms for the defense of a good cause"—who could go to war "fierce to the nth degree and meek to the nth degree."[16] Such a person recognizes that it is not war that threatens our salvation, but our lack of confidence in God's promise of salvation.

The perspective Lewis brought to his engagement with pacifism—"If it has got to be it's got to be"—is at the heart of how he understood moral rationality. His argument against pacifism nicely illustrates that contention.

Why Lewis Was Not a Pacifist

"Why I Am Not a Pacifist" was a talk Lewis gave sometime in 1940 to a pacifist society in Oxford.[17] In the essay, Lewis develops his most considered case for the "facticity" of war by first making clear how he understands the character of moral reason in general. He thus begins by asking, "How do we decide what is good or evil?"[18]

The usual answer to that question, Lewis observes, involves some appeal to the conscience; but this does not resolve the matter because conscience can be changed by argument. Argument is but another name for reason, which, according to Lewis, involves three main elements: (1) the reception of facts about which to reason, (2) the simple and intuitive act of perceiving self-evident truths, and (3) the art and skill of "arranging the facts so as to yield a series of such intuitions which linked together produce a proof of the truth or falsehood of the propositions we are considering" (65–66).

Lewis suggests that correcting error in our reasoning involves the first and third elements. Particularly important is the role authority plays in the reception of facts, because most of what we reliably believe is based on authority.

15. Darrell Cole, "C. S. Lewis on Pacifism, War, and the Christian Warrior," *Touchstone*, April 2003, 48.

16. C. S. Lewis, "Letter," in *Theology* 27 (May 1939), 373–74. The internal quote is from *Mere Christianity*, 119.

17. We do not have a copy of the original, so we are fortunate that Lewis gave a copy to his friend, George Sayer. Walter Hooper, introduction to Lewis, *Weight of Glory*, 18.

18. Lewis, "Why I Am Not a Pacifist," 64. References to this essay will appear in the text.

We are right to rely on the authority of our common sense because it reflects a law that constitutes our nature, a law that we did not need to be taught. Thus Lewis believed that we rightly think the idea of decent behavior is obvious to everyone. That does not mean that there are not differences between moralities but that such differences have never amounted to anything like a total difference.[19]

Lewis will, therefore, base his case against pacifism on the natural law he thinks is enshrined in the common conscience of our humanity. He is quite clear that all three elements of reason are also found in the conscience, but believes the inarguable intuitions of the conscience are much more likely to be corrupted by the passions in matters of good and evil than in questions of truth and falsehood. That is why authority is so important for checking and superseding our grasp of the facts (68–69). Our judgments as to right and wrong are a mixture of inarguable intuitions and arguable processes of reasoning or submission to authority. Accordingly, nothing is to be treated as an intuition unless it is such that no good man has ever dreamed of doubting it (70).

Therefore Lewis rules out any pacifist presumption that their disavowal of killing can be based on an intuition that taking life is always wrong. A person may think they should not kill by appealing to an authority, but not to an intuition. The former are open to argument but the latter are not. A pacifist who would base his position on an intuition is simply someone who has excommunicated himself from the human race (71). Lewis does not think, however, that most pacifists base their position on intuitive grounds.

He therefore begins systematically to characterize and then critique the arguments he understands pacifists to make. He begins by observing that everyone agrees that war is very disagreeable, but pacifists seem to hold the view that wars do more harm than good. Lewis argues that such a view is speculative, making it impossible to know what might count as evidence for such a conclusion. He happily concedes that rulers often promise more than they should, but that is no argument that no good comes from war (73–74). In fact Lewis asserts that history is full of both useful and useless wars.

The pacifist case also seems to be committed to the idea that we can do good to and for some without harming others. But according to "the law of beneficence," as Lewis calls it, doing good means that we cannot avoid showing preference to some over others. It is certainly true, Lewis acknowledges, that the lesser violence and harm is to be preferred, but that does not mean that killing *x* or *y* is always wrong or can be avoided (76).

Lewis also argues against the pacifist notion that war is always a greater evil. Such a view, he argues, seems to imply a materialistic ethic, which understands death and pain to be the greatest evils—but surely Christians cannot

19. Lewis, *Mere Christianity*, 5–6.

believe that. Only people parasitic on liberal societies can afford to be pacifists, believing as they do that the miseries of human suffering can be eliminated if we just find the right cures. Lewis contends that it is a mistake to think we can eradicate suffering; rather we must "work quietly away at limited objectives such as the abolition of the slave trade, or prison reform, or factory acts, or tuberculosis," rather than think that we "can achieve universal justice, or health, or peace" (79).

The pacifist case, furthermore, cannot be made by appeals to authority. The special human authority that should command our conscience, Lewis argues, is that of the society to which we belong. That society has decided the issue against pacifism through figures such as Arthur and Alfred, Elizabeth and Cromwell, Walpole and Burke. Even the literature of his country—represented by *Beowulf*, Shakespeare, Johnson, and Wordsworth—stands against the pacifists. Lewis concedes that the authority of England is not final, but because its citizens are indebted to their country by birth, upbringing, and education, national authority works against the pacifist (80–81).[20]

Not only the authority of England but the authority of all humanity is against the pacifist. To be a pacifist means one must part company with Homer, Virgil, Plato, Aristotle, Cicero, and Montaigne, with the sagas of Iceland and Egypt. Those who would appeal to human progress to dismiss such voices, Lewis simply dismisses as hopeless. He is willing, however, to argue with those who would dismiss human authority on grounds of divine authority (82).

Those who defend pacifism using divine authority do so almost exclusively by appeal to certain sayings of our Lord. But, according to Lewis, they pass over the authority of the Thirty-Nine Articles, Thomas Aquinas, and St. Augustine—for each of these authorities thought it lawful for Christians at the command of the magistrates to serve in wars. The whole pacifist case, therefore, rests on a doubtful interpretation of the dominical saying "Resist not evil: but whosoever shall smite thee on thy right cheek, turn to him the other also" (Matt. 5:39 KJV).

Lewis acknowledges the possibility of a pacifist interpretation of this text given that it seems to impose a duty of nonresistance on all men in all circumstances (85). He argues that the text means what it says but with an understood reservation of obvious exceptions that the hearer would understand without being told. Thus, for example, confronted by a homicidal maniac attempting murder against a third party, we must come to the aid of the innocent (86). According to Lewis, our Lord simply did not think that his call not to resist evil would apply to those with the duty to protect the public good. How otherwise could we explain Jesus's praise of the Roman centurion?

20. In "Learning in War-Time," Lewis observes, "A man may have to die for our country, but no man must, in any exclusive sense, live for his country" (53).

Lewis ends his case against pacifism by acknowledging that moral decisions do not admit of certainty, so there is a chance that pacifism may be right. But he concludes: "it seems to me very long odds, longer odds than I would care to take with the voice of almost all humanity against me" (90).

Why Lewis Should Have Been a Pacifist

I have spelled out Lewis's arguments against pacifism not only in an effort to be fair to him but because he gives voice to what many assume are the knock-down arguments against any account of Christian nonviolence. I hope to show, however, that his case against pacifism is not persuasive. It is unconvincing first and foremost because he made little effort to understand the most defensible forms of Christian pacifism.

As far as one can tell from his text, he seems to think pacifism can be equated with a general disavowal of war. Pacifism is, of course, a stance against war, but how that stance is shaped by more constitutive practices makes all the difference. Lewis seems to have understood pacifism by way of its liberal forms, which view war as so horrible that it has to be wrong. Liberal pacifists often, as Lewis's critique presupposes, thought war must be some kind of mistake or the result of a conspiracy, because no right-thinking human being can believe war to be "good." Such a view may seem naive, but it was a very common position held by many after WWI.[21] Lewis, therefore, had a far too easy target for his critique of pacifism.

What Lewis does not consider—an avoidance that I fear touches the heart of not only his understanding of pacifism but of his account of reason and Christianity—is that Christian nonviolence does not derive from any one dominical saying, but from the very character of Jesus's life, death, and resurrection. John Howard Yoder identifies this Christological nonviolence as the pacifism of the messianic community. Christian nonviolence must be embodied in a community that is an alternative to the world's violence. Accordingly, Jesus's authority is not expressed only in his teachings or his spiritual depth, but in "the way he went about representing a new moral option in Palestine, at the cost of his death."[22] Christians are nonviolent, therefore, not because we believe that nonviolence is a strategy to rid the world of war, but because nonviolence is constitutive of what it means to be a disciple of Jesus.

To be sure, such an account of nonviolence draws on an eschatological understanding of the relation of the church to the world, an account that is foreign to Lewis's theology. Lewis, as is clear from his appeal to common

21. There are, of course, diverse forms of liberal pacifism. John Howard Yoder provides an extraordinarily helpful analysis of different forms of pacifism in his *Nevertheless: Varieties of Religious Pacifism* (Scottdale, PA: Herald, 1992).

22. Yoder, *Nevertheless*, 134.

sense, assumes a strong identification between what it means to be a Christian and what it means to be a human being. Throughout his work Lewis emphasized the difference being a Christian makes for belief in God, but how he understood that difference did not shape his thinking about war. I think he failed to draw out the implications of his theological convictions for war because of his conviction that a natural-law ethic was sufficient to shape how we should think about war.

Lewis's flatfooted interpretation of "resist not evil" nicely illustrates his inability to recognize the difference Christ makes for the transformation of our "reason." He dismisses any readings of the Matthew passage that might be constructed through historical criticism, because he has learned as a scholar of literature that such methods are no way to read a text (88). But Lewis's suggestion that those hearing Jesus's words were "private people in a disarmed nation" and, therefore, would have not thought "our Lord to be referring to war" is as nice an example as one could wish for the kind of speculative reading sometimes associated with historical criticism (86–87).

Lewis's account of practical reason in "Why I Am Not a Pacifist" drew on his general view that "prudence means practical common sense, taking the trouble to think out what you are doing and what is likely to come of it."[23] The problem is not in his account of the three elements of reason, but rather in his failure to see how reason and conscience must be transformed by the virtues. Such a view seems odd given his claim that though every moral judgment involves facts, intuitions, and reasoning, regard for authority commensurate with the virtue of humility is also required (71–72). That seems exactly right, but then I cannot help but wonder why Lewis does not include the lives of the martyrs as authorities for the shaping of Christian practical reason.

In "Learning in War-Time" Lewis observes that before he became a Christian he did not realize his life after conversion would consist in doing most of the same things he had done prior to his conversion. He hopes he is doing things in a new spirit, but they are still the same things.[24] There is wisdom in what he says because we believe that Christians are to embody the way of life that God intended for all of humanity. Therefore there is some continuity between the natural moral virtues and the theological virtues; but Lewis is wrong to think what he is doing is "the same thing" he used to do, because what he does as a Christian is part of a different narrative.

Pacifists, at least pacifists shaped by Christological convictions, can agree with most of the arguments Lewis makes in "Why I Am Not a Pacifist." We have no stake in arguments that try to ground pacifism on an immediate intuition that the killing of a human being is an absolute evil. We believe, however, that we were not created to kill, so we will not be surprised if non-Christians

23. Lewis, *Mere Christianity*, 77

24. Lewis, "Learning in War-Time," 51.

also find pacifism to be rational. But Christian pacifism does not appeal to such intuitions for its justification.

Nor is Christian pacifism grounded in claims about the "disagreeable" character of war. Any serious moral conviction may entail disagreeable consequences—so Lewis is quite right that we simply cannot know whether wars do more harm than good. Even after rightly naming the speculative character of questions concerning the good or bad results of war, Lewis states his belief that history is full of useful wars (74). I assume, however, that he does not mean that observation to be a justification for war. For if he did so it would have the same speculative character that he rightly criticized the pacifist for assuming.

Lewis is quite right, moreover, to criticize liberal pacifists for underwriting the presumption that death and pain are the greatest evils we encounter. Indeed, Christological pacifism is determined by the conviction that there is much for which it is worth dying. In particular, those shaped by the presumptions of Christological pacifism assume it is better to die than to kill. Lewis is quite right, therefore, to remind us in "Learning in War-Time" that we face death every day, and wartime is no exception. The only difference war makes is to help us remember we are destined to die.[25]

Pacifists also have no reason to disagree with Lewis's concern that the innocent be protected from homicidal maniacs—but there are nonviolent alternatives to protect innocent people from unjust attack. It is, moreover, quite a logical leap from using force to stop a homicidal maniac to justifying war. At best Lewis has given a justification for the police function of governing authorities. But war is essentially a different reality than the largely peaceable work of the police.

Lewis's strongest argument against pacifism is quite simply that war is a "fact" of life. We cannot imagine a world without war. How would we have the resources to read Homer, Virgil, Plato, or Montaigne if we have disavowed war? War must remain a permanent possibility because without war we will lack the resources to sustain lives of gallantry. Michael Ward, I think, excellently sums up Lewis's most determinative position about war by characterizing Lewis's basic view as the attempt to sustain an ethic of chivalry. Lewis well knew that the innocent suffer in war, but you cannot alleviate the suffering of the peasant by banishing the knight.[26]

Lewis's view of the imaginative power of war for making our lives morally significant should not be dismissed lightly. I suspect that such an account of war is what compels many to think it unthinkable to disavow war. Yet I also believe that the gospel, as Lewis often argued, requires us to think the

25. Ibid., 62.

26. Michael Ward, *Planet Narnia: The Seven Heavens in the Imagination of C. S. Lewis* (Oxford: Oxford University Press, 2008), 95.

unthinkable by refusing to think that the way things are is the way things have to be. To conceive a world without war is the kind of imaginative challenge befitting a mind like that of Lewis.

Lewis was also quite right to suggest that we do much better working away at limited objectives than trying to eliminate evil qua evil. Christian nonviolence believes war has been ended, making it possible for Christians in a world of war to do the small and simple things that make war less likely. So the refusal to go to war is the necessary condition to force us to consider possibilities that would not otherwise exist.

In his wonderful sermon "Learning in War-Time," Lewis struck a note for a Christian understanding of nonviolence by insisting that war does not create a new situation of crisis to which all activities must be subordinated. War should not prevent students from pursuing knowledge, from recognizing beauty, from trying to see that God is working for peace. The intellectual life, Lewis observes, may not be the only road to God, nor the safest, but it is the road the student has been given. Failure to take that road makes war more likely.[27] He encourages students who must begin their work in a time of war not to worry about having time to finish. According to Lewis, "a more Christian attitude . . . is that of leaving futurity in God's hands. We may as well, for God will certainly retain it whether we leave it to Him or not."[28] Such a stance, though, could instead provide the patience to sustain the work of nonviolence.

The *Chronicles of Narnia* are war-determined stories, and I do not think Lewis could have written well or truthfully if he had tried to avoid the reality of war. Christians are, after all, in a battle with "the enemy," and Lewis rightly wanted Christians to recognize that we live in a dangerous world—a world all the more dangerous because we are Christians. I wish, however, that Lewis had imagined what it might have meant for the conflicts in the *Chronicles of Narnia* to have been fought nonviolently.

There are some hints that Lewis's imagination could see alternatives to war. Consider, for example, the story of Reepicheep in *Prince Caspian*.[29] Reepicheep may seem like an unlikely source for support of nonviolence. This honor-obsessed mouse is one of Lewis's most militaristic creations in the most war-centered book of the *Narnia Chronicles*. But it is just here that we meet the possibility of an "imaginative moment." After the great battle in which he has fought bravely, Reepicheep, who has had his wounds healed by Lucy, bows before Aslan. In the process he discovers, because he has difficulty keeping his balance, that he has lost most of his tail. He is confounded, explaining to Aslan that "a tail is the honor and glory of a mouse," which prompts Aslan to

27. Lewis, "Learning in War-Time," 57.

28. Ibid., 61.

29. C. S. Lewis, *Prince Caspian: The Return to Narnia* (London: Geoffrey Bles, 1960).

say: "I have sometimes wondered, friend, whether you do not think too much of your honor." Reepicheep defends himself by noting that, given their small size, if mice did not guard their dignity some might take advantage of them. But what moves Aslan is that all the other mice have drawn their swords to cut off their tails so that they will "not bear the shame of wearing an honor which is denied to the High Mouse."[30]

Aslan restores Reepicheep's tail, not for the sake of his dignity, but "for the love that is between you and your people, and still more for the kindness your people showed me long ago when you ate away the cords that bound me on the Stone Table."[31] Surely such love and service is at the heart of the gifts God has given that make possible an alternative to violence.[32] I believe Lewis, a man of war, could see that.

30. Ibid., 209.

31. Ibid.

32. Michael Ward provides a wonderful analysis of *Prince Caspian* in his book *Planet Narnia*, 93–99. He interprets Aslan's response to Reepicheep primarily as a rebuke, suggesting that "martyrdom, not knighthood, is the summit of Martial achievement and contains no worldly dignity or honor, only crucifixion-like shame that must be 'despised' (Heb. 12:2). In *Prince Caspian* Lewis gives us three martyrs, that is, three characters who witness to the truth and suffer for it: Caspian's Nurse, Dr. Cornelius, and Lucy Pevensie" (97).

7

Martin Luther King Jr. and Christian Nonviolence

How King Became Nonviolent

John Howard Yoder delivered thirteen lectures in 1983 designed to introduce Catholics in Poland to Christian nonviolence. He began the first lecture, "The Heritage of Nonviolent Thought and Action," with this observation:

> One of the most original cultural products of our century is our awareness of the power of organized nonviolent resistance as an instrument in the struggle for justice. One characteristic of this instrument is that its operation is often informal and decentralized. By the nature of the case it does not create institutions of great visible power. Therefore it is not easy for the historians to take account of, as they can tell the stories of military battles and the changing of regimes. Even those who see happening some of the visible phenomena of nonviolent action are often not sufficiently aware of the history behind them to recognize that this phenomenon is not an oddity or an accident, but the product of a religious and cultural historical development.[1]

I begin with Yoder's observation for two reasons. First, I hope to show that Martin Luther King's journey to nonviolence—a journey in which he was forced by circumstances to forge a remarkable understanding of nonviolence—is of

1. John Howard Yoder, *Nonviolence—A Brief History: The Warsaw Lectures*, ed. Paul Martens, Matthew Porter, and Myles Werntz (Waco: Baylor University Press, 2010), 17.

lasting significance. In particular, as Yoder goes on to suggest in these lectures, King found the means to wed nonviolent resistance to the search for justice, which belies the assumption by many that if you are committed to nonviolence, you must abandon attempts to achieve justice. Yoder's positive appreciation of King's (and Gandhi's) achievement, moreover, makes clear that Yoder's Christological pacifism and King's Gandhian campaign of nonviolent resistance are not, as many assume, in principle incompatible.[2]

Secondly, I think Yoder is right to suggest that the difficulty historians have in telling the story of nonviolence is one of the reasons many assume that there is no alternative to violence[3]—which makes it all the more important how King's story is told. For as Vincent Harding has argued, the price for a national holiday to honor a black man increasingly seems to be a national amnesia designed to hide from us who that black man really was.[4] In particular Harding suggests the last years of King's life, in which he campaigned against the war in Vietnam as well as on behalf of the poor, are too often forgotten. King's commitment to nonviolence, his controversial decision to oppose the war in Vietnam, and his concern for the poor were for him inseparable.

King's understanding as well as his commitment to nonviolence was hewn in the midst of conflict. Bernard Rustin, who helped King in the early stages of the Montgomery boycott to better understand Gandhi, observes:

> I do not believe that one honors Dr. King by assuming that somehow he had been prepared for this job. He had not been prepared for it: either tactically, strategically, or his understanding of nonviolence. The remarkable thing is that he came to a profoundly deep understanding of nonviolence through the struggle itself, and through reading and discussions which he had in the process of carrying on the protest. As he began to discuss nonviolence, as the newspapers throughout the country began to describe him as one who believed in nonviolence, he automatically took himself seriously because other people were taking him seriously.[5]

2. In the third of the Poland lectures, "The Lessons of the Nonviolent Experience," Yoder makes clear his admiration for King, noting that "there is no such thing as one nonviolent strategy to be used for liberation anywhere and everywhere. The essence of nonviolent action includes charismatic creativity. It needs prophetic insight into timing and symbolism which is more like the artist than the strategist. It demands precise analysis of social systems that is more like the sociologist than the ideologue. Nonetheless it is possible to say that in the labors of King we have seen the maturity or the roundedness of an understanding of nonviolent liberation which could illuminate and give direction in other cultures for ways to work in favor of other causes" (*Nonviolence*, 46).

3. See, for example, Linda Hogan, Enda McDonagh, and Stanley Hauerwas, "The Case for the Abolition of War in the Twenty-First Century," *Journal of the Society of Christian Ethics* 25 (2005): 17–31.

4. Vincent Harding, *Martin Luther King: The Inconvenient Hero* (Maryknoll, NY: Orbis, 1996), 60.

5. Rustin's comment is from Stewart Burns, *To the Mountaintop: Martin Luther King Jr.'s Sacred Mission to Save America: 1955–1968* (San Francisco: HarperSanFrancisco, 2004), 81.

Rustin rightly suggests that King's understanding of nonviolence was, so to speak, always a work in progress, but that is why Yoder rightly insists that King forged an account of nonviolence from which we have much to learn. King was not a philosopher, but ideas were important to him. He made use of ideas from sources many might think incompatible, but by doing so he exemplified a complex understanding of nonviolence that offers an alternative to the assumption that we must choose between using violence in the name of political responsibility or being nonviolent but politically irresponsible.

In *Stride toward Freedom: The Montgomery Story*, King provides a wonderfully candid account of the diverse influences that shaped his understanding of nonviolence. He reports that as a college student he was moved when he read Thoreau's essay on *Civil Disobedience*.[6] Thoreau convinced him that anyone who passively accepts evil, even oppressed people who cooperate with an evil system, are as implicated with evil as those who perpetrate it. Accordingly, if a righteous man is to be true to his conscience and true to God, he has no alternative but to refuse to cooperate with an evil system. In the early stages of the boycott of the buses in Montgomery, King drew on Thoreau to help him understand why the boycott was the necessary response to a system of evil.

Thoreau was not the only resource King had to draw on. He had heard A. J. Muste speak when he was a student at Crozer, but while he was deeply moved by Muste's account of pacifism, he continued to think that war, though never a positive good, might be necessary as an alternative to a totalitarian system.[7] During his studies at Crozer he also traveled to Philadelphia to hear a sermon by Dr. Mordecai Johnson, the president of Howard University, who had just returned from a trip to India. Dr. Johnson spoke of the life and times of Gandhi so eloquently that King subsequently bought and read books on or by Gandhi. The influence of Gandhi, however, was qualified by his reading of Reinhold Niebuhr and in particular *Moral Man and Immoral Society*. Niebuhr's argument that there is no intrinsic moral difference between violent and nonviolent resistance left King in a state of confusion.[8]

King's doctoral work made him more critical of what he characterizes as Niebuhr's overemphasis on the corruption of human nature. Indeed, King observes that Niebuhr had not balanced his pessimism concerning human nature with an optimism concerning divine nature.[9] But King's understanding of and commitment to nonviolence were finally not the result of these intellectual struggles. No doubt his philosophical and theological work served

6. Martin Luther King Jr., *Stride toward Freedom: The Montgomery Story* (San Francisco: HarperSanFrancisco, 1958), 51.

7. Ibid., 95.

8. Ibid., 98.

9. Ibid., 100.

to prepare him for what he was to learn in the early days of the struggle in Montgomery; but King's understanding of nonviolence was formed in the midst of struggle for justice, which required him to draw on the resources of the African American church.[10]

King was, moreover, well aware of how he came to be committed to nonviolence, not simply as a strategy, but as, in Gandhi's words, his experiment with truth.[11] For example, in an article entitled "Pilgrimage to Nonviolence" for *The Christian Century* in 1960, King says by being called to be a spokesman for his people, he was

> driven back to the Sermon on the Mount and the Gandhian method of nonviolent resistance. This principle became the guiding light of our movement. Christ furnished the spirit and motivation while Gandhi furnished the method. The experience of Montgomery did more to clarify my thinking on the question of nonviolence than all of the books I had read. As the days unfolded I became more and more convinced of the power of nonviolence. Living through the actual experience of the protest, nonviolence became more than a method to which I gave intellectual assent; it became a commitment to a way of life. Many issues I had not cleared up intellectually concerning nonviolence were now solved in the sphere of practical action.[12]

In the same article, King observes that he was also beginning to believe that the method of nonviolence may even be relevant to international relations. Yet he was still under the influence of Niebuhr, or at least at this stage in his

10. In his magnificent article "Prophetic Christian as Organic Intellectual: Martin Luther King Jr.," Cornel West argues that four sources fundamentally shaped King's thought: (1) the prophetic black church tradition; (2) prophetic liberal Christianity; (3) the prophetic Gandhian method of nonviolent social change; and (4) prophetic American civil religion. West argues, however, that it was the black church tradition that fundamentally shaped how King drew on the other three sources. West's article is in *The Cornel West Reader* (New York: Perseus, 1999), 425–34.

11. "My Experiments with Truth" is, of course, the subtitle of Gandhi's *Autobiography* (Boston: Beacon, 1957). King shared Gandhi's willingness to be ready to learn in the midst of struggle. In particular he admired Gandhi's "amazing capacity for self-criticism. This was true in individual life, in his family life, and was true in his people's life. Gandhi criticized himself when he needed it. And whenever he made a mistake, he confessed it publicly. Here was a man who would say to his people: I'm not perfect. I'm not infallible. I don't want you to start a religion around me. I'm not a god." King says he thinks there would have been a religion formed around Gandhi if he had not had the capacity for saying both in his personal life and in public life, "I made a mistake" (*The Autobiography of Martin Luther King Jr.*, ed. Clayborne Carson [New York: Warner, 1998], 128). It is, of course, not hard to see King's worry that many had expectations about his life that he knew he could not meet.

12. Martin Luther King Jr., *Testament of Hope: The Essential Writings and Speeches of Martin Luther King Jr.*, ed. James M. Washington (San Francisco: HarperSanFrancisco, 1986), 38. This passage can also be found in *Stride toward Freedom* but without the problematic observation about Christ furnishing the motivation and Gandhi the method. As we shall see, that way of putting the matter betrays King's own understanding of nonviolence.

thinking he could not escape Niebuhr's language. Thus, even after he argues that nonviolence is the only alternative we have when faced by the destructiveness of modern weapons, he declares: "I am no doctrinaire pacifist. I have tried to embrace a realistic pacifism. Moreover, I see the pacifist position not as sinless but as the lesser evil in the circumstances. Therefore I do not claim to be free from the moral dilemmas that the Christian nonpacifist confronts."[13]

That would not, however, be his final position. In an article entitled "Showdown for Nonviolence," which was published after his assassination, King says plainly, "I'm committed to nonviolence absolutely. I'm just not going to kill anybody, whether it's in Vietnam or here. . . . I plan to stand by nonviolence because I have found it to be a philosophy of life that regulates not only my dealings in the struggle for racial justice but also my dealings with people with my own self. I will still be faithful to nonviolence."[14]

King, the advocate of nonviolence, became nonviolent—which means it is all the more important to recognize how he understood nonviolence.

King's "Philosophy" of Nonviolence

In a 1957 article for *The Christian Century* entitled "Nonviolence and Racial Justice," King developed with admirable clarity the five points that he understood to be central to Gandhi's practice of nonviolent resistance.[15] The next year saw the publication of *Stride toward Freedom,* in which he expanded the five points to six.[16] The six points of emphasis are (1) nonviolent resistance is not cowardly but is a form of resistance, (2) advocates of nonviolence do not want to humiliate those they oppose, (3) the battle is against forces of evil not individuals, (4) nonviolence requires the willingness to suffer, (5) love is central to nonviolence, and finally (6) the universe is on the side of justice.

Though these points of emphasis are usefully distinguished, they are clearly interdependent. This is particularly apparent given King's stress in *Stride toward Freedom* that nonviolence requires the willingness to accept suffering rather than to retaliate against enemies. King approvingly quotes Gandhi's message to his countrymen—"Rivers of blood may have to flow before we gain our freedom, but it must be our blood." Then he argues that the willingness to accept but never inflict violence is justified "in the realization that unearned suffering is redemptive."[17]

13. King, "Pilgrimage to Nonviolence," *Testament of Hope*, 39.

14. King, *Testament of Hope*, 69.

15. The article is reprinted in *Testament of Hope*, 5–9.

16. King, *Stride toward Freedom*, 101–7. King either used what he had written for the book for the article or expanded the article for the book. I will use his presentation in the book because he was able to be more expansive there than in the space constraints required by the article.

17. King, *Stride toward Freedom*, 103.

King identified Gandhi as the primary source of his understanding of the "method" and "philosophy of nonviolence."[18] But he could not help but read Gandhi through the lens of the gospel, as his use of the word "redemption" makes clear.[19] Gandhi read Tolstoy, who convinced him not only that the Sermon on the Mount required nonviolence, but, equally important, that the willingness to suffer wrong is finally a more powerful force than violence. Gandhi's understanding of *satyagraha*, the belief that truth and suffering have the power to transform one's opponent, was Gandhi's way to translate Tolstoy into a Hindu idiom.[20] King read Gandhi and learned as a Christian how to read the Sermon on the Mount—or, put more accurately, he learned to trust the faith of the African American church in Jesus to sustain the hard discipline of nonviolence.[21] In King's own words,

> It was the Sermon on the Mount, rather than the doctrine of passive resistance, that initially inspired the Negroes of Montgomery to dignified social action. It was Jesus of Nazareth that stirred the Negro to protest with the creative weapon of love. As the days unfolded, however, the inspiration of Mahatma Gandhi began to exert its influence. I had come to see early that the Christian doctrine of love operating through the Gandhian method of nonviolence was one of the most potent weapons available to the Negro in his struggle for freedom.[22]

Gandhi's "method," moreover, gave King what he needed to challenge Niebuhr's argument that a strong distinction must be drawn between nonresistance and nonviolent resistance. Niebuhr had argued that Jesus's admonition

18. Ibid., 105. King had obviously read Gandhi when he was in seminary, but he seems to have depended on Glen Smiley, a Methodist minister from Texas who came to Montgomery in the early stages of the struggle, for learning the basic principles of Gandhi's nonviolence. See Stewart Burns's account in *To the Mountaintop*, 88–91. Burns rightly suggests that during 1956 King "forged an amalgam of Gandhian nonviolence and black Christian faith, in oratory and mass action" (91).

19. In *Bearing the Cross: Martin Luther King Jr. and the Southern Christian Leadership Conference* (New York: Vintage, 1988), David Garrow quotes King from an interview with a black interviewer in which King stressed that the nonviolent method used in Montgomery was not principally from India. "I have been a keen student of Gandhi for many years," King says. "However, this business of passive resistance and nonviolence is the gospel of Jesus. I went to Gandhi through Jesus" (75).

20. Gandhi's account of the significance of Tolstoy for his understanding of *satyagraha* can be found in his *Autobiography*, 90, 137, 160. For a well developed account of Gandhi and his significance for Christian theology, see Terrence Rynne, *Gandhi and Jesus: The Saving Power of Nonviolence* (Maryknoll, NY: Orbis, 2008).

21. In *The Preacher King: Martin Luther King Jr. and the Word That Moved America* (New York: Oxford University Press, 1995), Richard Lischer quotes King: "I am grateful to God that, through the influence of the Negro church, the way of nonviolence became an integral part of our struggle" (239).

22. King, "An Experiment in Love," in *Testament of Hope*, 16.

not to resist the evildoer in Matthew 5:38–42 means any attempt to act against evil is forbidden. Niebuhr, therefore, maintained that Gandhi's attempt to use nonviolence for political gains was really a form of coercion.[23] Through his study of Gandhi, King says he learned that Niebuhr's position involved a serious distortion because "true pacifism is not unrealistic submission to evil power. It is rather a courageous confrontation of evil by the power of love, in the faith that it is better to be the recipient of violence than the inflicter of it, since the latter only multiplies the existence of violence and bitterness in the universe, while the former may develop a sense of shame in the opponent, and thereby bring about a transformation and change of heart."[24]

King is well aware that such a commitment entails a massive metaphysical proposal. The willingness to accept suffering without retaliation must be based on the conviction that the universe is on the side of justice.[25] King acknowledges that there are devout believers in nonviolence who find it difficult to believe in a personal God, but "even these persons believe in the existence of some creative force that works for universal wholeness."[26] For King, however, it is the cross that is "the eternal expression of the length to which God will go in order to restore broken community. The resurrection is the symbol of God's triumph over all the forces that seek to block community. The Holy Spirit is the continuing community creating reality that moves through history. He who works against community is working against the whole of creation."[27]

23. Reinhold Niebuhr, *Moral Man and Immoral Society* (New York: Scribner, 1960), 240–52. Niebuhr thought nonviolence to be a particularly useful strategy for "an oppressed group which is hopelessly in the minority" and suggested that the "emancipation of the Negro race in America probably waits on the development of this kind of social and political strategy" (252). Niebuhr, however, insisted that nonviolent resistance was a type of coercion that betrayed the gospel demand not to resist in any fashion. Paul Ramsey continued to insist on the validity of Niebuhr's distinction between nonviolent resistance and pacifism in order to defend his account of just war. See, for example, his attempt to do justice to Yoder's critique of Niebuhr in his *Speak Up for Just War or Pacifism* (University Park, PA: Pennsylvania State University Press, 1988), 116–23.

24. King, *Stride toward Freedom*, 98–99. Yoder commends King's refusal to accept Niebuhr's contention that nonviolent resistance is equivalent to violence, noting that King (and Gandhi) had a threefold response: "(1) They agreed that nonviolent action could be unloving, and took measures against that danger. They disciplined their people to maintain respect for the adversary in the midst of conflict. (2) They denied that all forms of 'coercion' are morally equivalent. (3) They maintained that the physical integrity of the adversary is an important variable, both tactically and morally" (*Nevertheless*, 177).

25. These claims may seem to be too "idealistic," but King was a firm realist. That the universe is on the side of justice may sound far too highblown, but in effect it shaped King's deep pragmatism. For example in a "Statement at the Sixteenth Street Baptist Church in Birmingham," in 1963, King said, "Wait a minute, Birmingham. Somebody's got to have some sense in Birmingham" (*Autobiography*, 163). Saying that someone's got to have some sense in Birmingham indicates a belief that the universe is on the side of justice.

26. King, *Stride toward Freedom*, 106–7.

27. King, "An Experiment in Love," in *Testament of Hope*, 20. The use of the language of "symbol" betrays King's indebtedness to Protestant liberalism and, in particular, Tillich. When King

Love, therefore, becomes the hallmark of nonviolent resistance, requiring that the resister not only refuse to shoot his opponent but also refuse to hate him. Nonviolent resistance is meant to bring an end to hate by being the very embodiment of *agape*. King seemed never to tire of an appeal to Nygren's distinction between *eros*, *philia*, and *agape* to make the point that the love that shapes nonviolent resistance is one that is disciplined by the refusal to distinguish between worthy and unworthy people. *Agape* begins by loving others for their own sake, which requires that we "have love for the enemy-neighbor from whom you can expect no good in return, but only hostility and persecution."[28]

Such a love means that nonviolent resistance seeks not to defeat or humiliate the opponent, but to win a friend. The protests that may take the form of boycotts and other noncooperative modes of behavior are not ends in themselves, but rather attempts to awaken in the opponent a sense of shame and repentance. The end of nonviolent resistance is redemption and reconciliation with those who have been the oppressor. Love overwhelms hate, making possible the creation of a beloved community that would otherwise be impossible.

Nonviolent resistance therefore is not directed against people but against forces of evil.[29] Those who happen to be doing evil are as victimized by the evil they do as those who are the object of their oppression. From the perspective of nonviolence, King argued that the enemy is not the white people of Montgomery, but injustice itself. The object of the boycott of the buses was not to defeat white people, but to defeat the injustice that mars their lives.[30] The means must therefore be commensurate with the end that

---

preached, however, the cross was never a "symbol." See, for example, Richard Lischer's *Preacher King*, 52–62, for an astute analysis of the similarities and differences between Protestant liberalism and the African American church.

28. King, *Stride toward Freedom*, 104–5.

29. King insisted that nonviolence required a close study of one's opponents. For example in a speech in 1963 recorded by the police, King stressed four steps of nonviolent action: (1) collect the facts in order to understand the evil you are battling; (2) negotiate with your opponent, which will require "self-purification" because you must recognize your own anger, hatred, and other mistakes; (3) through direct action create enough tension to draw attention to the conflict in order to get to the conscience of your adversary; and (4) refuse to give in both to more militant calls for violence or to white pleas for moderation. Reported in Lischer, *Preacher King*, 261. King provides a similar account of the four basic steps of a nonviolent campaign in *Why We Can't Wait* (New York: Signet, 1964), 66. King's tactical brilliance I think is often underrated. He understood that the capacity to surprise your opponents was one of the strengths of nonviolence. He was, therefore, quite critical of the Albany movement because he mistakenly let the protest be targeted against segregation in general rather than a single and distinct facet of it. The protest was so vague that "we got nothing" (*Autobiography*, 168). One of King's criticisms of the Black Power movement was the lack of specificity of its demands. In short King found the Black Power movement insufficiently political.

30. King, *Stride toward Freedom*, 102–3. The often-made observation that Gandhian nonviolence only works if your opponent is as civilized as the British has a far too positive view of Gandhi's opponent. In like manner I suspect that there has been a "forgetfulness" about the forces that opposed King.

is sought—for the end cannot justify the means, particularly if the means involve the use of violence, because the "end is preexistent in the means."[31] This is particularly the case if the end of nonviolence is the creation of a "beloved community."[32]

It should now be apparent why nonviolent resistance is "not a method for cowards; it does resist."[33] There is nothing passive about nonviolence since it requires active engagement against evil. Nonviolence requires not the courage of the hero, but the courage that draws its strength from the willingness to listen, for the willingness to listen forms a basis for the organization necessary for a new community to come into existence. A people who are unwilling to resort to violence must create imaginative modes of resistance to injustice.

King learned not only what nonviolence is but how to be nonviolent, because he saw how nonviolence gave a new sense of worth to those who followed him in Montgomery. *Stride toward Freedom* begins with the lovely observation that though he must make frequent use of the pronoun "I" to tell the story of Montgomery, it is not a story in which one actor is central. Rather it is the "chronicle of 50,000 Negroes who took to heart the principles of nonviolence, who learned to fight for their rights with the weapon of love, and who, in the process, acquired a new estimate of their own human worth."[34]

King's account of nonviolence reflects what he learned through the struggle in Montgomery. He never wavered from that commitment to nonviolence, and, if anything, the subsequent movement in Birmingham, the rise of Black Power, and the focus on the poor only served to deepen his commitment to nonviolence. But these later developments also exposed challenges to his understanding of the practice of nonviolence, challenges that require our attention.

King's Dilemma

Martin Luther King believed in as well as practiced nonviolent resistance because he was sure that to do so was to be in harmony with the grain of the universe. The willingness to suffer without retaliation depended on that deep conviction. King certainly drew on the rhetoric of American democratic traditions to sustain the goals of nonviolence, but American ideals were not the basis of his hope. Rather, as John Howard Yoder contends, King and

31. King, "Love, Law, and Civil Disobedience," in *Testament of Hope*, 45.

32. King's understanding of the relations of means to ends should have required him to rethink his earlier characterization of nonviolent resistance as a lesser of two evils. He used that language rightly to distance himself from accounts of nonviolence that attempt to avoid acknowledgement of complicity with evil. But the language of the lesser of two evils assumes that the end can justify the means, which he was quite right to reject.

33. King, *Stride toward Freedom*, 102.

34. Ibid., 9.

Gandhi shared "a fundamental religious cosmology" based on the conviction that unearned suffering can be redemptive. This is a Hindu truth that Gandhi recovered, but Yoder observes that it is also "a Christian truth, although not all the meaning of the cross in the Christian message is rendered adequately by stating it in terms that sound like Gandhi."[35]

The Christian truth that Gandhi's understanding of *satyagraha* does not adequately express, according to Yoder, is "if the Lamb that was slain is worthy to receive power, then no calculation of other non-lamb roads to power can be ultimately authentic."[36] According to Yoder, because King understood nonviolence to be the bearing of Jesus's cross, King was able to choose the path of vulnerable faithfulness with full awareness that such a path would be costly. King operated with the conviction that the victory had been won, but also with the realization that the mopping up might take longer than expected.

Yet the success of Montgomery meant King could not avoid becoming the leader of a mass movement. To sustain the movement with a people who were not committed to nonviolence as King was meant results had to be forthcoming. For example, in the article "Nonviolence: The Only Road to Freedom," in which King defended nonviolence amid the riots of the 1960s as well as the stridency of the Black Power movement, he acknowledged the importance of results for sustaining the movement.[37] Results are necessary because King knew he could not assume that everyone who followed him understood that nonviolence was not simply a tactic to get what you want, but a way of life. But results can take months or even years, which means those committed to nonviolence must engage in continuing education of the community to help them understand how the sacrifices they are making are necessary to bring about the desired changes.[38]

35. Yoder, *For the Nations*, 127.

36. Ibid., 135. Yoder is not claiming, however, that King mistakenly adopted Gandhi to shape his account of nonviolence. In the third of his Polish lectures, "The Lessons of the Nonviolent Experience," Yoder observes that Gandhi and King each in their own way said the means and end cannot be separated because they believed that the means is the end in the process of becoming. Therefore Gandhi and King shared the following conviction: "When in the service of even the most valuable cause one chooses to resort to violence, that disregard for the dignity of the neighbor, and that disrespect for the social fabric have planted the seeds for the failure of one's own enterprise. Only fidelity to love as means can be an instrument for love as end" (*Nonviolence*, 46).

37. In *Why We Can't Wait* King observes that "the religious tradition of the Negro had shown him that the nonviolent resistance of the early Christians had constituted a moral offensive of such overriding power that it shook the Roman Empire." He also appealed to the American boycott that confounded the British as well as Gandhi's "muzzling of the guns of the British Empire" (23). It is by no means clear, though, that Christian nonviolent resistance shook the Roman Empire, and these kind of examples can mislead King as well as his followers to the extent that they suggest that these results are consistent with the means. Of course the American Revolution was not a boycott, but an armed conflict.

38. King, *Testament of Hope*, 60.

King suggests, then, that the most powerful nonviolent weapon, but also the most demanding, is the need for organization. He observes:

> To produce change, people must be organized to work together in units of power. These units might be political, as in the case of voters' leagues and political parties, they may be economic units such as groups of tenants who join forces to form a tenant union or to organize a rent strike; or they may be laboring units of persons who are seeking employment and wage increases. More and more, the civil rights movement will become engaged in the task of organizing people into permanent groups to protect their own interests and to produce change in their behalf. This is a tedious task which may take years, but the results are more permanent and meaningful.[39]

Yet Stewart Burns suggests King discovered that nothing fails like success. King, and those close to him in the Southern Christian Leadership Conference (SCLC), had been captured by the need to produce results. They had no time for the "tedious" work of organization.[40] The movement had become a trap. Every "success" required upping the ante in the hope that those who followed King would continue to do so even if they did not share his commitment to nonviolence. In Montgomery, King had been able to rely on the black churches and, in particular, the women leaders of those churches for the "organizing miracle" that made Montgomery possible.[41] But the further he moved beyond Montgomery, the more he had to depend on results in the hope that through results, community might come into existence.

King was well aware of this dilemma, as is evident from his anguished reflections on the destructive riots in Watts:

> Watts was not only a crisis for Los Angeles and the Northern cities of our nation: It was a crisis for the nonviolent movement. I tried desperately to maintain

39. Ibid., 60–61. Burns notes that King had hired Ella Baker to organize SCLC's operations, but he did not support her efforts to grow the grassroots movement that he rhetorically advocated (Burns, *To the Mountaintop*, 154). For the significance of Ella Baker, see Romand Coles's chapter "'To Make This Tradition Articulate': Practiced Receptivity Matters, Or Heading West of West with West and Ella Baker," in Stanley Hauerwas and Romand Coles, *Christianity, Democracy, and the Radical Ordinary: Conversations between a Radical Democrat and a Christian* (Eugene, OR: Cascade, 2007), 45–86.

40. The nonviolent character of King's leadership of the Southern Christian Leadership Conference (SCLC), however, should not be overlooked. There were often deep differences about strategic issues among those who made up King's inner circle. King had the capacity for what Burns (*To the Mountaintop*, 108) describes as "compassionate listening," which served to defuse conflicts that threatened to divide the movement. Again, nonviolence was not for King a tactic in the movement, but a way of life. Crucial to that way of life was a capacity for self-criticism. As I mentioned above, King admired Gandhi's ability to publicly confess he had made a mistake. It is hard to resist speculating how King might have been thinking about his own personal behavior when he so described Gandhi. King's capacity for self-criticism was remarkable and surely is a hallmark of his commitment to nonviolence. King's reflections on Gandhi are in his *Autobiography*, 128.

41. The phrase "organizing miracle" is Burns's. See *To the Mountaintop*, 152.

> a nonviolent atmosphere in which our nation could undergo the tremendous period of social change which confronts us, but this was mainly dependent on the obtaining of tangible progress and victories, if those of us who counsel reason and love were to maintain our leadership. However, the cause was not lost. In spite of pockets of hostility in ghetto areas such as Watts, there was still overwhelming acceptance of the ideal of nonviolence.[42]

But as King well knew, nonviolence is not just an "ideal" but must be embedded in the habits of a people across time in order to make possible the long and patient work of transformation necessary for the reconciliation of enemies. King was a creature of the African American church. In the "Letter from Birmingham Jail," even as he expresses his disappointment concerning the failure of the church, he declares, "Yes, I love the church."[43] For understandable reasons, however, King did not see that his understanding of nonviolence required the existence of an alternative community that could sustain the hard and "tedious" work of organization.

From Yoder's perspective, therefore, some of the later tactics of the civil rights movement designed to secure results without transformation of those against whom the protest was directed may have made King vulnerable to Niebuhr's critique that nonviolent resistance is but disguised violence.[44] King's attempt to combine nonviolent resistance with a social movement that aimed to make America a "beloved community" did not fundamentally challenge the Constantinian assumption that America is a Christian nation.

Christian nonviolence presupposes the resources of faith. King assumed those resources were available in Montgomery, and they were. However, the more he became a "civil rights leader" rather than a black Baptist minister—two offices that were indistinguishable in his own mind—he could not presume his followers shared his faith, making the demand for results all the more important. Yet King was sustained by his faith. In the last speech he gave before he was assassinated, King began by observing,

> I guess one of the great agonies of life is that we are constantly trying to finish that which is unfinishable. We are commanded to do that. And so we, like David, find ourselves in so many instances having to face the fact that our dreams are not fulfilled. Life is a continual story of shattered dreams. Mahatma Gandhi labored for years and years for the independence of his people. But Gandhi had to face the fact that he was assassinated and died with a broken heart, because that nation that he wanted to unite ended up being divided between India and Pakistan as a result of the conflict between the Hindus and the Moslems.[45]

42. King, *Autobiography*, 295–96.
43. King, *Why We Can't Wait*, 80.
44. Yoder, *For the Nations*, 116–19.
45. King, *Autobiography*, 357.

King is obviously thinking about his own life and dreams. He seems to know that he too will die of a broken heart. Yet King tells the congregation that he can testify not because he is a saint but because he is a sinner like all of God's children. And yet, he writes, "But I want to be a good man. And I want to hear a voice saying to me one day, 'I take you in and I bless you, because you tried. It is well that it was within thine heart.' "[46] It is, moreover, well with us who live after King, as he remains a great witness to the power of nonviolence. As Yoder observed, we have much to learn from this extraordinary man.

46. King, *Autobiography*, 358–59.

Part 3

The Ecclesial Difference

8

Jesus, the Justice of God

Justice: A Theological Proposal

A gift that comes with growing old, at least for me, is the discovery that your students say better what you think or should think than you are able to say. I once chided Herbert McCabe for not writing the book on Aquinas many of us thought only he could write. Herbert responded by noting that he had learned that if you wait long enough your students will do it for you. I should have written more about justice, but now I do not need to do so because a former student, Dan Bell, has said what I should have said.[1] By calling attention to Dan's work I am not trying to be humble, but rather to do what justice requires, that is, to tell the truth.[2]

1. I stole the title of this chapter, as well as most of what I have to say, from Dan Bell's reflections on justice, which can be found in his articles: "Jesus, the Jews, and the Politics of God's Justice," *Ex Auditu* 22 (2006): 87–111, and "Deliberating: Justice and Liberation," in *The Blackwell Companion to Christian Ethics*, ed. Stanley Hauerwas and Samuel Wells (Oxford: Blackwell, 2004), 182–95.

2. MacIntyre observes that Aquinas's account of justice is not only at odds with the accounts of justice characteristic of liberal modernity but also involves a challenge to the conventional standards of his own age. For example MacIntyre directs attention to Aquinas's views on truth-telling and lying, which require that we never assert anything except what we believe to be true. We are not required to tell all that we know because it is rightfully a matter of prudence when to or not to speak in terms of the duties and obligations we may have. But Aquinas, from MacIntyre's perspective, rightly maintains that we may "never lie, not for profit, nor convenience, nor pleasure, nor to cause pain or trouble. Lying is evil, and lying with malice is a mortal sin (S.T. IIa–IIae, 109 and 110)" (Alasdair MacIntyre, *Whose Justice? Which Rationality?* [Notre Dame: University of Notre Dame Press, 1988], 203).

In the epilogue to *Performing the Faith: Bonhoeffer and the Practice of Nonviolence*, I tried to respond to Stout's criticism of my alleged view that "justice is a bad idea."[3] I pointed out that my suggestion that justice is a bad idea was meant to call into question abstract accounts of justice often associated with liberal political theory, which assumes a just social order is possible without the people who constitute that order being just. My worry about appeals to justice in advanced capitalist societies has been that such appeals can blind us to the ways our lives may be implicated in fundamental forms of injustice.

However, my deeper worry about appeals to justice has been theological. Reinhold Niebuhr, in the interest of making Christians politically responsible, argued that in matters political Jesus must be left behind, because the political work necessary for the achievement of justice requires coercion and even violence. For Niebuhr, "justice" names the arrangements necessary to secure more equitable forms of life when we cannot love all neighbors equally. Good Barthian that I am, I worry that justice so understood becomes more important than the justice of God found in the cross and resurrection of Christ.[4]

3. Stanley Hauerwas, *Performing the Faith: Bonhoeffer and the Practice of Nonviolence* (Grand Rapids: Brazos, 2004), 215–41.

4. Ibid., 230. One of the reasons I suspect my rhetorical gestures concerning why justice or freedom are "bad ideas" is that some, particularly those who think of themselves as "ethicists" rather than theologians, fail to see how these seemingly outrageous claims reflect fundamental theological commitments. Francesca Murphy gets it just right in her book *God Is Not a Story: Realism Revisited* (New York: Oxford University Press, 2007). Noting Barth's insistence that Anselm's argument in the *Proslogion* was not trying to prove God's existence, she asks why Barth thought what Anselm did was so important. She puts the matter this way:

> To write a systematic theology about divine revelation, Christ, the Trinity, reconciliation, and creation, one needs to use an immense number of *words*, words like good, flesh, incarnation, generation, procession, sin, and human. But if everything we know about God comes from God, one cannot take those words in their ordinary usage, or as from their apparent human origin. One must assume that one is using them *not* only with the truth imparted to them by their correspondence to ordinary objects, but also and crucially with the truth imparted to them by God, the first Truth. Barth says that Anselm is not concerned with the *existence* of faith—bringing it into being by showing its object exists—but with the *nature* of faith. What kind of *understanding*, or *intelligence* can use theological language appropriately? Only one according to Barth, which, through grace, attains a "participation" "in God's mode of Being." In his discussion of Anselm's proof, Barth is looking for a divine anchor onto which to hook theological language. There are no philosophical or naturally known "analogies" between creatures and God, according to Barth, only analogies made known by the Revealer: he called analogies known by the revelation of God in Christ the analogy of faith, the *analogia fidei*. . . . Since he has chosen an eleventh-century Platonizing Benedictine monk as his paradigm, the *analogia fidei* is very much an *analogy of participation*, the "truing" of the theologian's words about God through their participation in the first Truth. (114–15)

Of course one of the words that must be subject to such a "truing" is "justice." For a similar account of Barth (and Aquinas), see Timothy Furry, "Analogous Analogies? Thomas Aquinas and Karl Barth," *Scottish Journal of Theology* 6 (2010): 318–30.

I do not pretend that these brief remarks in response to Stout provide an adequate account of justice. More needs to be said, but this has been done by Dan Bell. So I begin by introducing Bell's account of justice because, as I suggested, he says better what I think I should say. Bell, moreover, provides the basis for an engagement in the second part of this chapter with Nicholas Wolterstorff's account of justice in his extremely impressive and important book *Justice: Rights and Wrongs*.[5] By putting Bell and Wolterstorff into conversation, I hope to show the strengths of Bell's position. Finally, I will end by trying to show why, if as Bell argues Jesus is the justice of God, Christians cannot help but have a passion for justice.

Bell begins his article "Jesus, the Jews, and the Politics of God's Justice" with the observation that though Christians disagree about much, we are in agreement that God does justice and so should we. Yet he thinks such an agreement is part of the problem, just to the extent that the Christian enthusiasm for justice distorts our reading of Scripture. He is particularly critical of an approach he characterizes as "social justice advocacy" for how its adherents approach Scripture.[6] For according to Bell, advocates of social justice read Scripture for values and principles they think crucial to motivate Christians, in Bell's words, "to get off their pews, leave the stained glass bliss of the congregation and its liturgy behind, and go out into the world to do justice."[7]

Such an approach, Bell notes, presents justice as an external standard to which Christianity is accountable. Indeed it is assumed, and therefore it is also assumed that justice can be understood apart from Christian theological convictions and practices. Human rights, for example, are defended in a manner that renders irrelevant what Christians believe or do not believe about God. Such a view of justice, as well as the approach to Scripture associated with justice so conceived, Bell argues, is determined by the modern political context.[8]

That context, moreover, is one in which the church is assumed to be apolitical and, therefore, not relevant for determining how to know as well as do justice. Such a view of justice thus reinforces the politics of modernity, in which "the church is consigned to the role of cultural custodian of values tightly cordoned off from political practice, which finds its highest expression and guarantor in the nation-state."[9] Desperate to show the social relevance

5. Nicholas Wolterstorff, *Justice: Rights and Wrongs* (Princeton: Princeton University Press, 2008).

6. You know something has gone wrong when the phrase "social justice" is used. What kind of justice would not be "social"? The very description "social justice" reproduces the public/private distinction characteristic of liberal political regimes. I also think the phrase "restorative justice" has the same problems as the locution "social justice." Justice is or must be restorative if it is to be justice.

7. Bell, "Jesus, the Jews, and the Politics of God's Justice," 89.

8. Bell notes that it is not accidental that the historical-critical methods emerged simultaneously with the advent of modern politics as statecraft (ibid., 88).

9. Ibid, 90.

of the church, Christians ironically underwrite in the name of justice an account of social relations that presumes a privatized account of Christian convictions and the church.

But if such a view of justice displaces the church, it also results in a subtle displacement of Jesus. Jesus is relegated to being a motivator to encourage Christians to get involved in struggles for justice. Even if Jesus is thought to have practiced justice in his ministry, he is appealed to as a symbol or example. For what really matters is not Jesus, but justice. This understanding of justice not only displaced Jesus, but also displaces the Jews as crucial for determining what we mean by justice. Social justice advocates often direct attention to the call for justice made by the prophets, but the justice for which the prophets called is assumed to be universal in a manner that has no particular or intrinsic relation to the Jewish people.

The universalistic presumptions that inform such a call for justice are but a correlate of the political vision that assumes the task is to manage the inevitable conflict characteristic of societies in which people share no goods in common other than the necessity to pursue their subjective desires and interests.[10] It is a given that such a political order is pluralistic, which means no goods in common can be discerned through the exercise of practical reason.[11] It is, therefore, not surprising that such a view of justice, whether it is utilitarian or contractarian, whether it is a libertarian or egalitarian vision of rights, whether it be capitalist or socialist, ends up using Scripture to underwrite a distributive vision of justice determined by the presumption that the best we can do is to secure a plethora of discordant private goods.

10. In his article "Deliberating," Bell puts it this way:

> Liberalism re-imagined society as a teeming mass of individuals, each with their own interests, ends, and conceptions of what constitutes the good life. Consequently, justice was reconfigured; in contemporary parlance, now the right was given priority over the good. What constitutes justice is arrived at apart from any substantive agreement about what constitutes the good or *telos* of humanity. Justice in modern liberal social orders becomes essentially procedural. Under the sigh of modernity, justice is a matter of arriving at a procedure for securing effective cooperation between and security among discrete individuals pursuing irrepressibly diverse plethora of self-determined interests and private goods. In this situation, justice is no longer conceived as a unitive force. Indeed, with the arrival of modernity, the general virtue of justice is invariably reduced to "legal justice" and equated simply with following positive laws of the state, or it is discarded altogether. (183–84)

Bell's analysis obviously reflects the influence of Alasdair MacIntyre and, in particular, his *Whose Justice?*

11. Bell puts the matter more forcefully in "Deliberating," noting that the loss of a robust sense of the common good with the concomitant elevation of the individual means that theological calls for justice reproduce an account of justice understood primarily as the institution of procedures by which the regulation and exchange of goods is conceived as an aggregate of autonomous individuals. Bell observes, "noteworthy is the absence of justice as a general virtue concerned with nurturing a community's solidarity in a shared love" (185).

Bell identifies an alternative to this view of justice as social advocacy as one that at first seems more theologically determined, one which he calls "justice as justification." This approach recognizes the importance of social justice, but makes the achievement of social justice secondary to the individual entering into a saving relation with Jesus Christ. Such a view often presupposes satisfaction theories of the atonement in which Christ's death is thought to render due the debt incurred by our sin. Yet this understanding of justice is individualistic, which makes it congruent with the politics of modernity.[12] As a result the church remains an apolitical space assumed to be "spiritual" in contrast to the world of politics.

This understanding of justice also displaces Jesus as God's justice because Jesus must be the victim of divine justice. As a result the justice that is assumed to require Jesus's death is not remarkably different than the justice presupposed by the social advocacy approach. For it is a justice derived from the *suum cuique* conception that assumes that we can know what justice means apart from Christian convictions.[13] The justice God must enforce turns out to be thoroughly secular and, in particular, retributive, in a manner that reinforces modern statist forms of politics. Such a view not only continues the displacement of the Jews, who at best become representatives of the futility of attempting to fulfill the demands of divine justice, but also reinforces a vision of redemption analogous to modern political hopes that despair of a renewal of communion and seek rather for the state to provide defeat of one's enemies.[14]

In contrast to these views of justice, Bell provides a Christocentric rendering of justice that is, in his words, "robustly ecclesial and in the service to discipleship."[15] For according to Bell a proper theological reading of justice must be Christological in a manner that forgets neither the Jews nor the canonical plot of redemption. Such a view he thinks is exemplified by Paul, particularly in Romans, in which justice is displayed "as the divine redemptive solidarity that has as its end the restoration and renewal of the communion

12. In a letter responding to an earlier draft of this essay, David Aers observes that justification only becomes "individualistic" when divorced from incorporation into the body of Christ made possible through the sacraments of baptism, penance, and Eucharist.

13. Bell argues that though this view is often attributed to Anselm's account of the atonement, he thinks such a reading of Anselm to be a mistake. According to Bell, "Anselm describes how humanity is taken up into the communion of love that is the life of the blessed Trinity (*theosis*, deification). In other words, according to Anselm, God became human not in order to meet the demands of an implacable justice before which even God must bow, but so that humanity might be restored to the place of honor that God from the beginning intended for humanity, namely, participation in the divine life" ("Jesus, the Jews, and the Politics of God's Justice," 96).

14. For a quite different account of Paul on righteousness, see A. Katherine Grieb, "'So That in Him We Might Become the Righteousness of God' (2 Cor. 5:21): Some Theological Reflections on the Church Becoming Justice," *Ex Auditu* 22 (2006): 58–80.

15. Bell, "Jesus, the Jews, and the Politics of God's Justice," 94.

of all in God."[16] In contrast to worldly notions of justice that demand a strict rendering of what is due, the justice of God, that is, Jesus, requires the endurance of offense and the offer of forgiveness in the hope that the unjust has been made just by being gathered back into communion.

Thus at the heart of God's justice is God's fidelity to the promise to Abraham, which requires from Gentile converts a recognition of their dependence on the promised people called Jews. Bell argues that Paul provides, therefore, a crucial turning point for how we are to understand justice. For the Gentiles would rightly be suspicious if Jesus was but a sacrificial victim to satisfy the demands of a pagan justice or if he were the establishment of a justice completely divorced from God's promises to the Jews. In contrast, Paul argues that Jesus is not the victim of God's justice, but the very embodiment of God's justice through his faithfulness and obedience in manifesting God's unrelenting desire for reconciliation.

For Bell, Jesus does not exemplify a justice that can be known apart from his life, nor does he provide a motivation for us to underwrite some secular version of justice. "Rather, Jesus in his person *is* the justice of God."[17] Justice so understood obviously has significant implications for how Christians understand their place in the world. For Christians, the work of justice first and foremost begins with their participation in Christ's work. The liturgy, particularly baptism and Eucharist, becomes the form justice takes because through those rites we are incorporated into Christ, becoming God's justice for the world.[18] In Bell's language, Jesus does "not justify individuals who then go do justice on their own; rather, Jesus justifies persons in communion. Jesus justifies his body, the church. Being made just and doing justice are a matter of being immersed in the life of the ecclesial community; to do justice is to be a part of the community whose life is centered in and ordered by Jesus, God's justice."[19]

Bell thinks such a perspective illumines Augustine's contention in *The City of God* that true justice is to be found in the Christian community, because

16. Ibid., 95.

17. Ibid., 97.

18. Nathan Mitchell has written a wonderful account of the importance of liturgy as constitutive of justice. He observes,

> The solution to poverty isn't ugly art and sappy music in our worship. On the contrary, "the more striking (the) beauty and integrity and careful celebration of the Sunday liturgy, the deeper 'Rilke's rule' sinks in: *You must change your life*. We must change our lives—*together*. The solution to hunger, homelessness, oppression, racism, homophobia, and the host of other social evils that destroy lives isn't careless liturgy, it's repentance, it's *changing our lives*; it's the voluntary renunciation of those addictions—to power, money, and control—that continue to divide the world into 'haves' and 'have-nots.' We won't feed the world's hungry by neglecting the liturgy." (Nathan Mitchell, "Being Beautiful, Being Just," in *Toward Ritual Transformation: Remembering Robert W. Hovda* [Collegeville: Liturgical Press, 2003], 81)

19. Bell, "Jesus, the Jews, and the Politics of God's Justice," 97.

there, in contrast to Rome, the one true God is rightly worshiped. Justice, according to Augustine, is "where God, the one supreme God, rules an obedient city according to his grace, forbidding sacrifice to any being save himself alone."[20] Augustine, Bell suggests, praises Christianity not because Christians are able to do more than the pagans, but because Christians are liturgically incorporated into Christ, rendering praise and worship to the one alone worthy to be praised and worshiped.[21]

Bell draws on Aquinas's contention that charity is the form of all the virtues to suggest how his understanding of Jesus as the justice of God transforms what the actual operation of justice will look like. Aquinas certainly begins his account of justice with the classical notion that justice entails "rendering what is due," but what is due turns out to be shaped by the love that is Christ. Justice is, for Aquinas, a general virtue that nurtures solidarity in the shared loves that constitute the common good, but Aquinas locates the solidarity justice enacts within the divine order of charity. Justice therefore is no longer a matter of rendering what is due, but has as its *telos* the establishment of our humanity by making us friends with God.[22]

20. Augustine, *City of God*, 19, 23.

21. Bell's account of Augustine may strike some who have learned to read Augustine through Reinhold Niebuhr as quite problematic. But Robert Dodaro's account of Augustine in his book *Christ and the Just Society in the Thought of Augustine* (Cambridge: Cambridge University Press, 2004) supports Bell's account. Dodaro says, "Augustine maintains that justice cannot be known except in Christ, and that, as founder (*conditor*) and ruler (*rector*) Christ forms the just society in himself. United with Christ, members of his body constitute the whole, just Christ (*Christus totus iustus*), which is the city of God, the true commonwealth, and the locus for the revelation of justice" (72). Later Dodaro argues that Augustine thought that the civic virtues must be transformed by the virtues of faith, hope, and love, as otherwise the statesman will pursue a false peace and prosperity for the earthly city (209). The transformation of the virtues is required because the virtues, if they are to be true, must lead the soul to adhere to God, as only those who adhere to God can overcome the consequences of sin—suffering, temptation, toil, and death (210).

22. Though I think Bell is generally right about Aquinas's understanding of justice, as I point out in *Performing the Faith*, Aquinas does say that an act of justice can be thought to have "rectitude" "without taking into account the way in which it was done by the agent" (*Summa Theologiae*, trans. Fathers of the English Dominican Province [Westminster, MD: Christian Classics, 1947], IIaIIae.57.1). Therefore the "Treatise on Prudence and Justice" deals with a wide range of issues that might be thought "institutional," in which the standards of evaluation derive from expectations not always directly determined by theological considerations. I assume that any account of justice will, like Aquinas's account, draw on expectations and manners that have been honed from a people's peculiar history. Crucial to Aquinas's account of justice is his understanding of part to the whole. Thus he says, "all who are included in a community, stand in relation to that community as parts to a whole; while a part, as such belongs to a whole, so that whatever is the good of a part can be directed to the good of the whole. It follows therefore that the good of any virtue, whether such virtue directs man in relation to himself, or in relation to certain other individual persons, is referable to the common good, to which justice directs; so that all acts of virtue can pertain to justice, in so far as it directs man to the common good" (IIaIIae.58.5). This is the basis for Aquinas's judgments that it is lawful to kill sinners if they threaten the health of the whole body (IIaIIae.64.2).

Justice may, therefore, entail mercy and forgiveness by forgoing a strict accounting of what is due.[23] In Bell's words: "Justice and mercy are not opposing logics; rather they share a single end—the return of all love, the sociality of all desire, in God. Justice attains its end by enacting mercy to overcome sin."[24] Accordingly Bell thinks Aquinas provides expression to Paul's understanding of Christ's work, that is, that Christ's sacrifice was perfectly just, not because it satisfied a debt, "but because it renewed the communion of humanity in God; it was an expression of the divine fidelity to the redemptive promise made to Abraham."[25]

To so understand justice as being ordered by and to charity, Bell argues, has the effect of reconnecting justice with its Jewish roots, because justice in the Old Testament defies retributive accounts as well as those that are shaped by a strict rendering of what is due. *Mishpat* and *sedaqah*, the words we translate as justice or righteousness, rightly indicate that justice is a matter of judgment linked closely with righteousness.[26] Accordingly, justice for Israel cannot be procedural, but rather is orientated by the commitment to establish a right relation between people and God. Justice is not the impartial administration of laws, but rather imitates the divine partisanship on behalf of the poor, the widow, and the orphan. But it is equally important to remember that God's penchant for the poor, the widow, and the orphan is an expression of God's unrelenting desire to liberate us from sin.[27]

23. In his article "Deliberating," Bell develops this understanding of Aquinas, noting that Thomistic justice is not only a matter of protecting the rights of strangers in the absence of shared love, but is about nurturing the communion of saints in a shared love. Accordingly the Niebuhrian often presumed contrast between justice and peace is a mistake from a Thomistic point of view. For from Aquinas's perspective, justice redeems and is therefore predicated on peace. In other words justice is not merely the regulation of conflict but rather presumes the priority of peace. "Thus the common canard is transposed: 'Without peace there is no justice'" (189). Such an understanding of justice and peace has obvious implications for how one understands the "justice" that governs war.

24. Bell, "Justice and Liberation," 99.

25. Ibid.

26. Bell's emphasis on the place of judgment for understanding the work of justice in the Old Testament is the heart of O'Donovan's understanding of justice in *The Desire of the Nations: Rediscovering the Roots of Political Theology* (Cambridge: Cambridge University Press, 1996) and *The Ways of Judgment* (Grand Rapids: Eerdmans, 2005). It would be an extraordinarily fruitful enterprise to explore the similarities between Bell's and O'Donovan's understandings of justice. I am thinking, in particular, of O'Donovan's account of praise in *Desire of the Nations* and his treatment of mercy in *Ways of Judgment*.

27. Bell, "Jesus, the Jews, and the Politics of God's Justice," 100. Bell argues that this understanding of justice is necessary for the right reading of Scripture because justice is inseparable from the scriptural drama of redemption. "We see that God is just precisely as God is faithful to that redemptive intent. We see, as Paul argues, Jesus is the climax of the covenant, the promise of redemption, the justice of God who in his person breaks down the wall of hostility and restores the communion of all in God. Thus, the call to justice is the call to be joined to Christ and so to Christ's body, the church, whose life is just insofar as its life is centered in and ordered by Jesus who is the justice of God."

Bell acknowledges that his account of Jesus as the justice of God is not without its difficulties. It attempts to be at once particularistic and universal. Justice is tied to a particular people and a person yet seeks also the restoration of human communion. The latter is thought to be impossible without the former. Does that make this account sectarian? Does it mean that Christians must abandon the world if Jesus is our justice? Bell answers these challenges by directing attention to Jeremiah's admonition to seek the welfare of the city even when you are in exile.[28] I am deeply sympathetic with Bell's use of Jeremiah, but I want to test his account, an account that I take as my own, by trying to draw out the differences between Bell's and Wolterstorff's accounts of justice. I do so because I think the contrast will be extremely instructive since Wolterstorff, like Bell, claims that his understanding of justice is consistent with the Scriptural witness.

Justice: A Philosophical Proposal

Nicholas Wolterstorff's *Justice: Rights and Wrongs* is a major attempt to develop an account of justice that is at once theologically and philosophically defensible. I have little doubt that his book will rightly set the terms for discussion of justice, particularly among Christians, for some time. Bell's account of Jesus as the justice of God sounds homiletical when compared with Wolterstorff's careful and intricate arguments. Yet it will be the burden of my remarks not only to show why Bell's account of justice is more scriptural than Wolterstorff's account, but also to argue that Bell's understanding of justice helps illumine some of the limitations intrinsic to Wolterstorff's account.

It may be objected that the attempt to put Bell and Wolterstorff into conversation is not unlike trying to compare apples and oranges. If nothing else, Bell's position is to be found primarily in two articles and, therefore, lacks the detailed development Wolterstorff provides. Moreover, Wolterstorff is primarily a philosopher and Bell is a theologian. They can be interpreted, therefore, as addressing different audiences, which makes any comparison difficult. Though Wolterstorff is a philosopher, he is clearly writing for Christians, so I think it not unjust to suggest that as a philosopher he might have something to learn from Bell the theologian.

Wolterstorff not only writes for Christians, but much to his credit he engages scriptural and theological issues in his book. To be sure, he does so in an attempt to develop a theory of primary justice as inherent rights as an alternative to theories of justice as right order.[29] I hope to show that the

28. See Jeremiah 29:7. Bell intentionally chooses Jeremiah 29:7 because it seems to suggest that justice cannot be as narrowly circumscribed as Bell may seem to have done. Of course you need to ask what politics would suggest that Jesus as the justice of God should be described as "narrow."

29. Wolterstorff, *Justice*, ix–x.

distinction between primary justice, which Wolterstorff claims deals with distributive and commutative issues, and rectifying justice, which consists in response to breakdowns in distributive and commutative justice, is scripturally problematic. I also hope to show that the alternatives of justice as inherent rights and justice as right order are not fully consistent with Scripture. But I need first to give an overview of Wolterstorff's argument.

The structure of *Justice: Rights and Wrongs* is determined by Wolterstorff's contention that "rights" language has been wrongly dismissed by Oliver and Joan O'Donovan and Alasdair MacIntyre on the grounds that the notion of inherent rights is the result of the nominalist philosophical developments, which resulted in the sheer assertion of subjective rights as ends in themselves. The O'Donovans and MacIntyre further argue that inherent human rights are implicated in a perverse possessive individualism correlative of liberal and capitalist social orders, which have no place for understanding justice as right order.[30] In order to rebut this narrative, Wolterstorff develops a counter-narrative in which he tries to show that a conception of justice as inherent rights was not born in the fourteenth or seventeenth centuries but rather goes back to the Hebrew and Christian Scriptures.[31]

Wolterstorff acknowledges that the need to provide this counter-history means that *Justice: Rights and Wrongs* is a very different book than the one he set out to write. In order to make his case for an understanding of justice as inherent rights, he has been forced to provide a historical counter-narrative to that of justice as right order. Therefore on page 241 of this four-hundred-page book he says, "We now leave narrative behind and attend exclusively to theory." But the assumption that "theory" can be separated from the narrative—and I confess I remain unclear how Wolterstorff understands the status of his narrative for his theory—is exactly the kind of move that worries the O'Donovans and MacIntyre. If you are able to show that inherent human rights must be acknowledged to exist on philosophical grounds, why do you need to find them in Scripture?[32]

30. Ibid, 30–33.

31. Ibid., xii.

32. Wolterstorff does not engage the work of John Rawls because he thinks Rawls simply assumes the existence of inherent natural rights and therefore he does not develop an account of such rights (15–17). I find it odd, however, that Wolterstorff ignores MacIntyre's argument in *Whose Justice?* that conceptions of justice and practical reason are necessarily interrelated. To be sure, Wolterstorff has an extended discussion of why eudaimonistic ethical positions cannot sustain a theory of rights, but his arguments dealing with that issue do not take up MacIntyre's defense of an ethic of the virtues. In fact Wolterstorff provides no account of justice as a virtue. He may not think he needs to do so because of his arguments concerning eudaimonism, but a more direct discussion of why he thinks the question of justice as a virtue can be ignored would have been welcome. One of the reasons he does not treat justice as a virtue is his presumption "that the concept of a moral virtue is conceptually posterior to the concept of a morally admirable act" (289). His position on this involves complex questions about philosophical psychology as well as how act descriptions work that he does not develop in this book. Needless to say I have quite a different understanding of the significance of the virtues than Wolterstorff.

Wolterstorff does not argue that the idea of justice as right order—a conception he thinks first articulated by Plato in the *Republic*—is without relevance for an account of justice. According to Wolterstorff, right-order theorists need not and should not deny the existence of natural rights in general, just as inherent-natural-rights theorists should not deny the existence of natural laws of objective obligation.[33] Yet Wolterstorff's strong argument is that in contrast to justice as right order—a theory espoused by those who argue for human rights as conferred by agreements—the inherent-right theorists rightly maintain that we possess some rights that are not conferred. These nonconferred rights are inherent to our "possessing of certain properties, standing in certain relationships, performing certain actions," and they reveal that "each of us has a certain worth."[34]

Wolterstorff does not deny that rights language may have been put to perverse uses, but misuse does not undermine the necessary priority of justice as inherent rights over justice as right order. Contrary to MacIntyre's claim that rights assume an asocial individualism, our natural rights "are not the rights one would have if one were not living in society."[35] Rather our sociality is built into rights because a right is a right *with regard* to someone who is usually someone other than oneself, though it is also the case that someone may be oneself. But the crucial point is that rights are normative bonds that are not, for the most part, generated by the exercise of will on one's part.[36]

Drawing on the work of Charles Reid and Brian Tierney, Wolterstorff argues that such a view of justice as inherent rights can be found in developments in canon law as early as the twelfth century.[37] He also argues that such

I confess I find Wolterstorff's account of Augustine, to say the very least, odd. He argues that Augustine finally came to the view that virtue is not sufficient for happiness and as a result came closer to an "inherent rights" account of justice than good order (198). In the light of Bell's account above, particularly regarding Augustine's understanding of why worship is crucial for understanding the nature of justice, such a view as Wolterstorff's fails to do justice to Augustine's understanding not only of justice but of the virtues in general.

33. Ibid., 37. Wolterstorff, however, notes that though right-order theorists can and should concede the existence of natural rights, such a concession does not change the fact that natural rights will have a different significance for the right-order theorist than the natural-rights theorist. For the right-order theorist, the violation of someone's natural right is never in itself the treating of a human being with less than due respect. Rather it is an indication that some natural law has been disobeyed. For example, the right-order theorist may say that the rights of the poor are being violated, but that is simply to call attention from the right-order theorist perspective to the fundamental fact that the powerful and well-to-do are not fulfilling their obligation. "It is not a way of calling attention to the fact that the worth of those human beings who are poor is not being respected. The worth of human beings does not enter into his [right-order theorist's] way of thinking about rights" (43).

34. Ibid., 36. Wolterstorff distinguishes between inherent rights and human rights. A right may be inherent to a certain status and that status may be intrinsic to the human being that possesses that status but not to our nature as such. Thus the status of being a parent does not belong to human nature because one can be a human without being a parent (317–19).

35. Ibid., 33.

36. Ibid., 4.

37. Ibid., 53–59.

a view of rights is incipient in the thought of the church fathers, such as John Chrysostom's sermon on Lazarus and the rich man, but his case turns primarily on a certain reading of the Old Testament. Wolterstorff acknowledges that you cannot find in the Scripture "meta-level" talk about how to think about justice or rights. Yet he argues that the O'Donovans' claim that justice in the Old Testament, either in the form of judicial judgment or as the claim of a plaintiff before a judge, wrongly limits the work of justice in the Old Testament to rectifying justice rather than manifestations of a primary justice based in justice as inherent right.[38]

Wolterstorff notes that the striking feature of talk about justice in the Old Testament is how justice is connected to treatment of widows, orphans, resident aliens, and the poor. He observes that the prophets and psalmists do not argue the case for caring for the poor, but rather they assume it.[39] That they do so, Wolterstorff suggests, requires no special insight into why the writers of the Old Testament assumed the vulnerable to deserve particular attention. They saw quite clearly that the widow, the orphan, the resident alien, and the poor are not only often vulnerable to injustice but disproportionately actual victims of injustice.[40]

Such a "seeing," Wolterstorff contends, derived from Israel's memory that it too had experienced what it meant to be an alien in the land of Egypt (Lev. 19:33) as well as what it meant to be a slave (Deut. 24:22). Thus the assumption that "those with social power in Israel are to render justice to the vulnerable bottom ones *as a public remembrance, as a memorial*, of Yahweh's deliverance of Israel from Egypt. . . . Israel is to do justice as a memorial of its deliverance by God from the injustice of slavery."[41] Israel's commitment to justice is but the way she must live if she is to imitate and know Yahweh. Moreover, even though the law was given to Israel to make her a nation unlike other nations, a holy people, Israel's recognition of Yahweh's kingship meant all nations were held accountable to be just.

Wolterstorff acknowledges that though Israel's writers did not use the language of rights, to the extent that they assumed Yahweh holds humankind accountable for doing justice, they also assumed there was a normative structure of rights and obligations. Moreover, justice cannot be limited to God's commands, but rather we are held accountable to a "deep structure" that assumes justice as inherent rights based on the recognition of the worth of human persons.[42] Therefore the prohibition against murder found in Genesis 9:6—

38. Ibid., 68–75. Wolterstorff appeals to texts such as Isaiah 28:17 and 42:1–4 as well as Psalms 106:3 and 112:5 to argue that the rendering of juridical judgment presupposes an account of primary justice.

39. Ibid., 76.

40. Ibid., 78–79.

41. Ibid., 80.

42. Ibid., 91.

Whoever sheds the blood of a human,
By a human shall that person's blood be shed;
For in his own image
God made humankind

—is not grounded in God's law "but in the worth of the human being. All who bear God's image possess an inherent right not to be murdered."[43]

Wolterstorff argues that the narrative he has identified with the Old Testament is fundamentally continued in the New Testament.[44] The justice Jesus preaches when he opens the scroll in Luke 4:17–21 makes clear that Jesus identifies himself as God's anointed whose vocation is to proclaim to the poor, the blind, the captives, and the oppressed the good news of the inauguration of the year of the Lord that marks the time when justice shall reign.[45] Crucial for understanding the significance of Jesus's reading of the scroll is acknowledgement that Jesus does not merely proclaim the coming of God's kingdom, but is identified as the king of this kingdom.[46]

The acknowledgment of Jesus's kingship for Wolterstorff is the basis for the New Testament expansion of the scope of justice. Because Jesus is king, the justice he establishes goes beyond that envisioned in the Old Testament since now it is not enough that the powerful give to the poor what is their due. Jesus has the more radical view that a social inversion is required in which the lowly are lifted up and the high ones are cast down.[47] This does not literally mean that beggars are to become kings, but rather that justice will only be possible when the rich and powerful are cured of their attachment to wealth and power. Jesus, therefore, expands the Old Testament understanding of the downtrodden to include all those excluded from full participation in society because they are defective, malformed, or seen as religiously inferior.[48]

Jesus's expansion of those subject to injustice indicates recognition that human beings have inherent worth and that worth is to be grounded in how they are to be treated. Such a recognition of rights is clearly presumed when Jesus says, "Look at the birds of the air; they neither sow nor reap nor gather into barns, and yet your heavenly Father feeds them. Are you not of more

43. Ibid., 95.

44. Wolterstorff also deals with the theme of forgiveness, arguing that God too has rights because if God did not have rights God could not be wronged. Forgiveness requires that the one who is to forgive has been deprived of that to which they have a right. He argues against Nygren's account of *agape* exactly because it is "justice blind" just to the extent that Nygren fails to see that forgiveness necessarily incorporates the presumption of being wronged (105). But here, Wolterstorff argues, is one of the places that Jesus goes beyond the Old Testament because he regards our willingness to forgive those who wrong us as a manifestation of the repentance God requires for forgiving those who wrong God (130).

45. Ibid., 117.

46. Ibid., 120.

47. Ibid., 122–23.

48. Ibid., 126–27.

value than they?" (Matt. 6:26). Such statements imply that to be a human is to have worth. Though Jesus does not say what that worth is, Wolterstorff suggests that "it seems safe to infer" that Jesus presupposed the idea that the worth one has is that which comes from being qua human.[49]

Such is Wolterstorff's defense of an inherent-natural-rights theory of justice on scriptural and historical grounds. As I indicated, however, he does not seem to think the narrative he has provided is necessary for the justification of a natural-rights view of justice. Indeed the last third of his book is a defense of rights to show how, as he puts it, they "emerge from a certain interweaving of life- and history-goods and evils on the one hand, and the worth of human beings on the other."[50] But then one must ask: if a rights-based account of justice can be generated in such a fashion, why did he need to provide the account he does of the scriptural basis of a rights-based theory?

Put more contentiously, I think it is not at all clear why Wolterstorff assumes that justice as inherent rights—rather than a right-order account—is a necessary implication of calls for justice in Scripture. Indeed his suggestion that texts such as Leviticus and Deuteronomy cannot help but appear to us as "a bewildering mishmash of regulations concerning ritual cleanliness, instructions concerning cultic practices, and principles of justice"[51] betrays his desire to find in the Old Testament an account of justice that is not dependent on the practices of an actual people. The distinction between primary theories of justice and rectifying justice turns out to be a way to escape the historical particularity of the text.

The same problem is apparent in his treatment of Jesus. Jesus may initiate a more expansive understanding of justice, but that very way of putting the matter makes Jesus a representative of a theory of justice rather than, as Bell would have it, the very justice of God. I suspect Wolterstorff would find Bell's understanding of Jesus as the very justice of God "limiting" to the extent that such a view would imply that how Christians understand justice may well be in tension with the presumption that an account of justice, a theory of justice, is possible as such.

Wolterstorff wants to have it both ways; that is, he wants the viability of justice as inherent rights with and without his narrative. Late in his book he notes that he has reversed the narrative of those who understand natural rights to be born of individualistic and atomistic modes of thought, which climax in the UN Universal Declaration of Human Rights. In contrast, he has argued that not only did the moral vision of the writers of the Hebrew and Christian Scriptures implicitly recognize natural and human rights, but these rights were given explicit conceptualization by the canon lawyers in the twelfth century. He acknowledges that the recognition of such rights remained an "exceedingly

49. Ibid., 130–31.
50. Ibid., 288.
51. Ibid., 83.

slow and halting process, however, until, quite surprisingly, it burst forth after the horrors of World War II in the UN Declaration."[52] Scripture can now be used as a resource for grounding such rights, but to put the matter that way means Scripture serves to sustain a politics in which God does not matter. Wolterstorff may be correct that rights were discovered prior to the creation of the capitalist subject, but even if that is the case, I do not see how it can be denied that the language of rights, as used in the world in which we now find ourselves, underwrites an individualism that is not only possessive but agonistic.

Wolterstorff would find such criticisms odd, I am sure, because he argues that a secular grounding of rights is deficient just to the extent that it cannot account for respect for humans who do not possess the capacity for rational agency.[53] According to Wolterstorff, human rights require a theistic grounding because only by understanding ourselves as created in the image of God do we have sufficient reason for excluding no one from due respect. He observes that the biblical writers were well aware that some human beings were created by God who lacked the capacity to exercise dominion, but they still have a human nature sufficient to resemble God.[54] I am sympathetic with Wolterstorff's concern to make sure that those who seem to lack rational capacity are not excluded from claims of justice, but I remain unconvinced that his account of what it means for us to be in God's image can be sustained without a more robust Trinitarian account than he provides.[55]

Finally, I think the fundamental issue between Bell and Wolterstorff is one of theological method. That it is so is clear from Wolterstorff's quite charitable account of my claim in *After Christendom?* that justice is a bad idea. He suggests I could not have meant what I said, but rather that my point is that the vocabulary of justice and rights has been so corrupted by its use in the "larger social order" that the language cannot be redeemed. By contrast, Wolterstorff argues that not only can language be redeemed but "it must be redeemed—because, for one thing, to reject the language and conceptuality of justice would be to render the New Testament unintelligible. Pull justice out and nothing much is left. Justice understood in such a way, however, that it is not God or justice but God *and* justice—the justice of God and the justice God enjoins."[56]

That seems to me to put my problem with Wolterstorff about as clearly as it can be put. Wolterstorff is no foundationalist, but the move he makes here, a move that I think shapes the structure and form of his book, assumes that we must be able to secure an account of justice in and of itself if we are

52. Ibid., 361.

53. Ibid., 333.

54. Ibid., 350.

55. See, for example, Hans Reinders's account of the image of God and the disabled in his *Receiving the Gift of Friendship: Profound Disability, Theological Anthropology, and Ethics* (Grand Rapids: Eerdmans, 2008), 227–75.

56. Wolterstorff, *Justice*, 98.

to make sense of Scripture. Some forms of right-order theory could have the same problem, but it is usually the case that justice as right-order requires the naming of a history that makes unavoidable the existence of a concrete people for display of justice.[57] In other words, I am suggesting that there is at once a tendency to ignore the significance of history and politics by developing justice in terms of inherent rights.

Wolterstorff, for example, certainly has it right to point out Israel's understanding that the care of those most vulnerable is required if it is to rightly remember what God has done for it, but he fails to develop how this insight should affect our thinking about justice. That such a remembering is not constitutive of his understanding of justice as inherent rights is, I think, but a correlative of his attempt to develop an account of justice persuasive for anyone at anytime. I worry that such an account of justice may put him closer to John Rawls than he thinks. But then that may be where he desires to be.

I acknowledge that the difference between Bell and Wolterstorff cannot be settled by quoting this or that passage in the Scripture that explicitly uses the language of justice. Indeed I assume, as Bell suggests, that our understanding of justice will depend on passages of Scripture that make no mention of justice. Rather what is at stake is a construal of Scripture as a whole. I obviously think Bell is much closer to getting such a construal right just to the extent that his account of the relation between the two testaments as well as the status of and relation between Jews and Christians is crucial for how justice is to be understood.

A Passion for Justice

At the heart of Wolterstorff's account is an admirable passion for justice grounded in what he calls the "*Ur*-principle" of action: "one should never treat persons or human beings as if they had less worth than they do have; one should never treat them with under-respect, never demean them."[58] This principle once articulated can be put in even more general terms: "one should never treat *anything whatsoever* as having less worth than it is."[59] Wolterstorff is intent to sustain such principles in order to support what he calls the "moral subculture of rights." He worries that in the absence of such a subculture, the increasing secularism to which we may be subject will make appeals to justice as natural rights less compelling. If we lose the language of justice as natural rights, moreover, Wolterstorff thinks we cannot help but slide back into tribalism.[60]

57. Though I am more sympathetic with justice understood as right order, I hope it is clear that the account of justice articulated by Bell is not to be construed in terms of Wolterstorff's understanding of those two alternatives.

58. Ibid., 370.

59. Ibid.

60. Ibid., 393.

Like Wolterstorff, I too want those who suffer from Alzheimer's to have the care that befits their status as human beings. Such care, I believe, is a matter of justice. But I do not think such care is more likely to be forthcoming or sustained by a natural-rights theory of justice. Rather I think Bell rightly suggests that what is required is the recovery of communion made possible through the works of mercy. In particular, Bell argues that a text such as Matthew 25:31–45 makes clear that the works of mercy are not principles or values that then must be translated into a more universal or secular vision of justice. Rather, they summon us to participate in God's redemption by feeding the hungry, giving drink to the thirsty, clothing the naked, harboring the stranger, visiting the sick, ministering to prisoners, and burying the dead. Such is the way, Bell suggests, that we learn what it means for Jesus to be the justice of God.[61]

I know of no book that exemplifies better Bell's understanding of Jesus as God's justice than Hans Reinders's *Receiving the Gift of Friendship: Profound Disability, Theological Anthropology, and Ethics*. Reinders observes that much good has been done in the name of disability rights for creating new opportunities, as well as institutional space, for the disabled. But such an understanding of justice is not sufficient if we listen to the disabled. They do not seek to be tolerated or even respected because they have rights. Rather they seek to share their lives with us, and they want us to want to share our lives with them. In short, they want us to be claimed and to claim one another in friendship.

If you need an image for what it means for charity to be the form of the virtues and, in particular, justice, take this scene from Jennie Weiss Block's book *Copious Hosting: A Theology of Access for People with Disabilities*. She tells the story of Jason, a fourteen-year-old boy with profound intellectual disabilities who was born with spina bifida. He has an enlarged head and, because his arms and legs have often been broken due to a bone disease, his limbs are twisted. He cannot feed himself and must be carefully bathed and diapered. He is cared for by Felicia Santos, who is a professional caregiver. Weiss Block reports on a particular visit, a visit that she says changed her life, when she witnessed Felicia "leaning forward, talking softly to Jason. He was smiling. I stood for a few minutes before speaking and watched their interaction. What I witnessed between them was the purest love—the kind of love that asks for nothing in return."[62] That is what charity-formed justice looks like.[63]

61. Bell, "Jesus, the Jews, and the Politics of God's Justice," 106.

62. Jennie Weiss Block, *Copious Hosting: A Theology of Access for People with Disabilities* (New York: Continuum, 2002), 188. I am confident that Wolterstorff would claim that his account of justice would also identify Felicia's care of Jason as justice, but I do not see how justice understood as inherent rights can have such communion be constitutive of justice in the way Bell suggests it must be.

63. I am not "reading into" Reinders's account, as Reinders provides a quite extensive treatment of Aquinas's understanding of charity as the form of the virtues (ibid., 297–311). In doing so, however, he draws on the work of Paul Wadell to emphasize the primacy of God's grace. We are only able to acquire the virtues to make us God's friends because God has first befriended us.

Bell acknowledges that viewed through the lens of modernity's politics, such a view of justice—justice shaped by the works of mercy—will be dismissed as "philanthropy." But that is exactly the perspective that must be rejected if the justice that is the church is not to be identified with the justice of the nation-state. Wolterstorff worries that if justice is identified by Bell's "Spirit-blown mobile community," we will lack the universality necessary to sustain appeals to justice as such. But no theory of justice will be sufficient to do that work. Rather than a theory, God has called into the world a people capable of transgressing the borders of the nation-state to seek the welfare of the downtrodden.[64]

What we need is not a theory of justice capable of universal application. Rather what we need is what we have. What we have is a people learning again to live in diaspora. Bell concludes his article by observing that the broader argument concerning the necessity of attending to political context for a theological reading of Scripture converges with the development of a more focused argument concerning the nature of justice in Scripture. That it does so is crucial for understanding the political form God's restorative justice takes. For as it turned out, Israel's political vocation took the form of a politics of diaspora through which it becomes a blessing to all people. Bell suggests a similar political vocation has been given to the church insofar as it has been joined to Israel's Messiah, requiring it to be on pilgrimage to the ends of the world seeking reconciliation through the works of mercy. Such is the justice of God.

> Here is my servant, whom I uphold,
> my chosen, in whom my soul delights;
> I have put my spirit upon him;
> he will bring forth justice to the nations.
> He will not cry or lift up his voice,
> or make it heard in the street;
> a bruised reed he will not break,
> and a dimly burning wick he will not quench;
> he will faithfully bring forth justice. (Isa. 42:1–3)[65]

64. For an account of the radical implications of the works of mercy, see Kelly Johnson's *The Fear of Beggars: Stewardship and Poverty in Christian Ethics* (Grand Rapids: Eerdmans, 2007).

65. Wolterstorff also quotes this passage from Isaiah observing that Isaiah is not suggesting that the servant will establish a fair legal system, but rather that the servant will bring about a general social condition in which there will be no need for a judicial system to vindicate those who have been treated unjustly (Wolterstorff, *Justice*, 74). Wolterstorff does not explore the difference a Christological reading of this passage may make.

9

Pentecost

Learning the Languages of Peace

Being Particular about Particularity[1]

In his justly celebrated book *The Dignity of Difference: How to Avoid the Clash of Civilizations*, Jonathan Sacks, the Chief Rabbi of the United Hebrew Congregations of Britain and the Commonwealth, argues that the "greatest single antidote to violence is *conversation*, speaking our fears, listening to the fears of others, and in that sharing of vulnerabilities discovering a genesis of hope."[2] Some assume, according to Sacks, that if such conversations are to avoid becoming interminable debates between incommensurable positions, the participants must abandon their particularistic perspectives in favor of a more universal point of view.[3] A more universal perspective is required because it is assumed that if we are to speak truthfully to one another, we must do so from a position available to anyone.[4]

1. This chapter is adapted from a lecture first given at the Amnesty International Conference in Oxford, February 20, 2008.

2. Jonathan Sacks, *The Dignity of Difference: How to Avoid the Clash of Civilizations* (London: Continuum, 2002), 2. As much as I admire Sacks's book, I think he mistakenly underwrites the description "clash of civilizations." Talal Asad rightly argues that "there is no such thing as a clash of civilizations because there are no self-contained societies to which fixed civilizational values correspond" (*On Suicide Bombing* [New York: Columbia University Press, 2007], 12).

3. Sacks, *Dignity of Difference*, 83. One of the great virtues of Sacks's book is that he not only commends conversation but exemplifies what he commends. He writes unapologetically as a Jew yet in a manner that is accessible to those who do not share his faith. I am not as accomplished as Sacks, and I may even be more unapologetic as a Christian than he is as a Jew, but I hope nonetheless to follow his example in this chapter. Of course given the position I take, I assume some Christians may find themselves in deeper disagreement with me than those who are not Christian.

4. Ibid., 19.

Drawing on his own tradition, and in particular the story of Babel, Sacks argues that it is not true that truth is timeless or the same everywhere for anyone. It was at Babel that people, seduced by the technological breakthrough of learning to make bricks, concluded that they had become godlike because they were now free from the limitations of nature and their particular histories. For Sacks, therefore, Babel represents a turning point in history. For after Babel, God, who had first made a covenant with all creation, chooses to call out one people that they might be a witness to God's will for all people. The builders of Babel had tried to impose a human-made unity on a divinely created diversity, but after Babel, God "turns to one people and commands it to be different *in order to teach humanity the dignity of difference*."[5]

Sacks acknowledges that his refusal to abandon the distinctive perspective of Judaism means some will brand him a "tribalist."[6] Yet he argues that the very universalism that many assume to be the antithesis to the resurgence of tribalism, or worse terrorism, is an inadequate account of the human situation. A global culture may bring about much good, but from Sacks's perspective, such cultures, particularly when they take the form of empires, do much harm because they fail to be capable of acknowledging difference. That Sacks should distrust the universal pretensions of empires is not surprising, for, as he observes, Judaism was born as a protest against empire.[7]

I am extremely sympathetic with Sacks's attempt to recover the significance of conversation as an alternative to violence. I mentioned above the "Appeal to Abolish War" that Enda McDonagh and I drafted in order to try to begin such a conversation.[8] I confess, however, that I doubt such conversations can lead to peace without some specification of what such conversations should be about. It is my presumption that if conversing with an other for the sake of "diversity" becomes an end in itself, we are just as likely to want to kill each other as to make peace.[9] But I will state again that I am sympathetic with Sacks's attempt

5. Ibid., 53. Sacks's account of Babel has striking similarities with that of John Howard Yoder. See Yoder's essay "The Disavowal of Constantine: An Alternative Perspective on Interfaith Dialogue," in *The Royal Priesthood: Essays Ecclesiological and Ecumenical*, ed. Michael Cartwright (Grand Rapids: Eerdmans, 1994), 242–61.

6. One of the reasons I am sympathetic with Sacks may be because of the accusation that I am also a "sectarian, fideistic, tribalist." For my response to that charge, see the introduction to my book *Christian Existence Today: Essays on Church, World, and Living in Between* (Grand Rapids: Brazos, 2001), 1–23.

7. Sacks, *Dignity of Difference*, 60. One of the challenges for positions like Sacks's and my own is how the very descriptions used to critique us are part of the problem. For example, words like "religion" or "pluralism" are from my perspective problematic. See, for example, my chapter "The End of Religious Pluralism: A Tribute to David Burrell, C.S.C.," in *The State of the University: Academic Knowledges and the Knowledge of God* (Oxford: Blackwell, 2007), 58–75.

8. See chapter 4 above, "Reflections on the 'Appeal to Abolish War.'"

9. See, for example, my chapter entitled, "The Non-Violent Terrorist: In Defense of Christian Fanaticism," in my *Sanctify Them in the Truth: Holiness Exemplified*, 177–90 (Edinburgh: T&T Clark, 1998).

to recover "the dignity of difference" by resisting the presumptive universalism associated with liberal regimes, which allegedly stand for peace in contrast to terrorist attacks exemplified by September 11, 2001.[10]

Of course it may seem odd for a Christian to underwrite Sacks's claim that God loves difference. It has, after all, been the Christian conceit that the Jews are particularistic while Christians represent a universalistic faith. For example, in 1923 Ernst Troeltsch gave a lecture at Oxford entitled "The Place of Christianity Among the World-Religions." He argued that Christianity is the only "world religion" that can claim absolute and unconditional universality because it alone has produced a philosophy of history that recognizes that there is a historical development that promotes unconditional worthwhile goals. The name he gives that development is Europe. In Troeltsch's words,

> It is impossible to deny facts or to resist fate. And it is historical facts that have welded the civilizations of Greece, Rome and Northern Europe. All our thoughts and feelings are impregnated with Christian motives and Christian presuppositions; and, conversely, our whole Christianity is indissolubly bound up with elements of the ancient and modern civilizations of Europe. From being a Jewish sect Christianity has become the religion of all Europe. It stands or falls with European civilization; whilst, on its own part, it has entirely lost its Oriental character and has become hellenised and westernized. Our European conceptions of personality and its eternal, divine right, and of progress towards a kingdom of the spirit and of God, our enormous capacity for expansion and for the interconnection of spiritual and temporal, our whole social order, our science, our art—all these rest, whether we know it or not, upon the basis of this deorientalised Christianity. Its primary claim to validity is thus the fact that only through it have we become what we are, and that only in it can we preserve the religious forces that we need. Apart from it we lapse either into a self-destructive titanic attitude, or into effeminate trifling, or into crude brutality. . . . We cannot live without a religion, yet the only religion we can endure is Christianity, for Christianity has grown up with us and has become a part of our very being.[11]

10. Drawing on the work of Richard Tuck, Asad argues that there is a kind of violence inherent to liberal states not simply because such states require armies for their defense, but

> rather that violence founds the law as it founds political community. Violence is therefore embedded in the very concept of liberty that lies at the heart of liberal doctrine. That concept presupposes that the morally independent individual's right to violent self-defense is yielded to the state and that the state becomes the sole protector of individual liberties, abstracting the right to kill from domestic politics, denying to any agents other than states the right to kill at home and abroad. The right to kill is the right to behave in violent ways toward other people—especially toward citizens of foreign states at war and toward the uncivilized, whose very existence is a threat to civilized order. In certain circumstances, killing others is necessary, so it seems, for the security it provides. (*On Suicide Bombing*, 59–60)

11. Ernst Troeltsch, *Christian Thought: Its History and Application*, ed. and trans. Baron von Hügel (London: University of London Press, 1923), 24–25. For an insightful analysis of Troeltsch's understanding of Christianity among the world religions, indeed of the very creation of the idea of

As much as I should like to attribute Troeltsch's views to his commitment to the prejudices of the Enlightenment, it cannot be denied that Troeltsch gives expression to the Christian presumption that Christianity in contrast to Judaism represents a universal faith.[12] This presumption is based on a story Christians believe is the answer to Babel: Pentecost. Christians therefore have gone into the world with missionary zeal convinced that they possess the truth that all people desire even if they have not yet realized it.[13] The political form this presumption took is called Constantinianism, which has taken many different forms, but Troeltsch's claim for the inseparability of Christianity and Europe is as good an example as one could want for one of its most recent incarnations.[14]

"world religions," see Tomoko Masuzawa's *The Invention of World Religions: Or, How European Universalism Was Preserved in the Language of Pluralism* (Chicago: University of Chicago Press, 2005), 309–23. Troeltsch reflects Kant's judgment that Judaism is not really a religion at all "but merely a union of a number of people who, since they belonged to a particular stock, formed themselves into a commonwealth under purely political laws and not into a church" (*Religion within the Limits of Reason Alone*, trans. Theodore Greene and Hoyt Hudson [New York: Harper, 1960], 116). By "church" Kant meant the invisible church of reason, not the one "grounded on dogmas" and organized by men (140).

12. This, of course, raises the question to what extent the Enlightenment is the result of Christian presuppositions. It is my own view that the Enlightenment is a secularized form of Christianity and, in particular, of Constantinian Christianity—which, from my point of view, makes it all the more dangerous.

13. Troeltsch observes that the

> heathen races are being morally and spiritually disintegrated by the contact with European civilization; hence they demand a substitute from the higher religion and culture. We have a missionary duty towards these races, and our enterprise is likely to meet with success amongst them, although Christianity, be it remembered, is by no means the only religion taking part in this missionary campaign. Islam and Buddhism are also missionary religions. But in relation to the great world-religions we need to recognize that they are expressions of the religious consciousness corresponding to certain definite types of culture, and that it is their duty to increase in depth and purity by means of their own interior impulses, a task in which the contact with Christianity may prove helpful, to them as to us, in such processes of development from within. The great religions might indeed be described as crystallizations of thought of great races, as these races are themselves crystallizations of various biological and anthropological forms. There can be no conversion or transformation of one into the other, but only a measure of agreement and of mutual understanding. (*Christian Thought*, 29–30)

One could not wish for a more determinative expression of the racist presumptions that formed the thought world of the Enlightenment. My colleagues Willie Jennings and Jay Carter have written books I believe will force us to recognize the racialized character of much recent theology. See Willie Jennings, *The Christian Imagination: Theology and the Origin of Race* (New Haven: Yale University Press, 2010) and J. Kameron Carter, *Race: A Theological Account* (Oxford: Oxford University Press, 2008).

14. Popes and theological liberals are seldom thought to share common assumptions, but Benedict XVI's famous lecture "Faith, Reason, and the University," delivered at Regensburg on September 12, 2006 (available at http://www.vatican.va/holy_father/benedict_xvi/speeches/2006/september/documents/hf_ben-xvi_spe_20060912_university-regensburg_en.html), sounded themes quite similar to Troeltsch's. For example, Benedict described the rapprochement between biblical faith and Greek inquiry as one of "intrinsic necessity." He elaborated this claim, noting that

It is, of course, hard to know which came first, that is, the presumption that the Christian faith represents universal knowledge that only needs to be explained to those who are not yet Christian, or the politics of empire. Either way it is now clear that Christian presumption of universality either as knowledge qua knowledge or as a politics is—or at least should be—over.[15] This does not mean I believe the Christian faith is not true, but that what it means for it to be true cannot be secured by a theory of truth more determinative than the faith itself.

Interestingly enough, Christians now confronted by philosophical and political alternatives that claim universality as a necessary position to address the challenges of living in a global environment find themselves in the awkward position Jews have long occupied. From a cosmopolitan perspective, Christianity represents a parochial tradition that cannot pretend to be true as knowledge or as an ethic or politics. Thus the presumption that the language of rights and a faith based on revelation are in fundamental tension.

One strategy for Christians confronted by the challenge to pass muster as a faith compatible with more secular and universal alternatives is to criticize the arrogance of such presumption. As those long experienced in the exercise of such arrogance, it should not be surprising that Christians are able to spot it in

---

> this inner rapprochement between Biblical faith and Greek philosophical inquiry was an event of decisive importance not only for the standpoint of the history of religions, but also from that of world history—it is an event which concerns us even today. Given this convergence, it is not surprising that Christianity, despite its origins and some significant developments in the East, finally took on its historically decisive character in Europe. We can also express this the other way around: this convergence, with the subsequent addition of the Roman heritage, created Europe and remains the foundation of what can rightly be called Europe.

One cannot help but wonder what Benedict might mean by the phrase "despite its origins," as well as his suggestion that it was only with Europe that Christianity took on its "historically decisive character." Given Benedict's Augustinianism, you might think he would find the presumption that Christianity has assumed a final decisive character problematic. For an analysis and critique of Benedict XVI's position, see Dale F. Irwin, "Benedict XVI, the Ends of European Christendom, and the Horizons of World Christianity," in *The Pontificate of Benedict XVI: Its Premises and Promises*, ed. William G. Persch (Grand Rapids: Eerdmans, 2009), 1–20.

15. In *A Secular Age* (Cambridge, MA: Belknap, 2007), Charles Taylor provides the most compelling account we have that Christendom, that is, the attempt to imbue a civilization and society with the Christian faith, is over. He does not deny that the societies of the West will remain historically informed by Christianity, but he suggests "that it will be less and less common for people to be drawn into or kept within a faith by some strong political or group identity, or by the sense that they are sustaining a socially essential ethic" (314). I think Taylor is right for no other reason than that the Christianity so often represented by those who seek to maintain a Christian social order is little more than a parody of the gospel. From my perspective, I regard this development as a positive good because I assume that Christians made a decisive mistake when they thought they could use the power of the state or its equivalent to make the church secure. For my more extended reflections on Taylor's book, see Rom Coles's and my essay "Long Live the Weeds and the Wilderness Yet: Reflections on *A Secular Age*," *Modern Theology* 26 (July 2010): 349–62.

others. Put more philosophically, I think there are deep questions that bedevil attempts to develop a cosmopolitan perspective that is free of particularistic convictions.[16] Advocates of cosmopolitan perspectives too often fail to be as candid as Troeltsch's identification of Christianity with Europe. After all, who wants to acknowledge that the universalism they represent is that of the new Europe—that is, America?[17]

I think it is equally unlikely that a coherent account of natural rights has been given.[18] I have no difficulty with rights claims that express social and legal duties, but claims of human rights qua human rights involve philosophical difficulties that cannot be resolved. In particular, questions of what kind of human being we need to be to have rights are very troubling in relation to the mentally handicapped. Moreover, once rights language is legitimated in the abstract, rights seem to multiply faster than rabbits.

My deepest worry about rights, however, is how the language of rights can eviscerate more determinative moral descriptions. For example, during the civil rights campaign in the American South, the killing of a civil rights worker was described as a violation of his rights. If you think "rights" are more basic than the description "murder," you have an indication that language has gone on a holiday.

16. Kwame Anthony Appiah has provided, at least as far as I know, the best account of cosmopolitanism that negotiates this tension. According to Appiah, cosmopolitans hold in tension two ideas: (1) that we have obligations to others that reach beyond those that give us the resources for identity; (2) that the other is valued not just as human life, but as a particular human life. Appiah does not deny that these ideas are often in tension, which indicates that cosmopolitanism is not the name of a solution, or even a "position," but a challenge (*Cosmopolitanism: Ethics in a World of Strangers* [New York: W. W. Norton, 2006], xv). Appiah provides a more developed philosophical defense of his understanding of what he calls "rooted cosmopolitanism" in *The Ethics of Identity* (Princeton: Princeton University Press, 2005), 213–72. There he draws primarily on John Stuart Mill to sustain his defense of autonomy that allegedly does not undermine the "local." I remain unconvinced.

17. Oliver O'Donovan observes that publicity mediates universalism to the extent that its aspiration is to overcome differences in order to unify communications within a single world communication sphere. According to O'Donovan, modernity, which began its career with three centuries of conquest, produced colonialism, which, on being exhausted, found its new home in communications. The potential of globally transmitted images became the spearhead of an expansive movement which seemed to bypass obstacles posed by differences of language and national politics. O'Donovan notes it is hardly surprising, therefore, that these anarchistic aspirations, easily underestimated by Western observers, were identified in other parts of the globe with colonial intent. Accordingly it is not difficult to see the revival of radical Islamism as a protest against the universal ambitions of Western communications. He concludes, "In this universalizing thrust we may observe how Western society has forgotten how to be secular. Secularity is a stance of patience in the face of plurality, made sense of by eschatological hope; forgetfulness of it is part and parcel with the forgetfulness of Christian suppositions about history" (*Common Objects of Love: Moral Reflection and the Shaping of Community* [Grand Rapids: Eerdmans, 2002], 68–69). I am indebted to Adam Hollowell for drawing my attention to O'Donovan's argument.

18. For an attempt to provide a theological defense of "natural rights," see Esther Reed, *The Ethics of Human Rights: Contested Doctrinal and Moral Issues* (Waco: Baylor University Press, 2007).

I am not, however, going to pursue the conceptual issues surrounding the use of "inherent rights." Rather I want to explore the humanism that often informs the appeal to said rights, for I think there is an agony at the heart of that humanism to the extent that it is thought an effort must be made to remove all suffering from our lives. One result of this presumption is that many who assume the responsibility to create a better world in the name of eliminating suffering find that they themselves suffer from either doing too much or too little.[19]

For example, Sacks notes that the increasing awareness of our global interrelation tends to undermine our sense of moral responsibility. No longer able to identify who does what to whom, we are tempted to assume we bear no responsibility except for our immediate actions.[20] With his customary insight Zygmunt Bauman supports Sacks's suggestion, observing that as we become ever more knowledgeable about our and other people's plight, we are overwhelmed and become less able to respond with ethically inspired action. Paradoxically, according to Bauman, "our shared capacity to do harm seems infinitely greater than our shared capacity to do good."[21]

Joseph Amato, in his unfortunately little-known book *Victims and Values: A History and a Theory of Suffering*, suggests that this transformation in our consciousness, that is, that we know ourselves in relation to the suffering of the distant other, is inseparable from the "replacement of the traditional individual, who was attached by life and imagination to a single locality, by the modern individual, who by thought, opinion, and empathy is joined to a changing world."[22] The problem with such a consciousness, according to Amato,

19. Charles Taylor characterizes this form of humanism as "exclusive" in order to indicate that such a humanism, which may have come from a religious tradition, is now offered as the only alternative to religion. In short Taylor suggests that what it means to call our age "secular" is that now we live in a time in which "the eclipse of all goals beyond human flourishing" is conceivable (*Secular Age*, 18–19). Taylor's story of the development of this kind of humanism is complex, but his insight is crucial that as a correlative of the development of deism came a sense of invulnerability necessary to sustain a sense of self-possession (300–301). He then, like Foucault, suggests that the measures to ensure safety can make us insensitive to whatever lies beyond this human world. In particular, suffering becomes a threat to such a world, reminding us, as it does, that we are not invulnerable. Ironically the altruism that such a humanism produces can result in some humans being more "civilized" than others. The influence of Ivan Illich on Taylor's understanding of "modernity" has not been properly appreciated. For like Illich, Taylor does not think modern society is free of Christianity but rather it is an imitation of Christianity, and that makes it all the more demonic. Taylor, therefore, like Illich, thinks only "the best can become the worst." See Taylor's foreword to David Cayley's *The Rivers North of the Future: The Testament of Ivan Illich* (Toronto: House of Anansi, 2005).

20. Sacks, *Dignity of Difference*, 14.

21. Zygmunt Bauman, "The Liquid Modern Adventures of the 'Sovereign Expressions of Life,'" in *Concern for the Other: Perspectives on the Ethics of K. E. Løgstrup* (Notre Dame: University of Notre Dame Press, 2007), 133.

22. Joseph Amato, *Victims and Values: A History and a Theory of Suffering* (New York: Praeger, 1990), xxi. Amato thinks the development of sympathy for the distant other originates not in Christianity or humanism but more recently in Enlightenment and Romantic sensitivities.

is that not only are there more victims at our door than our front steps can hold, but the attempt to sympathize with those who suffer occurs at the same time when "people in ever greater numbers discard the notion that suffering is an inevitable part of human experience."[23] As a result those who refuse to be liberated from the particularity of their religious convictions, who suffer from traditions in which suffering is not assumed to be antithetical to being human, or who refuse to cease suffering, can only be ignored or eliminated.[24]

I hope to show that the Christian experience of Pentecost and what it means to learn to speak as well as understand another's language is a continuing resource God has given the church to sustain our ability to suffer as well as respond to those who suffer for the long haul. Our ability to communicate means we do not have to be isolated from one another by what we endure. There is, therefore, a crucial relationship between human suffering and the gift of speech. In order to develop that claim I want to direct our attention to Herbert McCabe's (OP) understanding of communication as the paradigm of ethics. I do so because McCabe's stress on the bodily character of communication challenges the presumption that communication can take place without people actually being present to one another.

Moreover, by focusing on McCabe's account of language I hope to show how, at least for Christians, the assumption that we must choose between membership in a particularistic community or some version of a more inclusive humanism is a false alternative. For the very presumption that we must so choose implies that such a choice makes sense in the abstract. But

23. Ibid., xxii. Talal Asad notes that the modern sufferer's sense of pain no longer has any moral significance, which may make it easier to bear. In contrast, modern poverty is experienced as more unjust, making it less tolerable. By calling attention to these developments, he denies he is suggesting that the distribution of pain engendered by modern power is worse than that of pre-modern societies. Rather he is only trying to suggest that they are different. Nor is he claiming that it is an undeniable social fact that there has been an amelioration of illness and improvements in public health. He calls attention to these differences to stress "that more is at stake in secularism than compassion for other human beings in plural democratic societies. And nothing is less plausible than the claim that secularism is an essential means of avoiding destructive conflict and establishing peace in the modern world. Secular societies—France among them—have always been capable of seeking solidarity at home while engaging in national wars and imperial conquests" ("Trying to Understand French Secularism," in *Political Theologies*, ed. Henri de Vries [New York: Fordham University Press, 2006], 24).

24. I think this stance toward suffering that is so defining of modern humanism helps explain the violence often characteristic as well as justified by appeals to our common humanity. Thus Asad argues "that the cult of sacrifice, blood, and death that secular liberals find so repellent in pre-liberal Christianity is a part of the genealogy of modern liberalism itself, in which violence and tenderness go together. . . . There is the imperative to use any means necessary (including homicide and suicide) to defend the nation-state that constitutes one's worldly identity and defends one's health and security and, on the other hand, the obligation to revere all human life, to offer life in place of death to universal humanity; the first presupposes a capacity for ruthlessness, the second for kindness" (*On Suicide Bombing*, 88). For the significance of the phrase "the refusal to cease suffering," see Daniel Bell, *Liberation Theology after the End of History: The Refusal to Cease Suffering* (London: Routledge, 2001).

we are never people in the abstract; we are people who are embedded in the narratives of particular linguistic communities. Our humanity depends on our ability to speak to one another, but that very ability is also the source of our differences. We are united by what divides us. Any attempt to overcome the reality of our linguistic constitution, and in particular any attempt to suggest that we suffer from that which constitutes our very being, threatens to hide from us a cruelty we perpetrate on one another in the name of a common humanity.

The "Humanism" of Herbert McCabe

In 1957, in response to the question "Does Oxford moral philosophy corrupt youth?" Elizabeth Anscombe answered that of course Oxford moral philosophy does not corrupt the youth. From Anscombe's perspective the problem is much deeper. Oxford moral philosophers do not corrupt the youth because their philosophy reflects as well as reproduces the corrupt moral presumptions of the spirit of the time. Such philosophy might be called, in Anscombe's words, "the philosophy of the flattery of that spirit."[25]

I have no stake in taking sides as to whether Anscombe's evaluation of Oxford moral philosophy was fair or unfair. I only call attention to it to suggest that while she was so judging Oxford philosophers, someone was developing an account of ethics in Oxford that was anything but a "flattery of the spirit of the time." His name was Herbert McCabe. McCabe was perhaps more theologian than philosopher, but as will become apparent, he was well acquainted with the philosophical alternatives of the day.

In 1968 McCabe published *Law, Love, and Language*, a book I believe should have changed the way we think about ethics.[26] Unfortunately that did not happen, but it is never too late to make use of a good thing. Indeed we may be in a better place to appreciate McCabe's position now because he argues, as Sacks's emphasis on conversation implies, that our ability to communicate, to be in conversation, makes us human. To be human, to share a common nature, according to McCabe, means we share a biological and linguistic nature. Humans are animals that talk (37).

McCabe avoids, therefore, any account of the human that might tempt us to forget our bodily nature. To be sure, to be human requires that at least in

25. Elizabeth Anscombe, "Does Oxford Moral Philosophy Corrupt Youth?" in *Human Life, Action, and Ethics: Essays by G. E. M. Anscombe*, ed. Mary Geach and Luke Gormelly (Exeter: Imprint Academic, 2005), 167.

26. Herbert McCabe, *Law, Love, and Language* (London: Continuum, 2003). Paginations will appear in the text. I wrote a foreword for the new edition of *Law, Love, and Language*, which the publisher forgot to include. For anyone interested, it has been published as "An Unpublished Foreword," *New Blackfriars* 86 (May 2005): 291–95.

principle we are able to communicate with other humans by using conventional signs. But if we came across any form of life that seemed to share our nature in only one of these ways, we would not be sure whether it could be called human. Creatures from Mars, for example, might be able to communicate with us, but if we could not breed with them, we should not call our guests human (38).

Our language, therefore, is the culmination of organic life (68).[27] "It is because I have this sort of body, a human body with a human life, that my communication can be linguistic. The human body is a source of communication" (90). McCabe puts it this way: "Instead of saying that I have a private mind and a public body, a mind for having concepts in and body for saying and hearing words, I say that I have a body that is able to be with other bodies not merely by physical contact but by linguistic communication. Having a soul is just being able to communicate; having a mind is being able to communicate linguistically" (86).[28]

Our shared bodily nature is not sufficient to sustain a common humanity, because as linguistic animals we can to some extent create responses to our world that constitute quite distinct worlds.[29] Our language not only distinguishes us from other animals, but it also distinguishes our animality from that of other animals as well as from each other (68). Therefore "there is no such thing on earth as a purely linguistic community" (46). Communication

27. McCabe was a great Aquinas scholar, and his emphasis on the body reflects not only what he learned from Wittgenstein, but also Aquinas's emphasis on our bodily nature. For example, Aquinas asks if the body of man was given an apt disposition, that is, was it appropriate that humans have an upright stature. He answers yes for four reasons: (1) our senses were given not only for procuring the necessities of life, but for knowledge, which means in contrast to animals, humans alone take pleasure in the beauty of sensible objects; (2) upright stature provides for greater freedom of the acts of the interior powers; (3) if humans were prone to the ground, they would need to use their hands as forefeet and thus lose their utility for other purposes; and (4) "because if man's stature were prone to the ground, and he used his hands as fore-feet, he would be obliged to take hold of his food with his mouth. Thus he would have a protruding mouth, with thick and hard lips, and also a hard tongue, so as to keep it from being hurt by exterior things; as we see in other animals. Moreover, such an attitude would quite hinder speech, which is reason's proper operation" (*Summa Theologiae* Iae.91.3.3).

28. McCabe's emphasis on the body obviously reflects the profound influence of Wittgenstein. Too often I fear that Wittgenstein is interpreted as assuming that all language is purely conventional if not arbitrary. John Bowlin, however, rightly argues that Wittgenstein thought that some of the moral and ontological commitments that constitute the foundation of our linguistic practices are set in place by custom or convention shared by those who inhabit a linguistic community that is not shared by all, but not all of our commitments are so constituted. Some are constituted by "nature," by what Wittgenstein calls in *On Certainty* "nature's grace" (505) by which we know anything at all (John Bowlin, "Nature's Grace: Aquinas and Wittgenstein on Natural Law and Moral Knowledge," in *Grammar and Grace: Reformulations of Aquinas and Wittgenstein*, ed. Jeffrey Stout and Robert MacSwain, [London: SCM, 2004], 154–74).

29. Appiah seems quite close to McCabe in this respect, arguing as McCabe does that we share a biology, "but that does not give us, in the relevant sense, a shared ethical nature" (*Ethics of Identity*, 252). Indeed in *Cosmopolitanism* he remarks, "Humanity isn't, in the relevant sense, an identity at all" (98).

requires sharing a common life that is intensified through language. We only become language users through the training provided by a particular language community in which we learn the ever-changing, and thus provisional, character of the language that speaks us.

The challenge facing linguistic animals, therefore, is to learn to live in a world in which the linguistic community is never co-extensive with the genetic community. We are not able to communicate with one another in virtue of our shared humanity, but rather our ability to communicate depends on being a member of a particular community.[30] Accordingly, the more concrete our discussion, the more work our language does, the more we become isolated from one another. As a result the story of human life is not and cannot be a single story. Indeed attempts to create a stable human community, to ensure we can communicate, have ended in failure (111).

You may begin to wonder what all this has to do with ethics. Ethics, for McCabe, is the study of human behavior as communication, because what we are able to accomplish or fail to accomplish is determined by what we can and cannot say (94). Just as literary criticism enables us to enjoy a poem or a novel more deeply, so the purpose of ethics is to enable us to enjoy life more fully "by entering into the significance of human action" (95). So ethics, like literary criticism, is never finished seeking, as it must, the deeper meaning of an action within the terms of a specific system of communication (98). Determining what we want, that is, to discover what it means to be free, is the great challenge that confronts us because we so seldom know what it is we desire (61).

To be sure, the dual character of human existence—that we are at once a natural and a linguistic community—provides a sufficient basis for what can be described as natural law. We do have a law in the depth of ourselves, and to act contrary to this law is to violate our nature (45). Yet that law is known primarily through what McCabe calls the "county council" understanding of natural law. For through the deliberation of county councils, decisions are made that create laws of expectation that allow life to flourish. But natural law so understood cannot be identified with the "highest common factor of the moral codes of different societies" (59).[31]

30. Sacks says something quite similar by observing,

> There is no universal language. There is no way we can speak, communicate or even think without placing ourselves within the constraints of a particular language whose contours were shaped by hundreds of generations of speakers, storytellers, artists and visionaries who came before us, whose legacy we inherit and of whose story we become a part. Within each language we can say something new. No language is fixed, unalterable, complete. What we cannot do is place ourselves outside the particularities of language to arrive at a truth, a way of understanding and responding to the world that applies to everyone at all times. That is not the essence of humanity but an attempt to escape from humanity. (*Dignity of Difference*, 54–55)

31. McCabe observes that Aquinas's account of natural law presumes such an understanding of the "county council" because he thought God, as "the inventor of mankind, the one who made

This means McCabe's account of ethics as communication cannot ensure anything like a common morality. Just as we have no basis to guarantee our ability in principle to communicate, neither do we have the innate ability to view the history of mankind as a dramatic unity. Of course some have tried to write such a history by utilizing the idea of progress or some analogue of that story, but such views inevitably come to grief when confronted by concentration camps and nuclear weapons.

Instead McCabe argues that the biblical view is that though we cannot now write a history of humanity we must live in the hope that in the end such a history can be written (112–13). However fragmented the human race may be, a people have been called into the world to sustain the hope for a common destiny (113).[32] The Bible, at least after the first eleven chapters of Genesis, does not try to be a history of humanity, but rather tells the story of a people whose history is a sacrament of the history of humanity.[33] The law, particularly the Decalogue, was given to these chosen people so they might learn to avoid the idolatrous temptation to assume, because they have been chosen, that they are the end of history.

---

the decisions about what sort of institutions mankind should have, had as a matter of fact issued the basic laws of mankind." Aquinas thought the Decalogue was God telling us the natural law, but McCabe suggests the matter is better put that God does not reveal to us the Ten Commandments, but the Ten Commandments reveal God to us. They do so because the Decalogue, particularly the prohibition against work on the Sabbath, is given to stop us from presuming we are our own creation (*Law, Love, and Language*, 57).

32. Sacks makes a similar point, suggesting that "the central insight of monotheism—that if God is the parent of humanity, then we are all members of a single extended family—has become more real in its implications than ever before. The Enlightenment gave us the concept of universal rights, but this remains a 'thin' morality, stronger in abstract ideas than in its grip on the moral imagination. Far more powerful is the biblical idea that those in need are our brothers and sisters and that poverty is something we feel in our bones" (*Dignity of Difference*, 112).

33. Oliver O'Donovan suggests that Israel's being so called means we "must allow that divine providence is ready to protect other national traditions besides the sacred one"—which implies, according to O'Donovan,

> something about the limits of collective identities. To be a human being at all is to participate in one or more collective identities. But there is no collective identity so overarching and all-encompassing that no human beings are left outside it. In that sense it is true that to speak of "humanity" is to speak of an abstraction. Only in that sense, for in fact "humanity" has a perfectly conceivable referent, and we should not hesitate to say that "humanity" is real. But it is not a reality that we can command politically. We do not meet it in any community, however great, of which we could assume leadership. We meet it only in the face of Christ, who presents himself as our leader and commander. The titanic temptation which besets collectives needs the check of a perpetual plurality at the universal level. There are always "others," those not of our fold whom we must respect and encounter. (*The Desire of the Nations: Rediscovering the Roots of Political Theology* [Cambridge: Cambridge University Press, 1999], 73)

I am obviously sympathetic with O'Donovan's suggestion, but I worry that his use of the language of "national traditions" may reproduce romantic understandings of politics.

Christians believe they have been grafted into the history of Israel by Jesus, who we believe is the very word of Yahweh. Thus in the Gospel of John the coming of Jesus is compared with the coming of a new language. McCabe writes, "Jesus is the word, the language of God which comes to be a language for man" (129). Accordingly McCabe makes the extraordinary claim that Jesus, not Adam, is "the first human being, the first member of the human race in whom humanity came to fulfillment, the first human being for whom to live was simply to love—for this is what human beings are for."[34] The witness of Jesus's love does not provide a utopian plan for a new society. Rather Jesus offers himself as the source that makes possible the creation of a community of communication in which the miracle of our common humanity occurs.

The crucifixion of Jesus displays our determination to be less than human. Yet, Jesus is risen. That his love conquered death, that he was able to achieve his mission through failure, means that whatever people may mean by ethics has been transformed into the problem of sin and holiness.

Pentecost marks the birth of a people through the restoration of communication between people of different languages and stories (111). At Pentecost we experience God's future which, according to McCabe, means "the business of the church is to 'remember' the future. Not merely to remember that there is to be a future, but mysteriously to make the future present" (141). Such a remembering is possible because Christ can be present through the work of the Spirit, offering the world an alternative mode of communication. It is in this sense that the church is the

> "sacrament of the unity of mankind," a continuing creative interpretation of human life; revealing and realizing in her proclamation of the gospel the presence of the risen Christ to the world; revealing therefore and realizing the revolutionary future of the world. The sacramental life as a whole, centering on the eucharist, is an articulation both of human life now in its real but only dimly discernible revolutionary depth and of the world to come. It is only by the utter openness implied in faith that the revelation of this depth and this future can be received. (145)[35]

Such a people cannot help but be revolutionary, calling into question as they must all revolutionary movements.[36] As a result the Christian moral position will always seem unreasonable based as it is on the virtue of hope. Christian

34. Herbert McCabe, *God Matters* (Springfield, IL: Templegate, 1987), 93.

35. By "sacrament" McCabe understands those actions that mark "the intersection of the world to come with this present world; or, as we say, the presence of the risen Christ" (ibid., 150).

36. In a recent interview Rowan Williams made the point this way: Jesus was "so revolutionary that he puts all revolutions into question. The change is so different that it is not so much a change from one system to another, but a change from one world to another. A new creation where our relations to each other are no longer mutually suspicious or exclusive or competitive, but entirely shaped by giving and receiving—building one another up by a community of transformed persons,

hope reaches out beyond this world toward a future world of freedom in which real communication is possible. Such freedom should not be confused with the autonomy promised by capitalist societies, that is, the freedom associated with the bourgeois secular city in which we suffer nothing other than having to endure our own desires. Rather the Christian seeks to transform the media of domination into the media of communication, in which people are free to love one another without fear (158).

The Church as God's New Language[37]

The strong Christological claims at the center of McCabe's work may seem to be exactly the kind of claims many assume should be avoided if Christians are to be responsible actors in a world of difference.[38] Yet according to McCabe what makes us human is the exemplification of the Christian conviction, in the words of Karl Barth, of the humanity of God.[39] It is in Christ we see our common humanity—a humanity that cannot avoid suffering if we are to be of service to one another.[40]

---

not just by a new legal system. That's revolutionary" ("Table Talk: The Archbishop of Canterbury," *Emel*, November 2007, 36).

37. For those interested, this is the title of a chapter in my book *Christian Existence Today*, 47–66. (The book was originally published in 1988.) I call attention to that chapter, which was originally written to honor Hans Frei, because when I reread it for this essay I was surprised I made no reference to McCabe. Yet I am sure I could not have written the essay without having learned from McCabe what it means for the church to be a "language."

38. As I mentioned in chapter 1, at the beginning of his *Stillborn God*, Mark Lilla gives voice to what I take to be the sentiment of many: "We are disturbed and confused. We find it incomprehensible that theological ideas still inflame the minds of men, stirring up messianic passions that leave societies in ruin. We assumed that this was no longer possible, that human beings had learned to separate religious questions from political ones, that fanaticism was dead. We were wrong" (*The Stillborn God: Religion, Politics, and the Modern West* [New York: Knopf, 2007], 3). I am more than happy to be identified with the "fanatics" because by being so identified I may at least be able to avoid the arrogance of Lilla's "we."

39. Karl Barth, *The Humanity of God* (Richmond: John Knox, 1963). Though many might doubt that McCabe and Barth could be made theologically compatible, I find in their work a common spirit. Theology in their hands is done with joy, which means all things human can be celebrated.

40. In a quite moving passage Charles Taylor observes that the self-giving of Christ reveals how God repairs the breach between God and humans. Such a view begins with the fact of human resistance to God, which we call sin, but it is God's initiative to enter, in full vulnerability, the heart of the resistance by offering humans participation in the divine life.

> But the nature of the resistance is that this offer arouses even more violent opposition, not a divine violence, more a counter-divine one. Now Christ's reaction to the resistance was to offer no counter-resistance, but to continue loving and offering. This love can go to the very heart of things, and open a road for the resisters. This is the second mystery. Through this loving submission, violence is turned around, and instead of breeding counter-violence in an endless spiral, can be transformed. A path is opened of non-power, limitless self-giving, full action, and infinite openness. On the basis of this initiative, the incomprehensible

Christians will do ourselves or our neighbors little good by trying to convince those who do not share our story that we also can be liberal cosmopolitans. Rather we must be what we are: the church of Jesus Christ. For if that church is not the anticipation of the peace God wills for all people then we are without hope.[41] To sustain that peace, to care for the stranger when all strangers cannot be cared for, to know how to go on in the face of our suffering, the suffering of those we love and the suffering of those we do not know, is possible because we believe God abandons no one. Our belief in God's persistence takes the form of a story which receives us as strangers and destines us to be friends.

The Christian word for universality is "catholic." Indeed that way of putting the matter can be misleading because it gives the impression that "catholic" is but another way to say "universal." But catholic is not the name of a logical category or a philosophical position. It is the name of a people sent into the world to discover places and people whose difference is a necessary condition for self-recognition.[42] Indeed the very presumption that we can identify something called the world depends on a people who have been separated from the world to be of service to the world. What the church offers is the patience and humility learned through the gospel, which teaches us how to live at peace although we cannot write the history of humankind.

If the church is rightly understood to be God's new language, it is crucial that it not displace our particular languages. At Pentecost the followers of Jesus came together in one place, and a violent wind filled the house in which they were sitting. Divided tongues, as of fire, rested on each of them, and "all of them were filled with the Holy Spirit and began to speak in other languages, as the Spirit gave them ability" (Acts 2:4). We are then told devout Jews from

---

> healing power of this suffering, it becomes possible for human suffering, even of the most meaningless type, to become associated with Christ's act, and to become a locus of renewed contact with God, an act which heals the world. (*Secular Age*, 654)

41. Miroslav Volf puts the matter just right in an article in the *Christian Century*. Volf says, "If we strip Christian convictions of their original and historic cognitive and moral content, and reduce faith to a cultural resource endowed with a diffuse aura of the sacred, we are likely to get religiously legitimized and inspired violence in situations of conflict. If, on the other hand, we nurture people in historic Christian convictions that are rooted in sacred texts, we will likely get militants for peace" ("Guns and Crosses: A Religion of Violence or Peace?" *Christian Century*, May 17, 2003).

42. Oliver O'Donovan puts it this way:

> No community should ever be allowed to think of itself as universal. It is essential to our humanity that there should always be foreigners, human beings from another community who have an alternative way of organizing the task and privilege of being human, so that our imaginations are refreshed and our sense of cultural possibilities renewed. The imperialist argument, that until foreigners are brought into relations of affinity within one cultural home they are enemies, is simply a creation of xenophobia. The act of recognition and welcome, which leaps across the divide between communities and finds on the other side another community which offers the distinctive friendship of hospitality, is a fundamental form of human relating. Xenophilia is commanded us: the neighbor whom we are to love is the foreigner whom we encounter on the road. (*Desire of the Nations*, 268)

every nation, Parthians, Medes, Elamites, residents of Mesopotamia, Judea, Cappadocia, Pontus, Asia, Egypt, visitors from Rome, Cretans, and Arabs, who were living in Jerusalem, heard each one speaking in their native language. "Amazed and astonished, they asked, 'Are not all these who are speaking Galileans? And how is it that we hear, each of us, in our own native language?' " (Acts 2:7–8). What they heard from these diverse speakers, moreover, was about God's deeds of power.[43]

What is remarkable about this account of Pentecost in the second chapter of Acts is that the Spirit does not replace the different language each person speaks.[44] They began to speak in other languages, but by the gift of the Spirit they were able to understand one another. This means that the language the church must be is not that which forces uniformity, but rather is shaped by the practices, as McCabe suggests, of love and vulnerability, which are necessary for the required patience that enables us to tell our different stories.[45] Pentecost has restored Babel not by mitigating the diversity granted by Babel but by creating a people who have learned how to be patient, how to be at peace, how to listen in a world of impatient violence.

But the gift of Pentecost entails slow, hard work. We must not only learn to suffer one another as Christians; we must learn how to suffer others whose stories might make us vulnerable. Indeed the gift of Pentecost is but the beginning of hard and painful lessons in failure. Yet even failure turns out to be a gift if through failure the church is reminded that others are included in

43. For confirmation of this reading of Acts in relation to Babel, see Joel Green, "In Our Own Language: Pentecost, Babel, and the Shaping of the Christian Community in Acts 2:1–13," in *The Word Leaps the Gap: Essays in Scripture and Theology in Honor of Richard B. Hays*, ed. J. Ross Wagner, C. Kavin Rowe, and A. Katherine Grieb (Grand Rapids: Eerdmans, 2008), 198–213. Like Yoder, Green argues that God's "scattering" of the people at Babel and their being determined by different languages was a gift, not a punishment. A single language, according to Green, suggested oppression by empire. Accordingly, Pentecost does not reverse Babel but parodies it, as multiple languages continued to be spoken.

44. Surely one of the most startling effects of Pentecost is the presumption that Christian Scriptures could be translated. The very language that Jesus spoke is not the language in which the New Testament was written. Accordingly, Christians have assumed that the Scriptures can be translated into other languages.

45. I am deeply sympathetic with Appiah's suggestion that what makes cosmopolitanism possible is not necessarily a shared "culture," nor even universal principles or values or a shared human understanding. Rather it is "stories—epic poems as well as modern forms like novels and films, for example—it is the capacity to follow a narrative and conjure a world: and, it turns out, there are people everywhere more than willing to do this. This is the moral epistemology that makes cosmopolitanism possible. . . . If there is a critique of the Enlightenment to be made, it is not that the *philosophers* believe in human nature, or the universality of reason: it is rather that they were so dismally unimaginative about the range of what we have in common" (*Ethics of Identity*, 258). One might then ask, how is the position I have taken in this paper different than Appiah's cosmopolitanism? I have no reason to emphasize the differences, but there is a difference: Pentecost. Put differently, it is not clear who is the agent of Appiah's cosmopolitanism. I hope it is clear I believe an agent exists that makes it imperative at least for Christians to listen to the stranger. We call that agent the Holy Spirit.

God's promise. At its best, the church learns to receive the stories of different linguistic communities and in the process discovers that our own speech requires constant revision.

Toward the end of his book, Sacks observes that retaliation is the instinctual response to perceived wrong. Since there seems to be no end to the wrongs that we have perpetrated on one another, the only way to end our endless violence, according to Sacks, is a willingness to be forgiven and to forgive. In a painful yet beautiful passage, Sacks writes:

> Forgiveness is the ability to let go, and without it we kill what we love. Every act of forgiveness mends something broken in this fractured world. It is a step, however small, in the long, hard journey of redemption. I am a Jew. As a Jew, I carry with me the tears and sufferings of my grandparents and theirs through the generations. The story of my people is a narrative of centuries of exiles and expulsions, persecutions and pogroms, beginning with the First Crusade and culminating in the murder of two-thirds of Europe's Jews, among them more than a million children. For centuries, Jews knew that they or their children risked being murdered simply because they were Jews. Those tears are written into the very fabric of Jewish memory, which is to say, Jewish identity. How can I let go of that pain when it is written into my very soul? And yet I must. For the sake of my children and theirs, not yet born.[46]

But learning the language of peace cannot, in the name of universality, require that Sacks forfeit the particularity of his tradition's memory. If forgiveness is the way to peace, then we cannot be asked to forget what has been forgiven; for it is impossible to remain forgiven if the memory of suffering no longer exists. Redemption requires memory.

Where does this leave us then? How can we begin the conversations Sacks talks about if there is no universal language with which to speak? I'd like to make a modest proposal: let us begin by learning to speak the language of peace within our own traditions. Perhaps the violence we perpetrate on those whose language is different than ours is the result of our losing our own language of peace. The greatest gift, I believe, that Christians can give the world is to refuse to kill other human beings because we are Christians. Until Christians understand that loving Christ means refusing to kill those he died for, until we recover our own language of peace, there is little hope that we will be able to engage others in conversation without it perpetuating a shallow discourse that leaves us all speechless.[47]

46. Sacks, *Dignity of Difference*, 190.

47. I am thankful to Sam Wells, Greg Jones, Adam Hollowell, and Carole Baker for reading and revising portions of this chapter.

10

A Worldly Church

Politics, Theology, and the Common Good

A Church in Diaspora

I begin with a quotation from a well-known theologian:

> Christianity exists everywhere in the world, and everywhere as a diaspora.
>
> It is effectually, in terms of numbers, a minority everywhere; nowhere does it fill such a role of effective leadership as would permit it to set upon the age, with any force or clarity, the stamp of a Christian ideal. Indeed, we are undoubtedly in an era which is going to see an increase in this diaspora character, no matter what causes we may assign to it. The new age of Jesus Christ is certainly not going to dawn for some considerable time. On the contrary, the Christendom of the Middle Ages and after, peasant and individualistic petty-bourgeois Christendom, is going to disappear with ever-increasing speed. For the causes which have brought about this process in the West are still at work and have not yet had their full effect. But that we are a diaspora throughout the world is not merely a fact to be recognized a posteriori and with dismay. It is something which on the basis of faith, we should have expected, in the sense of a "must" within the history of salvation. It is foretold, though of course only as an implication which could be made explicit only by reference to certain facts in the present world situation. It is a theological datum which can be interpreted according to faith. It is something which "ought not to be," in so far as all men ought to become Christians when the message of faith is preached to them (which to a certain measure has been done all over the world), and in so far as the peoples of the West ought not to have fallen away from Christianity. To this extent, the Christian desire not to be a diaspora remains, of course, an obligation on every

> Christian, a desire which cannot fail to inspire apostolic activity and witness. But between this grimly heroic desire and the merely dismayed recognition that it has very small success there can and should lie something intermediate: the knowledge of this diaspora situation as a "must" in the history of salvation, and the valid conclusion drawn from this historical knowledge.[1]

No, the theologian that insists that the church must learn to exist in diaspora is not John Howard Yoder.[2] It is Karl Rahner, and these reflections can be found in an essay entitled "Christians in the Modern World," written in 1963. I call attention to Rahner's claims about the church's diaspora because I hope to show that Rahner anticipated and constructively responded to the challenges many associate with globalization. It will be the burden of my remarks to suggest that in order to find a common good that can sustain a common morality, we will need the church—a church, Rahner rightly argued, that must recognize and learn to live as a worldwide communion.

It is often assumed that the challenge of living in a global world, that is, a world lacking any unity or agreement on moral norms that might be universally applicable, requires a natural law ethic. The norms of such an ethic are thought to be ones generally accessible to human reason but not dependent on human decision for their validity. Such an ethic is allegedly universal because it is available to anyone at any time or place.[3] Drawing on Alasdair MacIntyre's account of the politics required for the work of practical reason to discover goods in common, I will argue that a natural law ethic cannot be abstracted from the theological convictions necessary to make it intelligible.[4] I hope to show why a

1. Karl Rahner, *The Christian Commitment: Essays in Pastoral Theology* (New York: Sheed and Ward, 1963), 17–18.

2. Yoder begins *For the Nations* with this sentence: "The theme of this book is the tone of voice, or the style and stance, of the people of God in the dispersion" (1). Yoder assumes the diaspora characterizes the position in which the church, if it is faithful, will always find itself.

3. See, for example, Joseph Boyle's "Natural Law and Global Ethics," in *Natural Law and the Possibility of a Global Ethics*, ed. Mark Cherry (Dordrecht: Kluwer, 2004), 1–15.

4. It is not my intention to take sides in the current debate between Jean Porter and Martin Rhonheimer concerning how best to interpret Aquinas's understanding of natural law. I cannot resist, however, calling attention to Rhonheimer's claim that Porter's account of the theological presumptions necessary to sustain natural law is not sufficiently Christological. What I am attempting in this paper develops from Rhonheimer's suggestion at the end of his review of Porter's *Nature as Reason: A Thomistic Theory of the Natural Law* (Grand Rapids: Eerdmans, 2005) that natural law "needs a context of tradition, special practices, and religious faith in order to correctly grasp the truth to which natural reason is directed. Nothing is truer than that. It is in fact an empirical truth that traditions and social practices—as well as religious faith—decisively support moral knowledge rooted in natural law, and to some extent, as the Catholic Church actually teaches, this support is even necessary." He continues, suggesting that from a Christian and theological point of view, any natural law theory will only be a "torso" of an account of the moral life because a Christological perspective is indispensable (Martin Rhonheimer, *The Perspective of the Acting Person: Essays in the Renewal of Thomistic Moral Philosophy* [Washington, DC: Catholic University of America Press, 2008], 304–5).

natural law ethic requires Rahner-like ecclesial presuppositions—that is, why it requires concrete display by a community in time.

I am well aware that Rahner and MacIntyre are strange bedfellows. In quite different ways, however, they both challenge the presumption that the description "global" can be assumed by Christians to be unproblematic. Rather than weakening the nation-state—a state that represents the triumph of the particular over the universal—the process of globalization has served to increase the power of the state. For as Bill Cavanaugh argues, globalization is but the extension of capitalist markets that give the illusion of diversity by "juxtaposition of all the varied products of the world's traditions and cultures in one space and time in the marketplace. Mexican food and tuna hot-dish, mangoes and mayonnaise all meet the gaze of the consumer."[5] As a result, if MacIntyre is right that the discovery of the good through practical reason is a local affair, the particular practices necessary for the discovery of the common good are undermined by the processes associated with globalization.

Let me try to be as candid as I can about the strategy of this chapter. As someone identified with the work of John Howard Yoder, I bear the burden of the label "sectarian" because, like Yoder, I am critical of Constantinianism. Elsewhere I have tried to show, however, that Yoder is well aware that anti-Constantinianism can reproduce habits of Constantinianism.[6] The alternative to Constantinianism from Yoder's perspective is to recover the visibility of the church in its concrete localities. By drawing on Rahner's understanding of the diasporic character of the church after Vatican II and MacIntyre's account of practical reason, I hope to further that project.

Before turning to MacIntyre's account of practical reason, however, I need to say more about Rahner's understanding of what it means for the church to become a world-church. According to Rahner, the Second Vatican Council was the "first act in history" in which the world-church actually began to exist. Rahner acknowledges in the nineteenth and twentieth centuries that the church through missions moved slowly and tentatively from being a European and Western church to becoming a world-church. But he argues that for the first time at the Second Vatican Council, the responsibility for the council was in the hands of an episcopate from the whole world.[7]

The Second Vatican Council, therefore, for Rahner, signals the beginning of a new epoch of church history. The first epoch is the short period of Judeo-Christianity. The second period Rahner identifies with the development of

5. William Cavanaugh, *Theopolitical Imagination* (London: T&T Clark, 2002), 109.

6. Hauerwas, *The State of the University: Academic Knowledges and the Knowledge of God* (Oxford: Blackwell, 2007), 58–75. For a defense of Constantine and a critique of Yoder, see Peter Leithart, *Defending Constantine: The Twilight of an Empire and the Dawn of Christendom* (Downers Grove, IL: InterVarsity, 2010). For an appreciation of Leithart's book, see my review in the *Christian Century*, October 13, 2010.

7. Karl Rahner, *Concern for the Church* (New York: Crossroad, 1981), 91.

a church that was primarily characterized by a Hellenistic and European culture and civilization. The third period is when the church's living space is from the very outset the whole world.[8] Whatever one makes of Rahner's attempt to divide church history into these three periods—and I confess I find his account too simplistic—he rightly insists that he is trying to offer a theological reading of God's providential care of the world. That the church as a world-church is a church in diaspora, moreover, Rahner believes is a gift from God to the world.[9]

Rahner argues that if we are to discern what God is doing in our time to make us a world-church, we must recognize that there has never been a time that can be called *the* Christian age or any culture that is *the* Christian culture. That does not mean that Catholic teaching has not rightly thought in terms of church and state, redemptive history and secular history, nature and grace, and that these can never be united into one thing. But it does mean that it is not possible to deduce from Christian principles of belief and morality one single pattern of the way the world ought to be.[10]

Rahner observes that this may seem a truism, but the practical importance of this point cannot be overlooked. It means, according to Rahner, that nothing is ever *the* Christian culture, *the* Christian education, *the* Christian political system, *the* Christian party. Christians can in principle locate those developments that contradict Christian norms and they can develop Christian cultures, systems of education, and parties, "but there can never

8. Ibid., 82–83.

9. Nicholas Boyle develops a position quite similar to Rahner's in his book *Who Are We Now? Christian Humanism and the Global Market from Hegel to Heaney* (Notre Dame: University of Notre Dame Press, 1998). Boyle observes that

> the Church of the future will act as one global agency among others, and we shall be glad that it is there to do this for us; as our forefathers were glad that the church had the strength and presence to speak as a state to other states in an age when jurisdictions rarely crossed national boundaries and a man or woman at odds with their country had few friends. But in those days internationalism of itself gave a certain, almost suprahistorical aura of moral authority. In the future that will no longer be the case, and if the Church is to continue to be different, to continue to be unassimilated to the secular world which it nonetheless addresses, it will have to draw its authority from elsewhere. I suggest that the Church of the future will need to draw its moral strength not from its international presence but from its claim to represent people as they are locally and distinct from the worldwide ramifications of their existence as participants in the global market. Whatever currents may seem to be swirling temporarily in a contrary direction, the moral authority of the Church in the future will lie, as the Second Vatican Council foresaw, with the College of bishops. It will be the bishops, rather than specifically the papacy, which will challenge the claim of the global market to express and exhaust the human world. (91–92)

For a fuller account of why I think Boyle's book is so important, see my *A Better Hope: Resources for a Church Confronting Capitalism, Democracy, and Postmodernity* (Grand Rapids: Brazos, 2000), 35–51.

10. Rahner, *Christian Commitment*, 7.

(apart from the Church herself) be any single concrete thing in the sphere of world history and culture which can lay claim to be, in principle, uniquely and exclusively *the* Christian realization of anything."[11]

Rahner's qualification, "apart from the Church herself," however, is extremely important. Rahner, for example, observes that the leap from the church to the world-church occasioned by the Second Vatican Council means that Latin could no longer be the language of the world-church. "The victory of the vernacular languages in the Church's liturgy is a clear and urgent signal of the coming-to-be of a world-Church, with it particular churches each existing autarchically in its own cultural group, rooted in that culture and no longer exported from Europe."[12] Thus the church's challenge is to discover how a unity of faith can be maintained and established together with a plurality of liturgical forms shaped by different languages and cultures.[13]

For Rahner the church is the sacrament of the eschatological hope in the unity of humankind. The church must have, therefore, a historical presence in the world to the end of time, and must do its utmost to carry out this mission to establish its presence *everywhere*. No matter what the sociological significance or number of its members may be, the church becomes for the world what the world is meant to be, that is, one people united by the worship of God. The divided character of the church, our lack of unity, therefore is not only an embarrassment for the church but endangers the world.

That the churches now find ourselves in diaspora may well be a gift God has given us to help us rediscover the slow and hard work of Christian unity. That work, the work Rahner characterizes as "little local offensives," may not result in demonstrable statistical successes, but such successes are not the purpose of the church. He observes, "Beginnings may be disappointingly meager; but they may amount to a victory here and now with unforeseeable consequences. St. Benedict did not know that he was fathering a new western civilization when he went out with a few monks to refound monasticism on Monte Cassino."[14]

Benedict could found a monastic community, which surely did not seem at the time to be of great significance, because he thought he was doing the work of God. Faith in God, according to Rahner, is necessary to sustain our ability to hope that the work we do as Christians will be used by God to triumph even when all seems lost. That faith, moreover, must be "so strong that it is ready to purchase eternal life by the witness of earthly death."[15] The martyrs thus stand as a permanent challenge to the temptation, particularly in our time, to find some aspect of Christianity that will make it presentable in a world in

11. Ibid., 8.
12. Ibid., 80.
13. Ibid., 88.
14. Ibid., 36.
15. Ibid., 37.

which, in Charles Taylor's terms, it is assumed that no goods are conceivable beyond the good of human flourishing as an end in and of itself.[16]

MacIntyre on "Politics, Philosophy, and the Common Good"[17]

To introduce martyrdom and belief in eternal life in a chapter concerned with the development of a common morality for a global age may seem counterproductive. We have enough difficulty sustaining an account of any moral norms that might be universally acknowledged. To suggest that a confidence in eternal life may have something to do with morality would seem to make all the more unlikely any attempt to secure agreement on the basis of some goods thought to be held in common. Yet I think it no accident that John Paul II ended *Veritatis Splendor* with the claim that "martyrdom represents the high point of the witness to moral truth."[18]

By drawing on the work of Alasdair MacIntyre, and in particular his article "Politics, Philosophy, and the Common Good," I hope to show, however, that the "little local offensives" that Rahner rightly suggests are the task of the church are the condition for the necessary recognition of the common good. That is not necessarily a conclusion MacIntyre would draw, but I think it is one commensurate with MacIntyre's argument that we now inhabit social orders in which the heterogeneity of institutions and diversity of interest make it impossible for a politics of the common good to exist. That contemporary philosophy is now a specialized and professionalized academic activity assumed to have no political relevance MacIntyre takes to be an indication as well as a legitimization of the compartmentalized character of our politics. As a result our politics lack any place where ordinary persons are able to engage in the reasoned debate necessary to arrive at a common mind for answering questions "about the relationship of politics to the claims of rival and alternative ways of life, each with its own conception of the virtues and of the common good" (239).

MacIntyre, therefore, takes as his task to develop an account of the politics necessary for the discovery of the common good through the right functioning of practical reason and the virtues.[19] The common good is, first and foremost, the discovery of goods, through shared activities correlative of different human associations, that make common life possible. The common good may be pursued by individuals who belong to such associations, but there are associations

16. Charles Taylor, *A Secular Age* (Cambridge, MA: Belknap, 2007), 19.

17. Alasdair MacIntyre, "Politics, Philosophy, and the Common Good," in *The MacIntyre Reader*, ed. Kelvin Knight (Notre Dame: University of Notre Dame Press, 1998), 234–52. Paginations to this article will appear in the text.

18. See *Considering Veritatis Splendor*, ed. John Wilkins (Cleveland: Pilgrim, 1993). The quotation is from paragraph 93 of *Veritatis Splendor*.

19. For an attempt to provide an overview of MacIntyre's work, see my "The Virtues of Alasdair MacIntyre," *First Things*, October 2007, 35–40.

whose goods cannot be determined by the goods of its individual members. Instead, these goods must be discovered by the cooperative activity that leads to a shared understanding of their significance. Fishing crews, string quartets, farming households, and research scientists exemplify the kind of communities capable of sustaining the standards of excellence necessary to recognize goods internal to such practices (240).

Crucial to MacIntyre's account of the common good is the role the virtues must play for the discovery of the good. Only a practical education into the virtues can provide the skills required by the practices that constitute the goods of communities. Such an education is required because an individual must be able to discern how the goods of each practice fit within their life as well as the common life of the community. These questions can only be answered by an articulation of the common good of a community, in which individual goods and the goods of practices are inseparable and both contribute to the common good of the whole. A community capable of such a good is necessarily political because it is constituted by a practice that establishes a hierarchy of other practices (240–41).

Such a politics requires a shared culture in which the citizens share at least one language. They may well share more than one language, but one language is required because language is crucial to securing a common understanding of practices and institutions. Such a politics cannot be identified with a *volk* because in a politics capable of discerning common goods, individuals must always be able to question what custom and tradition have taken for granted. A *polis* in contrast to a *volk* "is always, potentially or actually, a society of rational enquiry, of self-scrutiny" (241).

MacIntyre argues that the politics of the *polis* makes a rational account of political authority possible. Such an authority requires a stable social order in which individuals can recognize how their own particular goods contribute to the common good. No political society can reasonably be expected to survive unless a significant portion of its members believe that there is a connection "between their own ends and purposes and the flourishing of their political society" (242).

Such an understanding of authority is quite different from that in which the good is assumed to be the sum of individual interest. A politics characterized by the attempt to satisfy the interests of individuals in the name of the common good cannot deal with the problem that some will take advantage of those committed to the social good by becoming free riders. Such a society cannot provide a rational justification of authority, and therefore certain figures, such as soldiers, police officers, and firefighters, have to pay an undue share of the costs for sustaining the social order.[20]

20. This is the basis of MacIntyre's high regard for the military in liberal social orders. Those who serve in the military represent a moral commitment incomprehensible on the basis of the moral presupposition of liberalism. I am a pacifist, but I am sure he is right about this. See, for

MacIntyre, therefore, concludes that political societies capable of rational justification must be those able to exhibit connections between the goods of individuals and the common good. Such connections are constituted by practical reason, which means that "practical rationality is a property of individuals-in-their-social-relationships rather than of individuals as such" (242). Practical reason requires, therefore, that I learn what my good is in different contexts through interaction with others who share a common learning.

According to MacIntyre, the modern state cannot justify the allegiance of those who constitute it because such states are deformed and fragmented, making rationality impossible. Politics in such fragmented societies is but one more compartmentalized sphere from which the most important questions are excluded. As a result, modern states try to maintain the allegiance of competing social groups by making promises that cannot be kept and by negotiating temporary peace treaties that eventually break down.

MacIntyre's analysis of the politics necessary for sustaining an account of practical reason sufficient to discover goods in common, he acknowledges, seems to have largely negative implications given modern political realities. Yet he argues that the kind of political reflection constitutive of the common good inevitably emerges as "local reflection, reflection upon local political structures, as these have developed through some particular social and cultural tradition, and moreover reflection guided by and limited by the conceptual and argumentative resources of that same tradition" (246). Such resources are the responsibility of philosophers who must develop the reflective skills to show the universal importance of questions framed in local terms.

MacIntyre contends that it could not be otherwise because there exist no cultures whose members do not treat the norms that guide their life and their conceptions of the human good as having more than local significance. MacIntyre wryly observes, "anthropologists, historians and philosophers may sometimes be relativist but those about whom they write never are" (246). Philosophers draw on their conceptual and argumentative resources to evaluate those norms that are claimed to represent the best for this society in an effort to understand how those norms are right and best for all human beings. As a result philosophers often cannot help but call into question the political order of their own society.

Given this account of practical reason, MacIntyre asks what kind of social and political conditions are necessary for individuals to learn how the goods that shape their lives can be justified as contributing to a society in which political authority is rationally acknowledged. He thinks such social orders will have three sets of characteristics: First, the community will be constituted by those who generally recognize that the standards of natural law, such as

---

example, William Willimon's and my account of the Marines in our *Where Resident Aliens Live* (Nashville: Abingdon, 1996), 67–87.

those articulated by Aquinas, make possible their ability to learn from and with each other. Thus ordinary persons will exhibit their commitment to truthfulness, respect and patience when caring for others, and faithful keeping of promises as requirements for learning what we most need to know.[21] Societies so constituted will display in their citizens' lives the relationship between goods, rules, and virtues (247).

Second, such societies must be small and as free as possible from the incursions of the state and the market economy. It is important to recognize that MacIntyre is not making a virtue of smallness for smallness' sake; rather he contends that politics needs to happen on a small scale so that everyone who has something to contribute can participate in a deliberative debate over important political questions and issues. He does not assume that he is describing something that does not already exist, but believes there are existing local enterprises characterized by such deliberative participation.

What is crucial about such local politics, however, is that politics cannot be, as it has become in modernity, a specialized area. To be sure, the activities of local communities will be differentiated by spheres such as the family, the workplace, and the parish, but MacIntyre argues the "relationship between the goods of each set of activities is such that in each much the same virtues are required and in each the same vices are all too apt to be disclosed, so that an individual is not fragmented into her or his separate roles, but is able to succeed or fail in ordering the goods of her or his life into a unified whole and to be judged by others in respect of that success or failure" (248–49).

Finally, the deliberative and other social relationships of such a society are violated by the misnamed "free markets" that forcibly deprive workers of productive work, condemn labor forces to economic deprivation, and enlarge inequities of wealth and income such that societies become largely made up of competing and antagonistic interest groups. So if a society is to sustain its ability to discover the common good through practical reason, it must renounce limitless development. For the conception of the common good presupposed by large-scale free-market economies is an individualistic one, even if individuals sometimes take the form of corporate entities. What must be recognized, according to MacIntyre, is that there is a conflict in practice and in theory between these rival conceptions of the common good.

Please note that MacIntyre is not suggesting that local communities can isolate themselves from nation-states or national and international markets. Indeed, local communities will need the resources such institutions can provide. But they must be careful to use those resources only on their own terms.[22] They

21. For an extraordinary account of the central role promising has for our lives, see Guy Mansini, *Promising and the Good* (Naples, FL: Ave Maria, 2005).

22. Benedict XVI argues a case quite similar to MacIntyre's by suggesting the relation of truth and freedom is best found not by "abstract philosophical consideration" but "inductively, starting from the realities of history as they are actually given. If we begin with a small community of

will always need to be wary adversaries in their dealings with the state and market economies, even challenging their protagonists to justify their authority—a challenge they cannot meet. For there is an intrinsic conflict between the state and market economies and local communities to the extent that the latter are often subverted and undermined by the former. It is all the more important, therefore, from MacIntyre's perspective, "to examine instructive examples of the politics of local community in a variety of social and cultural contexts, so as to learn better what makes such politics effective or ineffective" (252).

The Church and the Common Good of All People

On the jetways of airports around the world is written: "HSBC: The World's Local Bank." Such a sign confirms Cavanaugh's and MacIntyre's worry that international capital cannot help but make the "local" global. It is assumed by many that there is no alternative to such a development. But I believe Rahner's understanding of what it means for the church to be in diaspora offers an alternative to a globalized world, because the church has resources to sustain the kind of local politics, the cooperative work, that MacIntyre argues is constitutive of practical reason and of our ability to discover goods in common.[23]

Some worry that MacIntyre's politics of the local community fails to provide the kind of universal stance needed to sustain a global ethic. There is no question that for MacIntyre there is no shortcut to discovery of the common good. Rather, we only are able to build up a conception of the common good from particular local conceptions of the good. Yet as Luke Bretherton argues, MacIntyre's emphasis on the politics of the local community is not a withdrawal into a sectarian ghetto. "Rather, such local embodiments of conceptions of the

---

manageable proportion, its possibilities and limits furnish some basis for finding out which order best serves the shared life of all members, so that a common form of freedom emerges from their joint existence." He continues with the observation that no such community is self-contained but has its place within larger orders. It was customary at one time that the nation-state was the standard unit, but he says that the developments of the last century have made such a view inadequate. Appealing to Augustine he suggests that such states are not structurally different from well-organized robber bands ("Truth and Freedom," in *The Essential Pope Benedict XVI*, ed. John Thornton and Susan B. Varenne [New York: HarperCollins, 2007], 348–49).

23. Jacques Rancière argues that the reign of globalization is not the exemplification of the universal but its opposite. Rather globalization is the disappearance of places in which the universal might be found. In a manner quite similar to MacIntyre, he argues that "politics, in specificity, is rare. It is always local and occasional. Its actual eclipse is perfectly real and no political science exists that could map its future any more than a political ethics that would make its existence the object solely of will. How some new politics could break the circle of cheerful consensuality and denial of humanity is scarcely foreseeable or decidable right now" (*Disagreement: Politics and Philosophy* [Minneapolis: University of Minnesota Press, 1999], 139–40). For an attempt to imagine such a politics, see Stanley Hauerwas and Romand Coles, *Christianity, Democracy, and the Radical Ordinary: Conversations between a Radical Democrat and a Christian* (Eugene, OR: Cascade, 2007).

good seek, and are the source of, universal conceptions of the common good that can then be generalized as vision for the wider society."[24] It is the task of the philosopher, according to MacIntyre, to show how questions framed in local terms can be understood to have universal import (246).

While I have no reason to challenge MacIntyre's understanding of the philosopher's task, I do not think the philosopher qua philosopher is up to it. Drawing on the work of Oliver O'Donovan, Bretherton argues that what's missing in MacIntyre's account of practical reason is an eschatological horizon. According to Bretherton, the meaning of history for MacIntyre is immanent within history and is established only through human effort. In contrast, for O'Donovan, time and history are undergoing transformation by God's eschatological kingdom, making possible an "encounter with history and novelty without terror because God reveals the overall shape of things and their destiny in the life, death, and resurrection of Jesus Christ."[25] That is the story that I believe is at the heart of the life of the church, making possible the joining of Christians across time and space in the common endeavor to discern how our lives must be ordered to glorify God.[26]

In *A Secular Age* Charles Taylor makes the striking observation:

> At the heart of orthodox Christianity, seen in terms of communion, is the coming of God through Christ into a personal relation with disciples, and beyond them others, eventually ramifying through the church to humanity as a whole. God establishes the new relationship with us by loving us, in a way we cannot unaided love each other. (John 15: God loved us first.) The life-blood of this new relation is agape, which can't ever be understood simply in terms of a set of rules, but rather as the extension of a certain kind of relation, spreading outward in a network. The church is in this sense a quintessentially network society, even though of an utterly unparalleled kind, in that the relations are not mediated by any of the historical forms of relatedness: kinship, fealty to a chief, or whatever. It transcends all these, but not into a categorical society based on similarity of members, like citizenship; but rather into a network of ever different relations of agape.[27]

24. Luke Bretherton, *Hospitality as Holiness: Christian Witness amid Moral Diversity* (Aldershot, England: Ashgate, 2006), 97.

25. Ibid., 81.

26. Jana Bennett and I have argued that the theological convictions that make the social encyclicals intelligible are often missed by those who divorce the natural law from its proper theological home. See our "Catholic Social Teaching," in *The Oxford Handbook of Theological Ethics*, ed. Gilbert Meilaender and William Werpehowski (Oxford: Oxford University Press, 2005), 520–37. Consider, for example, the claim made in *Rerum Novarum* that for a society to be justly ordered, "the Church, with Jesus Christ for teacher and guide, seeks persistently for more than justice. She warns men that it is by keeping a more perfect rule that class becomes joined to class in the closest neighborliness and friendship. We cannot understand the goods of this moral life unless we have clear vision of that other life of immortality" (18).

27. Taylor, *Secular Age*, 282.

From this perspective the search for Christian unity is not only an imperative demanded by the gospel but an essential exercise of practical reason. If we are a church in diaspora, it is all the more important that local churches refuse to be isolated from one another. Our refusal to be isolated from one another, our willingness to share what we have learned from our attempts to faithfully worship God, is crucial if we are to exemplify for the world the peace that is essential for the discovery of the goods in common. The Christian refusal to kill surely is imperative if we are to sustain the conflicts necessary to learn from one another.

The work of practical reason so understood will be slow and hard, but it will also be good work. There are no shortcuts. We depend on the wisdom of the past being reclaimed, as it must be for each generation, to guide us into the future. But each reclaiming requires a courage no less than that required to sustain the original discovery of the goods.

Rahner is quite right, therefore, that if we are to learn to live as Christians in a world in which we are no longer in control, we must have "a faith so strong that it is ready to purchase eternal life by the witness of earthly death."[28] He has nothing against the hope that we can live a tolerably pleasant life in this world, but he suspects that if we live faithful to what we believe has been given us through Christ, the world may well think us mad. And this madness, moreover, may threaten those who would force a uniformity on the world in the name of humanity.

Rahner worries that if Christians forget that the only way they can live a happy life in this world is by not caring whether their lives are happy or not, they may think the only way to secure their existence is by withdrawing from the world. A church in diaspora, however, is not and cannot be a ghetto church. A Christian may be tempted, Rahner observes, to withdraw into a ghetto, "whether in order to defend himself, or to leave the world to the judgment of wrath as the fate it deserves, or with the feeling that it has nothing of any value or importance to offer him anyway,"[29] but to do so is to betray why we have been scattered among the nations.

Rather, as Christians we will best serve God and our neighbor by seeking to form a common life in the world as we find it. That may well mean we must attempt to develop institutions, such as the university, that make it possible to engage in the kind of exchanges MacIntyre thinks necessary for the development of practical reason. What we cannot fear or try to repress in the name of peace is conflict. Christians, particularly Christians in diaspora, owe one another as well as their neighbor truthful judgments that come only by having our convictions exposed to those who do not share them.

Language is obviously crucial for our ability to be a people capable of sharing judgments—thus MacIntyre's suggestion that a *polis* must share a

28. Rahner, *Christian Commitment*, 37.
29. Ibid., 28.

language if it is to be capable of reasoning together. Yet Rahner contends that the diaspora church's use of the vernacular cannot help but create differences between churches that may put them in tension. In particular Rahner observes, "as a result of the diversity of liturgical languages, there will be a necessary and irreversible process of development of a variety of liturgies, even though it is impossible to predict with certainty and accuracy the relationship between similarity and diversity of regional liturgies."[30]

The development of diverse liturgies will, of course, threaten the common work we have as Christians. Christians never seem more willing to kill one another than when locked in conflict with other Christians about how properly to worship God. For example, in his book *Divided by Faith: Religious Conflict and the Practice of Toleration in Early Modern Europe*, Benjamin Kaplan observes that incidents of religious violence in early modern Europe were often triggered by three types of events—processions, holiday celebrations, and funerals.[31] As so often is the case we find ourselves divided by what most unites us, that is, the worship of God.[32]

There is no "solution" to resolve the tension between the necessary *local* character of the church and the *universal* mission with which the church has been entrusted.[33] Locality, moreover, can produce perversions of the gospel

30. Rahner, *Concern for the Church*, 92.

31. Benjamin Kaplan, *Divided by Faith: Religious Conflict and the Practice of Toleration in Early Modern Europe* (Cambridge, MA: Harvard University Press, 2007), 78. Kaplan's challenge to the standard story shaped by the Enlightenment, that is, that tolerant regimes arose in response to religious violence, is important for the argument I have tried to make in this paper. According to Kaplan, "the story of the rise of toleration is an ideological construct that perpetuates our ignorance. It is a myth, not only in being at variance with known facts, but in being a symbolic story, with heroes and villains and a moral—a story told about the past to explain or justify a present state of affairs. According to this myth, toleration triumphed in the eighteenth century because reason triumphed over faith. It triumphed because religion lost its hold on people, and hence its importance as a historical phenomenon" (356). Kaplan's book provides extensive evidence that the practice of toleration between different religious groups long predated the Enlightenment because Christians found ways to live peaceably with one another despite their religious differences.

32. Kaplan, however, argues that the developments associated with the division of Christendom created a new form of Catholicism; that is, a new stress on the importance of confession became the hallmark of the church. As a result, to be in communion with other Christians was no longer sufficient to make one a Christian, but now the church was identified by declarations of fundamental doctrines—the most famous being the Augsburg Confession. Kaplan observes, "All early modern churches issued such documents, which embodied three of the most basic trends then in Christianity: the internalization of church teaching, the drawing of sharp dichotomies, and the quest for 'holy uniformity.' Each fueled intolerance" (*Divided by Faith*, 29).

33. Drawing on Rahner's account of the rediscovery of the significance of the diaspora for the recovery of the congregational element in Catholicism, Nicholas Lash observes, "Paradoxically as it may seem the more successful the recover of 'congregationalism' in Catholic Christianity, the clearer the indispensability of the 'great church' dimension, including the office and function of the papal primacy, will be" (*Theology for Pilgrims* [Notre Dame: University of Notre Dame Press, 2008], 217). I had written this chapter before reading Lash, to which I can only say, "Great minds . . ."

that are often rightly challenged in the name of justice. The problem with such challenges, however, is that they too often fail to see that the only way to confront perversions is through the concrete practices that give claims to justice's intelligibility.[34]

This makes it all the more urgent that Christians not become isolated from one another. The peace of Christ means we must love one another even if it means we must learn to listen and understand one another's language.[35] We are after all a Pentecostal church, and we do not believe the Holy Spirit has abandoned its work.[36]

I should like to think that the Holy Spirit can even use the work of theology for the upbuilding of the church. John Milbank begins *The Word Made Strange: Theology, Language, Culture* with the striking observation that "today, theology is tragically too important."[37] He explains that for all the current talk of theology as reflection on practice, we in fact do not know where to locate

34. I owe this emphasis to Sam Wells, who provides an account of Christian ethics based on a typology of universal, subversive, and ecclesial options. See Samuel Wells and Ben Quash, *Introducing Christian Ethics* (Oxford: Wiley-Blackwell, 2010).

35. Reflecting on the ethical ambiguities of the state of Israel, George Steiner observes that for Jews outside Israel, Jews in diaspora, survival signifies mission. It is so, according to Steiner, because diaspora forces Jews, and the rest of us who finally must recognize that we too are in diaspora, to acknowledge that we must learn to be one another's guest. Steiner notes, however, that the arts of being a guest are not easy.

> Prejudice, jealousy, territorial atavisms on the part of the host pose a constant threat. However warm the initial welcome, the Jew does well to keep his bags packed. If he is forced to resume his wandering, he will not regard this experience as a lamentable chastisement. It is also an opportunity. There is no language not worth learning. No nation or society not worth exploring. No city is not worth leaving if it succumbs to injustice. We are accomplices to that which leaves us indifferent. The password of Judaism is *Exodus*, the spur of new beginnings, of the morning star. . . . Nationalism, of which Israel is necessarily emblematic, tribal ingathering, seems to me not only foreign to the inward genius of Judaism and the enigma of its survival. It violates the imperative of Baal Shem Tov, master of Hassidism: "The truth is always in exile." This is the maxim of my morning prayer. I realize full well that a peregrine state is not for everyone. That the risks it incurs are extreme. The Shoah may have made a mockery of my persuasion. Yet I repeat: Let us survive, if at all, as guests among men, as guests of being itself. (*My Unwritten Books* [New York: W. W. Norton, 2008], 121–22)

I should hope Christians may learn to be such guests.

36. See, for example, Thomas Hughson, "Interpreting Vatican II: 'A New Pentecost,'" *Theological Studies* 69 (2008): 3–37. Hughson argues that to read Vatican II as an event of a "new Pentecost" "accents a diffused, underlying finality inherent in Vatican II toward mission, a finality in *Lumen gentium* and *Ad gentes* on the missionary activity of the church located in Trinitarian *missio Dei* and the nature of the church, as well as in Christ's mandate. A renaissance of the church's missionary nature as *missio Dei* is an essential dimension of the event and documents of Vatican II associated with 'a new Pentecost'" (35). Hughson does not cite Rahner's interpretation of Vatican II, but his argument seems quite compatible with it.

37. John Milbank, *The Word Made Strange: Theology, Language, Culture* (Oxford: Blackwell, 1997), 1.

true Christian practice. As a result the theologian "feels almost that the entire ecclesial task falls on his own head" because he must seek to imagine the repetitions necessary to perpetuate the original "making strange" that was the divine assumption of human flesh.

Milbank contends that the theologian must therefore try to compose a new theoretical music to remind the church that language is the inescapable means of truth. Accordingly, Milbank criticizes the modern theological penchant for seeking a foundation for Christian convictions prior to linguistic mediation. Rather, what is required is a theological account of language in which the human being as a linguistic creature participates in the very life of the Logos, the Word, that is, Trinity.[38]

Though I am not quite as ready as Milbank to give the theologian such a heroic role, I think he is right to remind us that theology itself is a form of practical reason necessary for maintaining Christian faithfulness. When theology became, like philosophy, a specialized discipline compartmentalized into subdisciplines, the church lost one of the resources it needs to be articulate. In short, Christians lost our ability to show how our faith is a linguistic performance making possible the recognition of what it means to be united by a common love of God.

If Rahner is right that we have become a world-church, it may well mean that our scattered character is now the resource we have needed to rediscover the goods we share in common as Christians. For as a world-church we will discover we need to learn from one another skills of survival.[39] The discovery that we need one another to survive is not to be minimized because it has been made necessary by a hostile environment. Often our most important relationships and discoveries result from the need to band together to survive—for it turns out that we never seek to survive simply to survive, but we seek to survive so that we might enjoy the goods survival makes possible.

MacIntyre is quite right that the virtues and correlative precepts of natural law must be embodied in the habits of a community if rational arguments for the discovery and articulation of goods in common can be sustained. I do not believe, as Joseph Boyle maintains, that a natural law ethic in and of itself has the "possibility of overcoming moral diversity and especially disagreement

38. Ibid., 2.

39. In particular Christians will need to learn from the Jews. It is quite interesting that MacIntyre, as he draws to the end of "Politics, Philosophy, and the Common Good," observes that the small scale political communities he thinks deserve our rational allegiance have within them those who hold dissenting views on fundamental issues. What is important is not to tolerate such dissent, but to enter into rational conversation with those who disagree in order to learn from them. He then observes, "this is a lesson to be learned from our own Christian past. For among the worst failures of Christianity has been the inability of Christian societies, except on the rarest of occasions, to listen to and learn from the dissenting Jewish communities in their midst, an inability that has been both a consequence and a cause of the poisonous corruption of Christianity by anti-Semitism" (251–52).

by means other than manipulation, force, or compromise."[40] Such an understanding of natural law, I fear, divorces it from the theological claims—and in particular the ecclesial context—necessary for the articulation of the natural law.[41] In short I do not find it at all absurd to think that the church, and in particular the office of unity, is the best interpreter of the natural law.[42]

Christians believe that God matters. We believe we are only able to know that there is a world, particularly a world that is allegedly "global," because there is a God who created the world. For those who do not believe that God created the world, no story can be told that can make the world intelligible. We believe that through Christ God has made us participants in God's story of the world, and that the community that constitutes that participation is the church. We believe that the world cannot know it is the world if a people do not exist across time and space who make the world the world. Whatever it means, therefore, for the world to be "global," that meaning requires a people who, having been scattered among the nations, have had to learn from one another's lessons in survival, making it possible for them to discover what it means to be human.

40. Boyle, "Natural Law and Global Ethics," 9.

41. I cannot pretend to have dealt adequately here with the complex questions surrounding the status and character of the natural law. For my most considered account of these questions, see my chapter "The Truth about God: The Decalogue as Condition for Truthful Speech" in my book *Sanctify Them in the Truth: Holiness Exemplified* (Nashville: Abingdon, 1998), 37–59.

42. For my most sustained attempt to give an account of natural theology, and by implication natural law, in terms of cross and resurrection, see my *With the Grain of the Universe: The Church's Witness and Natural Theology* (Grand Rapids: Brazos, 2001).

11

A Particular Place

The Future of Parish Ministry

Representing "No Place"

It was odd for me to be in England to deliver the following lecture, in which I reflect about the importance of place.[1] That I had flown from one country to another to present my argument that place is important might seem to suggest that I and my audience engaged in group self-deception; however, the verb "engage" suggests "trying," and if you try to be self-deceived you cannot be self-deceived. Self-deception is a condition you inhabit.

Toward the end of his Gifford Lectures, *Three Rival Versions of Moral Enquiry: Encyclopedia, Genealogy, and Tradition*, Alasdair MacIntyre raises the question of whether the very idea of a public lecture is any longer possible. According to MacIntyre, the lecture as a genre depended on the assumption of a common intellectual culture, which can no longer be presupposed.[2] Given the lack of frameworks that might make clear our differences, the lecture has become a relic from the past in which form does not match content.

The challenge I faced when delivering this lecture was not quite the same as the one that MacIntyre suggests confronts the Gifford lecturer, but they are not completely dissimilar either. I had to try to lecture on the importance of place from no place. But that cannot be quite right since we share in common a place called church. If the church is necessarily local, then we must test the

1. This chapter was originally delivered as a conference paper at Westcott House, Cambridge, England, September 16–18, 2009.

2. Alasdair MacIntyre, *Three Rival Versions of Moral Enquiry: Encyclopedia, Genealogy, and Tradition* (Notre Dame: University of Notre Dame Press, 1990), 220–21.

assumption that the conditions for communication exist. The giving of this lecture exemplifies the challenge before us—that is, the challenge to understand how the church can be both everywhere and at the same time embodied in the habits of a people and a place.

Habit is the heart of the matter.[3] Place must be inhabited because it is this inhabitation that creates memory, and memory is essential for a place to be a place.[4] Language is a particular habit crucial for memory, for there is no more fundamental form of habituation than the training of the tongue to speak. That we need the tongue to speak is a reminder that we are first and foremost bodies that inhabit place. Because we are bodies, we must be one place rather than another. Our bodies place us, give us a past, and require that we have a future. One of the major challenges before us concerning place, therefore, is the gnostic character of modern life.

But that brings to the fore another problem about my delivering of this lecture. I am an American, and therefore I represent the ultimate form of disembodied life. I often try to resist that description by recalling my identification as a Texan. It is true that I am a Texan, but this identification threatens to hide the more determinative identification, particularly when I am in England, that I am an American.[5] I am a representative of a place that is no place just to the extent that Americans believe that we are what anyone would want to be if they had our education and money. Americans represent what it means to be a "human being" and America is the first universal society.[6]

3. See, for example, Felix Ravaisson's *Of Habit*, trans. Clare Carlisle and Mark Sinclair (London: Continuum, 2008). Ravaisson's work is simply crucial for the recovery of the metaphysical significance of habit.

4. John Inge rightly calls attention to the role of inhabitation in his *A Christian Theology of Place* (Aldershot, England: Ashgate, 2003), 135–36. Memory is not only essential for a place to be a place, but place is equally essential for memory. To be "relocated" often means the loss or distortion of memory. Surely that is one of the reasons people refuse to be moved from their homes.

5. I do have an accent, which may or may not be discernable to the English. I think accent, moreover, is a quite telling indicator of place. Accents are, however, increasingly disappearing in America. I take it to be one of the strengths of England that accents are nourished. I understand that there are class implications involved in the ability to locate accents, but the loss of accents in America does not ensure that class is any less an invidious reality.

6. In his *American Babylon: Notes of a Christian Exile* (New York: Basic Books, 2009), Richard John Neuhaus describes what it might mean to say America is a universal nation this way:

> An academic friend who teaches religious ethics at a prestigious university fervently insists that she is not an American citizen but a "citizen of the world." You perhaps have friends like that. This is also a very American thing, thinking we have transcended being American. We are, after all, as some like to say, the world's first "universal nation." By that is meant that we are a "nation of immigrants," and therefore that American identity is an amalgam of identities of all the peoples of the world. The phrase *universal nation* is established not by national origin, ethnicity, race, religion, or other historically contingent features but by subscribing to certain *universal principles*—for instance, the principles set forth in the Declaration of Independence. (29–30)

To be sure, America has a history, but we think our history is but the outworking of the ideals that are available to anyone anywhere.[7] America is, of course, a country with a diverse and extraordinary geography that invites a sense of place. Yet as the most advanced capitalist social order, our history and geography, which at one time could and did supply some with quite distinct identities, are increasingly subject to the processes of modernity that require standardization.[8] You have to be able to build a Walmart and sell McDonald's anywhere.

To the extent that as an American I represent "no place," I may be able to help the English to place themselves. To be English now means you can rejoice that you are not an American. Of course that puts you in the peculiar situation of needing Americans in order to be English. In short, your particularity now depends on us, which means before too long you will realize that you are now "us."

This may not be bad news if you believe those who celebrate that phenomenon called "globalization." From their perspective we face the inevitable interconnectedness of the world, which will require us, if we are to live in peace, to become cosmopolitan citizens of nowhere so that we might be capable of negotiating difference. As John Inge suggests, some of the fundamental philosophical and political convictions of the West (interestingly enough a spatial designation) have conspired to convince many that "local embodied relations are to be transcended and left behind."[9] According to Inge, space and time,

---

Neuhaus seems to provide a qualified defense of such an understanding of America, though he emphasizes that the American story is but one story in the story of the world. He is sure, however, that "God is not indifferent toward the American experiment" (55). I am also sure God is not indifferent to the American experiment, but I do not believe God is indifferent to any people. God's judgment on that experiment, however, may be just that, that is, a judgment.

I think, however, that Neuhaus is quite right to worry about someone who might think they are a "citizen of the world." That is, of course, an attempt to be a citizen of "no where," which is a contradiction in terms. MacIntyre, for example, has argued that American notions of patriotism and citizenship as commitment to universal ideals are incoherent. See his "Is Patriotism a Virtue?" in *Theorizing Citizenship*, ed. Ronald Beiner (New York: SUNY Press, 1995), 209–28.

7. In his *Christianity and Contemporary Politics: The Conditions and Possibilities of Faithful Witness* (Oxford: Wiley-Blackwell, 2009), Luke Bretherton notes there is an inherent contradiction in modern liberal democratic nation-states insofar as they claim to uphold human rights. Such rights are allegedly to be extended to all humans, but in fact they are limited to the members of the nation-state itself. Bretherton's point is particularly relevant to the United States where the language of "rights" is simply out of control. Bretherton observes that Christianity and liberalism share a cosmopolitan outlook that seeks to universalize these rights, but liberalism, in contrast to Christianity, does this at the expense of the particular. For Christianity, particularity is constitutive of universality and is, therefore, appropriately called catholic. Bretherton develops this contrast in order to suggest the difference this might make for how immigration is understood.

8. One of the names that can be given to the process of standardization is, of course, capitalism. For an incisive analysis of the shift from use value to exchange value for the development of market societies, see Christopher Franks, *He Became Poor: The Poverty of Christ and Aquinas's Economic Teachings* (Grand Rapids: Eerdmans, 2009).

9. Inge, *Christian Theology of Place*, 5.

particularly in the academy, have replaced any serious consideration of place as having metaphysical or ethical significance.[10]

Many who are concerned about our increasing interconnectedness think it important that our religious and moral convictions not depend on the particularities of place and/or history. They argue that a universal ethic is required if we are to negotiate a mode of survival for the future. Philosophers are working overtime to develop the conceptual tools necessary to sustain an account of rationality that is free of contingency. Tradition-determined accounts of rationality, such as MacIntyre's, are from such a perspective seen not only as reactionary but dangerous.

These kinds of considerations are not irrelevant for questions concerning the future of the local parish in England. The very phrase "local parish" I assume is redundant because by its very nature a parish is local. The parish is the ecclesial form that has tied the church to place. Yet it seems that this form of the church may not have the resources to respond to an increasingly mobile population that is no longer tied to place. Again American developments beckon, because the church in America, with few exceptions, has not been tied to place. In America you do not belong to a parish, but you can be a member of a church.[11]

In her insightful article "Debate," in *Praying for England*, Grace Davie notes that the dominant mode of religious and political organization and power in Europe was territorial. Populations lived and many continue to live in "parishes." Parishes were not only ecclesial structures, but they were also a mode of administration for civil purposes. You were born in a parish, Davie observes, whether you liked it or not. That mode of administration worked well for pre-modern Europe, which was constituted by relatively stable social orders. The church was accordingly embedded physically and culturally in the everyday.[12] However, we are now living, according to Davie, in a different religious economy. She characterizes our current religious economy as one that has shifted from a culture of obligation to a culture of consumption or choice. What was once imposed or inherited has now becomes a matter of choice.[13] She notes,

10. Ibid., 10. Though I do not disagree with Inge on this point I think it is not time that has trumped place, but a particular understanding of time as speed.

11. The challenge of "locality" in America is nicely illustrated by an article in our "local" weekly paper in Durham, North Carolina, called the *Independent*. The article describes how national and international corporations are co-opting the current popularity of the "local." For example, Walmart has learned that the consumer interest in supporting companies they perceive to be responsible is best responded to by tossing around the word "local." They have even begun to encourage people to shop at their "local" Walmart. Local businesses are responding by using the word "independent" rather than local, but obviously any word can be co-opted. See Stacy Mitchell, "The Dirty Tricks Behind Local-Washing," *Independent*, July 8, 2009, 13–15.

12. Grace Davie, "Debate," in *Praying for England: Priestly Presence in Contemporary Culture*, ed. Sam Wells and Sarah Coakley (London: Continuum Books, 2008), 149–50.

13. Ibid., 155.

moreover, that in America "economic development and a freedom *to believe* interacted positively with voluntarist forms of religion, which—unlike their European counterparts—were able to move rapidly and effectively into the growing cities of North America."[14]

So again, your future, which may be already your present, is to be "us." But at least, if Davie is right, there is this difference, namely, that the church remains for many in Europe and England a "public utility." This means that many feel no need to attend the church, but are nonetheless glad that churches exist in which an active minority engage in and sustain religious practice. Davie describes this as a form of "vicarious religion." She, moreover, thinks "vicarious religiosity" may be compatible with the development of churches shaped by a culture of choice.[15]

I think I understand what Davie means by "vicarious religion." I lived in England in 1983 and was able to follow debates in the synod that year concerning the ethics of the possession of nuclear weapons. But also on the agenda of that synod was the question of whether all livings, that is, endowments that support a priest, ought to be under the control of the local ordinary. There was an editorial in *The Times* arguing against a change in the policy of letting livings be free of control by the bishop. It noted that of course not having the appointment of clergy under the control of the bishop has led to abuse. For example, atheists could be and in fact had been appointed to certain livings. But the editorial suggested that if all livings were brought under the control of the bishops then that would make the Church of England the possession of those who actually go to church. As a result the church could not be the cultural resource it is meant to be for the nation.

I am quite sympathetic with the position taken by *The Times*, because I think it important that the church is socially embodied. The problem is how a church in which all livings are not under the control of the bishop can also be a church capable of telling the state that it should not possess nuclear weapons. For it turned out that many of the bishops at the synod argued that the church had to defer to the state to make decisions about what was morally responsible for the state to do, in the face of the realities of international politics. The bishops, it seems, unable to distinguish between church and nation, had begun to think like the state.

Of course I am not supposed to be sympathetic with the editorial in *The Times*, nor am I thought to support the parish system or "vicarious religion." I am, after all, on record to be against all forms of Constantinianism. I hope I remain determinatively anti-Constantinian, but how I can do so while supporting a national church will take some explaining—and the explanation has everything to do with place. For I hope to show that the parish system can be

14. Ibid., 151.
15. Ibid., 154–55.

a form of resistance to the false universals that now represent the transmutations of Constantinianism into secular forms.

In order to know what such transmutations look like, you need to look no further than the voluntary character of the American church. More people may go to church in America than in England, but the church to which they go, exactly because it is a church of their choice, lacks the ability to resist accommodation to economic and political powers. The voluntary character of the church, enshrined in the language of "joining the church," turns out to be a perfect Constantinian strategy. A voluntary church cannot develop the disciplines necessary to distinguish the universalism of the gospel from allegedly universal presumptions of a democratic social order.

The rhetoric of Constantinianism and anti-Constantinianism can be quite misleading just to the extent that it can suggest a far too clear alternative. John Howard Yoder sometimes sounded as if the choice between those alternatives was and is clear.[16] In fact, however, he recognized that even when Rome made Christianity the only legal faith of the Empire, there were faithful forms of life that continued to shape the life of the church. Indeed Yoder observes, "The medieval church remained largely pacifist. The peace concern of the medieval church was institutionalized by the designation of holy times and places, which were to be completely exempt from the pressure of war."[17]

Yoder understood well, therefore, that you do not free yourself of Constantinianism by becoming anti-Constantinian. For him the alternative to Constantinianism was not anti-Constantinianism, but locality and place.[18] According to Yoder, locality and place are the forms of communal life necessary to express the particularity of Jesus through the visibility of the church.

16. Alex Sider provides an internal critique of Yoder's use of the language of "shift" or "fall" to describe Constantinianism. Such language, Sider argues, can reflect a "primitivist account of Christianity" inconsistent with Yoder's more considered views. Such a contrast can also see early Christianity as a contest between martyrs as representatives of Christian exclusivism and apologists who are allegedly representatives of hellenization and acculturation. Sider argues that Yoder's understanding of the eschatological character of history should have made him more critical of such tropes and dualism. See Alex Sider, *To See History Doxologically: Conflict, History, and Holiness in John Howard Yoder's Ecclesiology* (Grand Rapids: Eerdmans, 2011). Nathan Kerr also provides a helpful account of Yoder's understanding of Constantinianism in his *Christ, History, and Apocalyptic: The Politics of Christian Mission* (London: SCM, 2008). Kerr suggests that by Constantinianism Yoder was naming the temptation of the church to think the meaning of history is to be found in the ordered structure of a given society rather than in God's activity in the church (7–10). Kerr develops this theme in his article "Communio Missionis: Certeau, Yoder, and the Missionary Space of the Church," *The New Yoder*, ed. Peter Dula and Chris Huebner (Eugene, OR: Cascade, 2010), 317–35.

17. John Howard Yoder, *Christian Attitudes to War, Peace, and Revolution*, ed. Theodore Koontz and Andy Alexis-Baker (Grand Rapids: Brazos, 2009), 131.

18. For a fuller account of Yoder's understanding of Constantinianism, see my *The State of the University: Academic Knowledges and the Knowledge of God* (Oxford: Blackwell, 2007), 66–72 and 170–73.

Only at the local level is the church able to engage in the discernment necessary to be prophetic. The temptation is to denounce "paganism" in general or to decry the "secularization" of culture as an inevitable process without doing the work necessary to specify what "pagan" or "secular" might mean in the concrete. The church's prophetic role in Yoder's words must always be in "language as local and as timely as the abuses it critiques."[19]

Rowan Williams, I think, suggests something quite similar to Yoder's understanding of Christology and place in the epilogue to *Praying for England*. Williams observes that the New Testament testifies to the creation of a pathway between earth and heaven that nothing can ever again close. A place has been cleared in which God and human reality can belong together without rivalry or fear. That place is Jesus. It is a place where a love abides that is at once vulnerable and without protection. It is a place in which human competition does not count; "a place where the desperate anxiety to please God means nothing; a place where the admission of failure is not the end but the beginning; a place from which no one is excluded in advance."[20]

According to Williams the role of church is to take up space in the world, to inhabit a place, where Jesus's priesthood can be exercised. Such a place unavoidably must be able to be located on a social map so that it does not have to be constantly reinvented.[21] Williams even suggests that the Church of England, a church that has lost much of its substance and now occupies the shell of national political significance, "is peculiarly well placed to communicate something of the central vision of an undefended territory created by God's displacement of divine power from heaven to earth."[22]

That Williams provides a Christological understanding of place is extremely important if we are to avoid turning the local into an abstraction.[23] Appeals to locality and/or place can be every bit as destructive as the steam roller of universality that flattens all difference.[24] The local can not only be parochial, but the local can also be demonic. I am a Texan, which has its own problems, but it is the South which has left its mark on me. I am all too well aware of the

19. John Howard Yoder, "The Disavowal of Constantine: An Alternative Perspective on Interfaith Dialogue," in *The Royal Priesthood: Essays Ecclesiological and Ecumenical*, ed. Michael Cartwright (Grand Rapids: Eerdmans, 1994), 250.

20. Rowan Williams, epilogue in Wells and Coakley, *Praying for England*, 175.

21. Ibid., 176.

22. Ibid., 178–79.

23. Stephen Pickard observes that there is little consensus about the place of place in contemporary discussions in geography and discourse surrounding globalization, but what is "incontrovertible is that place is an essentially contested concept." See his "Church of the In-Between God: Recovering an Ecclesial Sense of Place Down-Under," *Journal of Anglican Studies* 7 (May 2009): 43.

24. In *Religion and English Everyday Life* (New York: Berghahn, 1999), Timothy Jenkins provides all the evidence one might need to avoid romanticizing place. His account of the "economy of fantasies" that grips parish life is particularly telling.

perversities of the so-called local church. But you do not avoid the perversities of place by escaping to some alleged universal. You can only avoid the perversities of place by being the church of Jesus Christ which, as I now hope to show, the Church of England has by God's good grace done.

Bruce Kaye's Account of "The Anglican Experiment"

In *Conflict and the Practice of Christian Faith: The Anglican Experiment*, Bruce Kaye provides a fascinating account of Anglicanism that puts flesh on Williams's suggestive comments about the relation of Christology and locality by focusing on the Anglican Communion.[25] Kaye's title rightly suggests that he does not mean to restrict his analysis only to the Anglican Communion, but rather he uses the Anglican Communion to illumine what he takes to be the essential character of the church catholic. That character is determined by our belief that Jesus of Nazareth is the incarnate Son of God, making possible and necessary the invitation to all humanity, without distinction of race or circumstance, to respond to the gospel. Those who respond to this invitation do so, according to Kaye, "in the particularities of their personal circumstance" (3). The challenge, therefore, becomes acknowledging the personal responses to the gospel, responses unavoidably determined by place, without threatening the church's unity.

Kaye develops his account of the place of the Church of England with the current controversies in the Anglican Communion clearly in mind. He explores how a "globalized" form of Anglicanism has emerged from a local form, with the result of deep divisions and conflicts dominating the common life of Anglicanism. He does not think, however, that this is a development unique to the Anglican Communion. According to Kaye, patterns of life that now characterize Anglican life were present in the New Testament. By fulfilling the hopes of Israel through a crucifixion of universal significance, as well as the call of the disciples, Jesus laid the foundation for a profusion of local diversity and cosmic belonging. Kaye quotes the second-century writer Diognetus to give evidence to the necessary relation between Christ's cosmic and universal reality as the background that makes locality not only possible but necessary. Diognetus puts it this way:

> For Christians are no different from other people in terms of their country, language, or customs. Nowhere do they inhabit cities of their own, use a strange dialect, or live life out of the ordinary. They have not discovered this teaching of theirs through reflection or through the thought of meddlesome people, nor do they set forth any human doctrine, as do some. They inhabit both Greek and barbarian cities, according to the lot assigned to each. And they show forth the

25. Bruce N. Kaye, *Conflict and the Practice of Christian Faith: The Anglican Experiment* (Eugene, OR: Cascade, 2009). Paginations will appear in the text.

> character of their own citizenship in a marvelous and admittedly paradoxical way by following local customs in what they wear and what they eat and in the rest of their lives. (11–12)

It is important to attend to the language Kaye uses to characterize Diognetus's description of Christians. Kaye refuses the contrast between the universal and particular and instead resorts to the language of the personal as a contrast to the universal to suggest why the gospel can only be received in context.[26] To be sure, the gospel is for prisoners, jailers, magistrates, philosophers, masters, slaves, men, and women, but that it is so requires that each person must respond by making the whole of their life subject to the everyday interactions of the community of the church. From the beginning, Christianity has struggled to sustain the creative tension between the personal appropriation of the gospel and the gospel's universal reach. The result has been the creation of a politics that sought not to overthrow the old political order, but to build a new order manifest in each church's peculiar circumstance (19).

The current divisions and controversies arising from locality that beset Anglicanism, from Kaye's perspective, are nothing new. Local diversity has always characterized Christianity and conflict is thereby inevitable. Kaye, for example, reminds us that Western Christianity is a local tradition within which other local traditions developed, creating continuing disputes (32). That Western Christianity names a "locality" is a nice reminder that all claims to place depend on contrast with another place.

Kaye, therefore, suggests that Anglicanism became identifiable as a place with a distinct history because Bede wrote his ecclesiastical history. For it was Bede's history that created what would become the idea known as England. Kaye suggests, therefore, that Anglicanism is best understood as a regional form of Christianity not unlike the church in Gaul.[27] Without becoming any less insistent on the cosmic lordship of Christ, the church in England developed a distinctive way to be church by maintaining a resilient call to personal discipleship to Jesus (36). From Kaye's perspective, Henry VIII is but a later expression of the resistance of Anglicanism to Rome's attempt to develop an imperial conception of catholicity.

Kaye identifies Anglicanism, therefore, as the attempt to maintain catholicity without Leviathan. The fundamental character of our faith means an

26. Yoder was fond of saying, "The gospel is not the gospel until it has been received." I think that is right, which means that those who have received the gospel have much to teach those from whom they received it.

27. Kaye's focus on Bede is consistent with Adrian Hastings's contention that ethnicities become nations or elements within a nation at the point "when their specific vernacular moves from an oral to written usage to the extent that it is being regularly employed for the production of a literature, and particularly for the translation of the Bible" (*The Construction of Nationhood: Ethnicity, Religion, and Nationalism* [Cambridge: Cambridge University Press, 1997], 12). For Hastings's explicit account of the influence of Bede, see 35–39.

extensive diversity is required not only within local community, but between communities. Each person and community must respond faithfully to the particularities of their situation; yet they must seek, if they are faithfully to be Christ's body, to remain interconnected. The necessity of such interconnectedness is called "catholicity."[28] To be "catholic" is to recognize that my particularity must serve to build up the whole (41).

Such building up has always been a challenge.[29] Kaye, in particular, calls attention to the ambiguity created by the attempt to impose order on the Anglican reality through the 1662 Act of Uniformity. From Kaye's perspective, the Act of Uniformity was an attempt to impose conformity on the church without respecting the diversity of gifts found in the parishes of England. In Kaye's words, "the Act of Uniformity did not serve well the tradition of Anglican Christianity. It narrowed the focus and failed to move the ecclesiastical structures in a direction that served the new social and political realities of the Christian citizens of England" (47).

Some seem to think that something like an Act of Uniformity is required in response to the current controversies in the Anglican Communion. Kaye thinks such a response would be ill advised[30] because it would deny the Anglican commitment to live faithfully in their local circumstance even though doing so establishes diversity, which creates difficulties for those in other places (66). Kaye is not suggesting that truth does not matter, but that truth demands that those whom we do not understand not be cast beyond the pale of fellowship (73). Anglicans have been committed to the local expression of the faith, which means that the challenge confronting its reality as an international fellowship of churches should not be how we can enforce uniformity, but rather how we can be known through our love of one another.

28. The office of the bishop is an office of hospitality, for it is the bishop's duty to share the stories of particular Eucharistic assemblies to ensure that when we move from one parish to another we can have some assurance we are worshiping the same God. That is why the church has discovered that some Christians must be on the move.

29. This is not simply a matter of how unity is to be discovered by churches in different places, but also how the church in a particular place avoids the temptation to think that the way church is church is by doing it the way it was done in England. Stephen Pickard describes Australian Anglicanism as a long history of a struggle to make a "home away from home." This was done, according to Pickard, by creating a conception of space in which homemaking was identified as transplantation. But that task proved to be impossible because even a colonial church generates modifications that it may not even notice. Pickard observes that the nature of Australia, "its sheer vastness and the immensity of the spaces in between, as well as the infinite expanse of surrounding oceans and limitless high skies contribute to a certain ecclesial character that is fearful of the new and untamed and more at home with the known from another place" ("Church of the In-Between God," 53).

30. Rowan Williams agrees. That he has refused the role of hero or martyr, but rather, in the words of Rupert Shortt, opted to play the role of "patient peacemaker," I take to be a gift to the Communion. See Rupert Shortt, *Rowan's Rule: The Biography of the Archbishop of Canterbury* (Grand Rapids: Eerdmans, 2008).

Catholicity is, therefore, that name we give to the priority of the local for the determination of faithfulness that can only be sustained by engagement with other local expressions of the faith as well as engagement with the whole. As Rowan Williams reminded us at the 2008 Lambeth Conference, "The entire Church is present in every local church assembled around the Lord's Table. Yet the local church alone is never the entire Church. We are called to see this not as a circle to be squared but as an invitation to be more and more lovingly engaged with one another" (169).

Such engagement, moreover, is crucial if the church is to be an alternative to the forces that threaten to destroy locality in the name of peace. We are in danger of confusing the universality of the cross with the allegedly inevitable process of globalization. We are in the odd situation of needing one another in our diverse localities in order not to be subject to the power of false universals. Kaye calls attention to Rowan Williams's claim in the final address at the 2008 Lambeth Conference as an expression of this understanding of catholicity. Williams said, "The global horizon of the Church matters because churches without this are always in danger of slowly surrendering to the culture around them and losing sight of their calling to challenge that culture" (165).

The culture that inhabits us—and by us I mean Christians—is a subtle and seductive one. It tempts us to believe we are free of place. It tempts us to believe that we do not have the time to do what needs to be done, so we must constantly hurry. These temptations are often assumed to be congruent with the gospel imperatives to have no permanent home; but in fact they cause us to lose the visibility necessary to be witnesses to the One who made it possible to be Christians—even in England.

"The Place That Jesus Is"

I believe the work of parish ministry is crucial for sustaining the visibility of the church in a culture that has no time for time and place. For as Ben Quash suggests in an article entitled "The Anglican Church as a Polity of Presence," the very presence of a priest, a presence that often has no use other than to be present, has everything to do with place. Quash observes that "the parish priest is often in the very privileged position of being able to describe what the truth of everyday life is in a particular locality."[31] I think it is no accident that Quash's essay is in a book modestly titled *Anglicanism: The Answer to Modernity*. For I think the task of describing "the truth of everyday life in a

31. Ben Quash, "The Anglican Church as a Polity of Presence," in *Anglicanism: The Answer to Modernity*, ed. Duncan Dormor, Jack McDonald, and Jeremy Caddick (London: Continuum, 2003), 47.

particular locality" is, in the words of Archbishop Williams, how "the place that Jesus is" becomes visible in modernity.[32]

To "describe the truth of everyday life in a particular locality" is not easily done. For example Wendell Berry, the Kentucky farmer and writer, observes:

> When one buys the farm and moves there to live, something different begins. Thoughts begin to be translated into acts. Truth begins to intrude with its matter-of-fact. One's work may be defined in part by one's vision, but it is defined in part too by problems, which work leads to and reveals. And daily life, work, and problems gradually alter the visions. It invariably turns out, I think, that one's first vision of one's place was to some extent an imposition on it. But if one's sight is clear and if one stays on and works well, one's love gradually responds to the place as it really is, and one's visions gradually image possibilities that are really in it. Vision, possibility, work, and life—*all* have changed by mutual correction. Correct discipline, given enough time, gradually removes one's self from one's line of sight. One works to better purpose then and makes fewer mistakes, because at last one sees where one is. Two human possibilities of the highest order thus come within reach: what one wants can become the same as what one has, and one's knowledge can cause one to respect what one knows.[33]

"At last one sees where one is" I take to be as good a description as any of the challenge of parish ministry. For one does not come to see by looking, but rather one only comes to see where one is, as Berry suggests, by living through the problems that the work that is to be done inevitably creates.[34] Yet it is love

32. There is an important connection between place and an appropriate appreciation for the "truth of everyday life" that deserves a more extended analysis than I have provided. Terry Eagleton notes that Christianity brings together the impossible and the everyday in a manner that makes possible a new esteem for the ordinary. He associates the discovery of the significance of the everyday with an ethics of virtue just to the extent that an ethics of virtue is a product of a concrete historical process in which people learn to live enjoyably. It turns out, moreover, that to learn to so live is to learn to do what you want to do—an incredibly difficult task (Terry Eagleton, *Trouble with Strangers: A Study of Ethics* [Oxford: Wiley-Blackwell, 2009], 300–303). I have tried to suggest something similar to Eagleton's point by explaining how apocalyptic makes the everyday livable.

33. Wendell Berry, *The Art of the Common-Place: The Agrarian Essays*, ed. Norman Wirzba (Washington, DC: Counterpoint, 2002), 187. I think it not accidental that John Inge turns to Berry in the last chapter of *Christian Theology of Place*.

34. One of the challenges, however, facing those in the ministry is how to understand "the work that is to be done" as work and, in particular, the work of their hands. Though seldom noticed, everything priests do depends on the work of their hands at the altar. The knowledges that shape ministry are, therefore, exemplifications of practical reason. If you need to ask how theological knowledge should be applied to the everyday tasks of ministry, then you have an indication that a mistake has been made. The ministry is a craft requiring apprenticeship through which wisdom is acquired through example. For a compelling account of the importance of craft knowledge, see Richard Sennett's *The Craftsman* (New Haven: Yale University Press, 2008). In his *Shop Class as Soulcraft: An Inquiry into the Value of Work* (New York: Penguin, 2009),

that shapes such clear vision, requiring that we respond to place as it really is rather than as our narcissistic fantasies of self-importance would have it be. To be in place is a discipline that can remove the self from one's line of sight so that we can finally be where we are. Yet to learn to be where we are, as Rowan Williams reminds us, is one of the hardest things to do.[35]

Berry observes that the good farmer comes to understand that how to farm well cannot be separated from questions of scale. A farm can be too big for the farmer to pay appropriate attention. Distraction is inimical to correct discipline and, Berry notes, "enough time is beyond the reach of anyone who has too much to do." But he says we must go farther to see that the propriety of scale must be associated with the propriety of another kind: "an understanding and acceptance of the human place in the order of Creation—a proper humility."[36] Such humility is born by the seventeen years it took Berry to reclaim a hillside which had been exhausted by over-farming.

Berry is not a romantic. He knows that all agricultural work will erode a place, making food production impossible. When we are no longer able to farm, life itself is threatened. Human continuity and good farming are, therefore, virtually synonymous. That they are so requires that good farming outlast the life of a good farmer. Farmers, like all of us, die, but it is critical that what they have learned about good farming not die with them. So to sustain good farming, a community must exist across time. Such a community is an order of memories consciously preserved in instructions, songs, and stories. "Culture" is the name Berry gives to the joining of land, work, and community through which knowledge is preserved in place and for a long time.[37]

Quash suggests that nowhere is the significance of such a knowledge of place more apparent than at funerals. For the parish priest at a funeral has the responsibility "to describe the truth of a single life. His presence to the locality and to individuals and families authorizes this kind of description. The clergy describe well because they are really present to the situation they describe."[38] That "situation" is, moreover, exactly that place that Williams describes as the pathway between earth and heaven that nothing can ever again close.

In his essay "Presence" in *Praying for England*, Edmund Newey provides an extraordinary account of the role of the priest when someone dies who may have only a tangential relationship to the church.[39] He observes that the priest's

---

Matthew Crawford observes, "If thinking is bound up with action, then the task of getting an adequate *grasp* on the world, intellectually, depends on our doing stuff in it" (164). The "stuff" we do is to worship God, which is the end of all work.

35. For my reflections on Williams's remark in his *Christ on Trial*, see my *State of the University*, 209–13.

36. Berry, *Art of the Common-Place*, 187.

37. Ibid., 189.

38. Quash, "Anglican Church as a Polity of Presence," 47.

39. Edmund Newey, "Presence," in Wells and Coakley, *Praying for England*, 85–106.

visit to the home of the dead is often a quite awkward encounter because the priest may be seen as but a professional spiritual emissary to give help beyond the usual channels. Yet he suggests, drawing on Robert Pogue Harrison's extraordinary book *The Dominion of the Dead*, that the very presence of the priest can create for the living the possibility of recognizing God's presence so that we can be "at home" with one another.[40]

Newey notes that being "at home" with one another does not mean the "awkwardness" disappears. The awkwardness may even become more pronounced as the priest ministers to the bereaved family after they confront the unfamiliar territory of funeral. Yet through these different moments of ministry to the family and friends of the dead, if they are marked by liturgical hospitality in which people are met where they are, some may come to be "at home" with themselves, their bereavement, and with God. In the process, Newey suggests that such a ministry brings all God's people—ministers and bereaved alike—to the foot of the cross "where the extremity of loss meets the consummation of love."[41]

That Quash and Newey direct our attention to the care of the dead as central to the ministry of a parish seems crucial for helping us understand what Rowan Williams means when describing the place that Jesus is. For if the parish is the place where Jesus is, we are invited as Christians, who are never to be at home in this world, to learn to be at home even in England.[42] By having our

40. In particular Newey draws attention to Harrison's observation that the origins of architecture are to be found in the attempt to provide shelter not for the living but for the dead. The modern penchant, therefore, of separating places that house the dead and the living may threaten our sense of home. For it may be that home is only found through the encounter with death. Newey suggests that Harrison's understanding of the "pedagogy of grief" by which we learn to be at home with the dead can be a pedagogy of hope by which a new home is found in God.

41. Newey, "Presence," 90.

42. I think, moreover, that there is a close connection between how Christians learn to die (which is embodied in our burial rites) and what some describe as the social ministry of the church. For only a people who are taught how to die can live at peace. A church that knows how to bury the dead may find the resources to challenge those who would try to secure their existence by possessing nuclear weapons. In his article "Anglicanism: The Only Answer to Modernity," Timothy Jenkins responds to the question concerning what role or vision the Anglican church should have by noting that any answer, because the church is embedded and conversational, must be worked out on site. But interestingly enough he then suggests that the basic issue has not changed since the time of Bede, that is, "the Church has a crucial role to play in the creation and maintenance of a just and peaceful society, so that people may live ordered, quiet, and faithful lives. Its concern is human flourishing, which we call salvation, or the Kingdom of God." Jenkins acknowledges some emphasize the eschatological element of the faith that he associates with the kingdom of God, which is not simply about human well-being, but he argues it is best to concentrate on such an eschatological future in a grounded way that deals with human particularities. Moreover, salvation is about such things that the human heart truly desires—such as health, and peace, and company, and dying well—and these must be comprehended in any account of salvation. I would only add that the account of salvation he defends is eschatological (in Quash, *Anglicanism*, 201–2).

home so established, moreover, we will hopefully discover how important it is that we are connected to Christians across time and place whose differences from us turn out to enrich our lives.

The work of the parish, like work on Berry's farm, is slow, hard, rewarding work. We can take the time such work requires because we believe we have been given all the time we need through Jesus's cross and resurrection to listen to as well as care for one another. From such a perspective, the question is not whether parish ministry has a future, but rather whether, without the parish, we, Christian and non-Christian alike, can have a future in England and elsewhere.

12

Beyond the Boundaries

The Church Is Mission

The political novelty that God brings into the world is a community of those who serve instead of ruling, who suffer instead of inflicting suffering, whose fellowship crosses social lines instead of reinforcing them. The new Christian community in which walls are broken down not by human idealism or democratic legalism but by the work of Christ is not only a vehicle of the gospel or a fruit of the gospel; it is the good news.[1] It is not merely the agent of mission or the constituency of a mission agency. It is the mission.[2]

1. I begin *In Good Company: The Church as Polis* (Notre Dame: University of Notre Dame Press, 1995) with a quote from C. L. R. James's book on cricket entitled *Beyond a Boundary* (Durham: Duke University Press, 1993). "Beyond the Boundaries" is meant to echo James's title because in this chapter I will attend to criticisms of the language of *polis* that I use to describe the church in *In Good Company*. The quotation from James I used as the epigraph to *In Good Company* is this: "The aesthetics of cricket demand first that you master the game, and, preferably, have played it, if not well, at least in good company. And that is not the easy acquisition outsiders think it to be." This chapter was originally an address given at the "Church and Mission in a Multireligious Third Millennium" international conference, Aarhus University, January 27–29, 2010.

2. Yoder, *Royal Priesthood: Essays Ecclesiological and Ecumenical*, ed. Michael Cartwright (Grand Rapids: Eerdmans, 1994), 91.

Setting the Context

The early years of a new millennium seem an appropriate time to address the future of Christian mission. After all, time is the heart of the matter. The missionary character of the church is constituted by—and constitutes—time. For if it is true, as I have argued, that the first task of the church is to make the world the world, then the world can only know itself to the extent that the church is led, which often means is forced, by the Holy Spirit to leave one time and place to go to an unfamiliar time and place. The very idea that there is "a world" and "a time" in which Christians and non-Christians alike must live depends on there being a church charged with the task to be a witness in the world.

It is also a good time for me to reflect on the continuing necessity of mission. In his book *Christ, History, and Apocalyptic: The Politics of Christian Mission*, Nathan Kerr has suggested that I have an inadequate account of mission.[3] I hope to clarify my understanding of the missionary character of the church by responding to Kerr's critique. I have always assumed that the church is in mission wherever it may be. My focus, however, has been on the recovery of the significance of the church in Christendom. Kerr rightly forces me to say why and how I think the first task of the church is to be the church in mission.[4]

In the preceding chapter I argued against the alleged necessity for the church to have a universal ethic if we are to respond to the challenge of living in a globalized world.[5] In particular I suggested the need to develop an understanding of the necessary locality of the church if we are to recognize as well as resist the false universalisms, particularly those associated with capitalism, spawned in modernity. The stress on locality, however, may seem to some to be in tension with the imperative for the church to be in mission.

By addressing Kerr's critique, as well as trying to understand how the church can be everywhere only if it is somewhere, I hope to advance our understanding of why the church does not have a mission, but rather *is* mission. I should like to think, moreover, that my stress on witness as the necessary condition for understanding what it means for the gospel to be true means that the

3. Nathan Kerr, *Christ, History, and Apocalyptic: The Politics of Christian Mission* (London: SCM, 2008).

4. The title of the conference, "Church and Mission in a Multireligious Third Millennium," seems to suggest that the Christian missionary task is facing a new challenge by using the adjective "multireligious." But the church has always faced a multireligious world, so I find it hard to understand what is new about the world in which we find ourselves. What is new, and I assume it is a good thing, is that Christians, at least in the West, are no longer assumed to be in control of the social orders in which we find ourselves.

5. Brian Goldstone, a graduate student in cultural anthropology at Duke, and I have written a paper entitled "Disciplined Seeing: Forms of Christianity and Forms of Life" for the *South Atlantic Quarterly's* issue on "Global Christianity, Global Critique" in which we argue that "catholic" is a more appropriate description than "global" for the missionary character of the church (*South Atlantic Quarterly* 109, no. 4 [Fall 2010]: 765–90).

way I have tried to do theology requires the church to be mission.[6] I am not a historian or theologian of mission, but I have assumed any account of Christianity in which mission is understood to be something the church does after it has become settled in a place and time cannot help but be an unfaithful account of the gospel.

The challenge that confronts anyone who would defend the church as mission is that many of us are held captive by the assumption that the great missionary effort of the church in the nineteenth and early twentieth centuries is definitive for understanding what it means for the church to be a missionary church. Defenders as well as critics of missionaries seem to assume that a missionary is a European or American going to Asia or Africa to "make Christians." I have great sympathy with revisionist accounts of the missionary efforts of the church in recent centuries, but, as Dana Robert observes, it must be acknowledged that "even many of the best missionary efforts of the era were tainted by paternalism and assumptions about the superiority of western culture."[7]

Robert, however, helpfully reminds us that the church's missionary efforts did not begin in the nineteenth century. For example, she challenges the stereotype of the missionary as a representative of Western colonialism by reminding us that over the history of Christianity the "missionary" is more likely to be a Korean couple working among university students in China; an Indian medical doctor caring for refugees; or monks, who intentionally or not, became the countercultural witness that spread Christianity across Europe.[8] Though the typical missionary in 1910 was a European, Robert observes, "what thrilled the delegates at Edinburgh in 1910 was the prophetic vision they glimpsed of worldwide Christian unity marked by human equality, justice, and a shared passion to spread the name of Jesus Christ."[9]

6. Though my account of witness owes much to Barth and Yoder, I think George Lindbeck's *The Future of Roman Catholic Theology* (Philadelphia: Fortress, 1970) had a decisive influence on me. For example, Lindbeck notes that he treats "church and mission" as a single topic in his book on the Second Vatican Council because the renewed eschatological vision of the Council means that the "church is mission." According to Lindbeck this means that in its essence the church "is to be a sacramental sign or witness to God's saving work in all that it is and does. It exercises this witnessing or missionary function in its *diakonia* or secular service of the world, its *leitourgia* or worship of God, and its *koinonia* or communal unity expressed both interpersonally and in institutional structures and in common faith and dogma" (5).

7. Dana Robert, *Christian Mission: How Christianity Became a World Religion* (Oxford: Wiley-Blackwell, 2009), 89. Robert observes, however, that compared with the overt racism of most Westerners at the time, missionaries come across as surprisingly enlightened.

8. Ibid., 1–2. Robert calls attention to the significance of monasticism on pages 25–26 of her book.

9. Ibid., 55. Yoder observes that

> one fruition of the modern missionary movement was that it reminded people "back home" in Christian Europe that most of the world was not Christian. Just as important was that it dramatized the unity of the globe. It is as much the missionary movement as the commercial and political imperialism of the same age that created for us today the possibility

That vision was, of course, soon shattered by the reality of World War I. Indeed Robert observes that the violence and brutality of World War I marked a decisive change in Christian mission—for the war discredited the presumption that Western culture was intrinsically Christian or superior to other cultures and religions. As a result she suggests that many missionaries assumed their task was not to change the culture of a people, but "to simply introduce them to Jesus Christ."[10]

"To simply introduce them to Jesus Christ" may seem like progress to the extent that the gospel so understood is assumed not to be burdened by the cultural presumptions of the West. But I fear "to simply introduce them to Jesus Christ" may be an expression of the rationalistic philosophical and political presumptions that shaped the character of Christianity in the West. Such an understanding of mission can even celebrate the "enculturation" of the gospel, but that too is an expression of liberal modernity.[11] If the church *is* mission, rather than simply having a mission, then it may well be the case—particularly if Robert is right to name monasticism as the exemplification of the missionary character of the church—that the presence of the church will or should be culturally disruptive wherever it finds itself.

In what follows I hope to develop why I think it so important to understand that the church is mission. My fundamental conviction is quite simple: I assume that the church is at its missionary best when it does those things that make it a faithful witness to the gospel of Jesus Christ. From time to time it may find it useful to send out missionaries, but its first missionary task is to be a witness in and to the worlds in which it finds itself. All missionary tasks are in that sense local.

Because mission is a local affair, there must be an essential relation between the catholic character of the church and what it means for the church to be

---

> of seeing our one world as a cultural family. *Christian unity is the true internationalism*, for it posits and proclaims a unification of humankind whose basis is not some as yet unachieved restructuring of political sovereignties but an already achieved transformation of vision and community. (*Royal Priesthood*, 179–80)

10. Robert, *Christian Mission*, 90.

11. In his fascinating book on Dutch missionaries in the Dutch East Indies, *Christian Moderns: Freedom and Fetish in the Mission Encounter* (Berkeley: University of California Press, 2007), Webb Keane observes that by the twentieth century it had become conventional for the missionaries he studied to advocate the preservation of local cultures. Appealing to Kuyper, the missionaries assumed that only the local religious practices needed changing. Of course, as Keane points out, this assumes that the difference between religion and culture can be established. Keane notes, however, that by so doing the missionaries "risked participation in the purification processes that had contributed to secularization in the West, by confining religion to a distinct sphere apart from other domains of social life—a risk of which many were aware" (106). Those who saw religion and culture as inextricably connected thought the question of what counted for culture and what counted for religion to be inescapable, which meant that considering how to understand such matters as burial sites, marriage exchanges, divorce, tooth filing, and polygamy could not be avoided.

mission. That church as mission must be "in place" requires the church to be connected in a manner that challenges "the boundaries" that threaten to divide Christians from one another. The catholic character of the church will not be secured through institutional means, but rather comes by way of mutual accountability and reconciliation. At the very least that means that the missionary task of the church depends on the refusal of Christians to kill one another.

Witness and the Missionary Imperative

If Christians are to be faithful to Jesus's command, found at the end of Matthew's Gospel, to "make disciples of all nations," then Christians must be missionaries (28:19). But I think it crucial to understand why without witnesses the gospel would not be the gospel. The reason is very simple: we must be witnesses because at the center of the Christian faith is a person, Jesus of Nazareth. You can only know who Jesus is because of those who have been witnesses to him. Karl Barth puts it this way:

> It is this ontological connexion between the man Jesus on the one side and all other men on the other, and between active Christians on the one side and merely virtual and prospective on the other, which is the basis of the fact that in the New Testament the gathering and upbuilding of the community, of those who know Him, is depicted as a necessity grounded in Himself, and that this community is sent out, again with a necessity grounded in Himself, and entrusted with the task of mission in the world. Jesus Christ would not be who He is if He had no community and if this community did not have or need not have missionary character. We can sum it up this way. The ontological connexion is the legal basis of the *kerygma* which forms the community and with which the community is charged. And this ontological connexion is also the basis of the fact that the *kerygma* does not indicate possibilities but declares actualities.[12]

The inseparable relation between who Jesus is and why who he is requires witnesses explains why attempts to say what the gospel is "about" so often result in attenuated and misleading accounts that fail to do justice to it. The gospel is a story because it is about a concrete human being.[13] Good stories—and the gospel is the good story of God's care of his creation—defy summaries.

12. Karl Barth, *Church Dogmatics* IV/2, trans. G. W. Bromiley (Edinburgh: T&T Clark, 1958), 275. Though Barth maintains that Christ is the community, he is insistent that there can be no reversing of this claim. "The community is not Christ, nor is it the kingdom of God" (669). I, of course, agree that the church "exists only as it points beyond itself" (623), that is, it exists to witness to Christ. Yet I suspect I have a much more "catholic" understanding of what it means for the church to make Christ known than does Barth.

13. Barth rightly, I think, worried that the orthodox account of the incarnation could result in a natural theology based in a generalized anthropology. He notes that we can use the term "human

To tell the story of the life, death, and resurrection of Jesus requires other stories to be told. The name given to the other stories that must be told to rightly tell the story of Jesus is "church."[14]

The stories that must be told to tell the story of Jesus, moreover, are discovered through witness. Through its witness the church finds that it often has said more than it realized by having the story retold by those who have received and made it their own. The name given to the memory necessary to retain what the church has learned through witness is "tradition." The tradition is an ongoing argument that requires those in the tradition to be hospitable to the new discoveries witness makes possible and even requires.

The story, therefore, cannot be abstracted from the people who embody it. Lives matter, which means that the missionary character of the story cannot help but render vulnerable the lives of those who are "sent out." For if they are to be that to which they witness then they must be as ready to receive as they are to give the witness the story requires.[15] Through the giving and receiving of the story, the whole church through the work of the Holy Spirit participates in that to which it witnesses.[16]

---

nature" as long as the expression is kept free from any idea of a generally known *humanum*. But we must remember if we speak of nature, or being, or essence, or kind, or of humanity,

> we should keep in the background for the moment the idea and concept of "a man." What became and is in the divine act of the incarnation is, of course, a man. It is the man Jesus of Nazareth. But its object, that which God assumed into unity with Himself and His being and essence and kind and nature is not "a man," i.e., one of many who existed and was actual with all his fellow-men in a human being and essence and nature and kind as opposed to other creatures, but who was and is also this one man as opposed to all other men. (Ibid., 47–48)

14. I can make the significance of this point concrete by observing that the New Testament would be incomplete without the Pauline epistles, the other shorter writings, Revelation, and, of course, Acts. For an account of Acts that I think supports my claim, see C. Kavin Rowe, *World Upside Down: Reading Acts in the Graeco-Roman Age* (Oxford: Oxford University Press, 2009).

15. Lesslie Newbigin observes that often missionaries have been guilty of a kind of speaking from a distance, which betrayed the incarnation by not speaking from within the situation of those to whom the gospel was proclaimed. We must remember, Newbigin argues, that when Jesus first commissioned the disciples to go out and preach the kingdom, he first authorized them to exercise the ministry of deliverance. Yet Newbigin maintains, "the Word remains sovereign. . . . The world sets the agenda in the sense that Christ's ministry is exercised in terms of human needs—hunger, sickness, blindness. Yet the action of Jesus always sets the human situation in a new perspective" (*Signs amid the Rubble: The Purposes of God in Human History*, ed. Geoffrey Wainwright [Grand Rapids: Eerdmans, 2003], 108). Wainwright notes that Newbigin expressed his understanding of the relation between listening and speaking with the epigram, "Words without deeds are empty, but deeds without words are dumb" (xii).

16. Our participation in Christ through witness is a major, but often overlooked, motif in Barth's theology. Adam Neder, however, has highlighted Barth's understanding of participation in his *Participation in Christ: An Entry into Karl Barth's Church Dogmatics* (Louisville: Westminster John Knox, 2009). Neder observes that Barth's account of participation does not use the language of the "infused virtues," but rather Barth talks of "an increase in the constancy with which the actions of one's life correspond to the truth of one's objective being in Christ." Neder observes,

It has been a constant temptation for Christians to find a way to avoid being witnesses. To be a witness demands that our lives be more than we think they can be. We should like to think that what we believe could be shown to be true no matter what might be the character of our lives. What God has done in Christ is true and good regardless of what we do or say, but that does not preclude the importance of faithful witnesses to Jesus. Finally, the teller and the tale are one.[17]

The loss of social status and political power by the church, with the correlative presumption that what Christians believe is incapable of intellectual justification, made the attempt to do theology in a manner that avoided the necessity of witnesses seem particularly attractive in modernity. Ernst Troeltsch, for example, assumed that the Christian missionary enterprise must be fundamentally transformed. The missionary enterprise of the church, according to Troeltsch, particularly if it is understood to bear witness to an "exclusive redemptive power of the truth to be preached," can no longer be sustained. Rather, he argued, the task of the church must be an attempt to attain mutual understanding based on the history and philosophy of religion.[18]

Troeltsch, of course, assumed that the "historical method" had made the Christian conviction that Jesus had been raised from the dead unintelligible.[19] Historicist though he may have been, Troeltsch thought some form of Platonism was required to sustain an account of truth that was not subject to the contingencies of history.[20] From Troeltsch's perspective missionaries did not have to be witnesses but rather quasi-philosophers who could help others discover that they already believed what the missionaries believed, once they had been properly educated. So, ironically, there was always a kind of ahistorical character to the liberal Protestant account of mission.

In contrast, I think the eschatological character of the gospel makes history the medium of a truthful witness. Thus my claim that if you need a theory of truth to assume that Jesus has been raised from the dead, worship that theory instead of Jesus Christ. There can be no truth more determinative than that known through Jesus's crucifixion and resurrection. But what it means "to believe" in that cross and resurrection requires being made a participant in a community whose existence depends on the miracle of the resurrection.

---

however, that Barth is in agreement with much that is valuable about the stress on the virtues, but he disagrees with the ontology that underlies most of the writing on the virtues (101).

17. See, for example, "The Church as God's New Language," in my *Christian Existence Today: Essays on Church, World, and Living in Between* (Grand Rapids: Brazos, 2001), 47–66.

18. Ernst Troeltsch, *Religion in History*, trans. James Luther Adams (Philadelphia: Fortress, 1991), 102–3.

19. Ibid., 20–23.

20. Troeltsch thought only Christianity could satisfy the needs of modernity because Christianity "integrates powerful prophetic theism with the intimate Christian sense of God's presence, the infinity of the soul with the brotherhood of love, the joyous assurance of God with the heroic hope of redemption, and, finally, the Platonic-Stoic humanism with the idealistic interpretation of the universe" (ibid., 53). I think Troeltsch's "mystical type" is an expression of his Platonism.

Evangelism, therefore, cannot be a theological afterthought. To be sure, as Julian Hartt observes in his *Toward a Theology of Evangelism*, a book published in 1955 and sadly overlooked by most who write on evangelism, there is a metaphysical background to the story of the gospel; but if that was all there was, the church would have no mission in and for the world. But the church's mission in and for the world is rooted in a concrete history in which God is acting. God has acted—and is acting—in a way that makes it absolutely desirable and imperative that we share what he has done with the whole world. "God acts: and whoever knows that he is grasped by this action becomes overpoweringly aware of the command, 'Go and tell!' This is the fate of the church; it can be resisted, but it cannot be eluded."[21]

Mission after Christendom: A Response to Kerr

In *Evangelism after Christendom: The Theology and Practice of Christian Witness*, Bryan Stone develops an understanding of mission I should like to think consistent with the account I have given above. Drawing on the work of John Howard Yoder, Stone argues that the loss of Christendom, that is, the loss of a "center" which Christians thought gave them a place to evangelize the rest of the world, is a positive development for the recovery of a missionary stance. From such a position Stone suggests the church is able to announce the peace that characterizes the kingdom of God in a manner that invites others to take seriously the "subversive implications" of that announcement.[22]

I call attention to Stone's account of the relation of evangelism and ecclesiology because he has articulated what I hope I think. According to Stone,

21. Julian Hartt, *Toward a Theology of Evangelism* (Eugene, OR: Wipf and Stock, 2006), 24–25. Some may think it a mistake to identify mission with evangelism, but I assume the former is a subset of the latter. What is crucial, however, is to heed Lesslie Newbigin's plea that "we stop arguing about whether or not other people are going to be saved. I do not believe that that is our business. I do not believe that we have a mandate to settle those questions. We know from the teaching of Jesus that one thing is sure—that at the end of time there will be surprises. . . . What then is the point of mission? That, I think, brings us to the very heart of the matter. What is the point of mission? And the answer I believe quite simply is the glory of God" (*Signs amid the Rubble*, 120). In his extremely important book *Eccentric Existence: A Theological Anthropology* (Louisville: Westminster John Knox, 2009), David Kelsey observes that God relates to us in three complexly interrelated but distinct ways: to create us, to draw us to eschatological consummation, to reconcile us (1:5). He argues throughout this work that too often the reconciling work of God is overdetermined in accounts of our relationship with God. He quite wonderfully develops Newbigin's claim that our task is to glorify God in a chapter entitled "Doxological Gratitude: Who We Are and How We Are to Be as Faithful Creatures" (1:333–56).

22. Bryan Stone, *Evangelism after Christendom: The Theology and Practice of Christian Witness* (Grand Rapids: Brazos, 2007), 11. For a similar account influenced by Yoder's work that draws out more radical ecclesial implications for mission, particularly in terms of race and class, see Derek Alan Woodard-Lehmann, "Being and Bearing the Witness of the Spirit: Toward a Postcolonial Missional Politics," *Pro Ecclesia* 18 (Fall 2009): 437–58.

what it means for the church to be mission is the recognition that salvation is ecclesial, that is, that the shape of salvation "in the world *is* a participation in Christ through worship, shared practices, disciplines, loyalties, and social patterns of his body."[23] That salvation is ecclesial is why the church does not *have* a mission but by being faithful to the gospel *is* mission.

Nathan Kerr, who like Stone has been influenced by John Howard Yoder's anti-Constantinianism, nonetheless argues that to make the church constitutive of mission is a mistake. According to Kerr the missionary imperative precedes the church. In his language, the church is not so much in mission; rather mission makes the church. In particular, Kerr thinks my emphasis on the church as *polis* is overdetermined because such an understanding of the church simply makes her an alternative to liberalism. As a result Kerr argues that I mistakenly privilege "the church itself as *subject* and *agent* of the Christ-story, such that it is the church's own narrative history that constitutes the 'storied' identity of Jesus."[24] Thus my suggestion that "the teller and the tale are one," according to Kerr, betrays a "transcendental narrativity" that displaces the man Jesus confessed as God and Lord. The narrative identity with which I am most concerned is not that of the unrepeatable event of Jesus Christ, but the church itself.[25]

In spite of my claim to do no more than represent John Howard Yoder's position, Kerr argues that in contrast to Yoder's, my understanding of the church harbors a pretension to universality inimical to Yoder's emphasis on the "vulnerability of the particular." My account of the church, therefore, is subject to ideological perversion just to the degree that the church I seem to envisage is but the mirror image of the liberalism I oppose. As a result, from Kerr's perspective, I ironically reproduce the error of Protestant liberals by positioning the church as necessarily an imperialistic community in order that it might be capable of challenging nationalistic and cultural imperialism.[26]

According to Kerr, by "integrating the history of Jesus into the ongoing narrative of the church," I have fundamentally betrayed Yoder's apocalyptic Christology. Apocalyptic has become for me an ecclesiological strategy to establish the church as *polis* against the nation-state, whereas for Yoder apocalyptic remains principally a tactic to negotiate the ordinary contingencies of the everyday world in which the truth of the gospel is made articulate.[27]

Though Kerr reads Yoder as an ally in his criticisms of me, he nonetheless worries that Yoder's emphasis on the central role of worship for the mission of the church, an emphasis also characteristic of my work, threatens to result in

23. Stone, *Evangelism after Christendom*, 15. Brad Kallenberg develops a similar account of evangelism in his *Live to Tell: Evangelism for a Postmodern Age* (Grand Rapids: Brazos, 2002).

24. Kerr, *Christ, History, and Apocalyptic*, 106.

25. Ibid., 109.

26. Ibid., 118–19.

27. Ibid., 130–31.

a "political *ontologization* of the church, on the one hand, and a concomitant *instrumentalization* of worship, on the other hand."[28] Yoder, therefore, risks making the church too concerned with its own identity by defining itself against the world. In contrast, Kerr, drawing on Herbert McCabe, suggests that the church is not so much an "alternative society" or even an "alternative to society," but rather is a kind of subversive challenge to society or to politics as such.[29]

Kerr's stress on mission as the necessary condition for the church to be the church is meant to ensure that Jesus is not made captive to the church. According to Kerr, Jesus cannot be given to us through "a given institution, a single historical narrative, or a set of achieved practices and habits, but only received ever again as the gift of another, at once unpredictably new yet recognizably strange."[30] An appropriate apocalyptic Christology is possible only through the encounter with the other in which the witness and the one who receives the witness are converted to the "more" that is Jesus. Accordingly, if we are to continue speaking of *ecclesia*, we must do so in terms of exile or diaspora, requiring that the contrast between church and world be determined not so much by contrast as by mutual implication.[31]

I am quite sympathetic with the general problematic Kerr develops, that is, to show how Yoder's Christology can be understood as a response to Troeltsch's historicism to the extent that Yoder refuses to escape history by appeal to a false transcendental universalism.[32] For Yoder there can be no guarantees to ensure that the church's witness to the gospel will be received. But that is exactly why the church must exist as witness; that is, witness presumes that there

28. Ibid., 169.
29. Ibid., 175.
30. Ibid., 179.
31. Ibid., 189.
32. Dan Barber rightly characterizes Yoder's position by observing that

> Yoder is claiming not simply that Jesus's messianic community has a particular emergence, but that it must exist in such a way that it is able to affirm the possibilities of particularity. Putting it otherwise, we can say that Jesus's messianic community is possible only insofar as it refuses the move toward universality. It is thus necessary to understand not just that the church is particular, but even more that it is one particular among other particulars. . . . If being-diasporic is an essential feature of the church, this means that the church's condition of possibility is a relationship between particularities—which is precisely the sort of relationship that is refused by the particularity-that-claims-to-be-universal. Jesus's messianic community finds its identity, therefore, not in the intersection between particularity and universality, but in the intersection—the encounter—between particularities. Accordingly, the church's identity must not be fixed. (Daniel Colucciello Barber, "Epistemological Violence, Christianity, and the Secular," in *The New Yoder*, ed. Peter Dula and Chris Huebner [Eugene, OR: Cascade, 2010], 289)

Barber suggests Kerr's stress that the church only becomes church in encounter is an expression of this understanding of particularity. I suspect he is right about that, which means that whatever differences there may be between Kerr's and my understanding of the church, they are more a matter of emphasis than fundamental disagreements.

is no "behind" to which we can retreat to guarantee that the proclamation of Jesus as the Son of God will be received.[33] Witness to Christ must be as he was, that is, nonviolent, in so far as no one can become his disciple through coercion.[34] If that is what Kerr thinks, moreover, I should like to think we are in fundamental agreement.

Yet I remain unclear as to what Kerr thinks is at stake in the contrast he draws between his understanding that mission makes the church and my, and I should like to think Yoder's, understanding of mission as constitutive of the church. He suggests the emphasis on the church as *polis* short-circuits the work of doxology and, therefore, betrays the missionary task. But the emphasis on doxology was first and foremost a way to remind the church that the worship of God is a politics of witness.

I confess I simply find it hard to understand or better have a sense what mission might look like for Kerr. He says that mission is a "sending" of the Spirit by which we are gathered into the priestly work of God's perfect agape. "So mission is the *form* in which Christ *gives* himself in the 'historicity' of the Spirit. 'Mission' thereby names the ongoing enactment of Jesus's non-territorial,

33. Thus Barth's claim that the statement "God was in Jesus Christ" is the sole point in which the New Testament witness originates, and therefore it is also the sole point from which a doctrine of revelation congruous with this witness can originate:

> We do not look for some higher vantage point from which our statement can derive its meaning, but we start from this point itself. This, of course, we cannot do by our own authority and discretion. We can only make it clear from the Evangelist and apostles what it will mean to start from this point, and then try to make clear what our own starting point is. But we cannot get "behind" this point. Therefore we cannot derive or prove the statement, in which this point is to be described, from a higher discernment. We can only describe it as a starting point. . . . If revelation is to be taken seriously as the revelation of God, and not just as an emphatic expression for a discovery which man has made in himself or in his cosmos by his own powers, then in any doctrine of revelation we must deal expressly with the point that constitutes the mystery of revelation, the starting-point of all thought and language about it. (*Church Dogmatics* I/2, 124).

34. Yoder puts it this way:

> The truth claim of the herald or witness must remain non-coercive if it is to be valid. You never *have* to believe it. For that there are two reasons: First, because the message concerns a contingent, particular event with the challengeable relativity of historical reporting. It will always be possible to believe that the Exodus and Sinai, or the Resurrection and Ascension did not happen or were imagined later, or were misreported. Secondly, you do not have to believe it because the herald has no clout. He or she cannot bring it about that if you refuse to believe you must be destroyed or demoted. In fact, it is the herald who is vulnerable, not a full citizen. It is not only that he or she is weak and cannot coerce assent. What makes the herald renounce coercion is not doubt or being unsettled by the tug of older views. The herald believes in accepting weakness, because the message is about a Suffering Servant whose meekness it is that brings justice to the nations. (*Royal Priesthood*, 256)

Yoder observes the problem with the age of Christian triumphalism was not that the missionary enterprise was tied to Jesus but that it denied him to the extent that it did not respect the neighbor to whom it witnessed.

subversive, apocalyptic historicity of the world."[35] But surely mission so understood begs for exemplification.

Too often I simply do not understand the significance of the alternatives Kerr thinks crucial to distinguish our positions. For example, I fail to see the difference between the church as an alternative society and what it might mean for the church to be a subversive challenge to society. Nor do I understand Kerr's contention that doxology as constitutive of Christian political action is not primarily moral, pragmatic, or metaphysical, but eschatological.[36] From where does such contrast come?

Little hangs, moreover, on whether the terms *polis* or "mission" are used to characterize the church.[37] To make any one image of the church control all other descriptions is always an understandable temptation as well as a danger to be avoided.[38] Kerr may well be right that the emphasis of the church as *polis* may fail to suggest the exilic character of the church. In an odd way, however, the emphasis on the church as *polis* was meant to suggest how the church should live as an exilic people—that is, the witness the church must make if it is to be a visible people who can provide an alternative to the world. I have assumed, as I think Yoder assumed, that doxology is constitutive of the visibility of the church.

35. Kerr, *Christ, History, and Apocalyptic*, 174.

36. Ibid., 162. In his book *Seek the Peace of the City: Christian Political Criticism as Public, Realist, and Transformative* (Eugene, OR: Cascade, 2009), Richard Bourne develops Yoder's understanding of doxology by calling attention to reconciliation as a communal practice. He notes that the "recovery of the fully missiological potential of the practice of fraternal admonition itself requires an act of penitence begun through the application of Yoder's anti-Constantinian historiography." I would like to think Kerr is making a similar suggestion, but his appeal to "doxology" remains too formal for me to know if that is the case. Below I will briefly develop the significance of binding and loosing for understanding the catholicity of the church.

37. For what it is worth I am sure I first thought to characterize the church as *polis* because I had read John Howard Yoder's use of *polis* to characterize the church in *The Christian Witness to the State* (Scottdale, PA: Herald, 2002), 18. Yoder used *polis* to indicate that the church is a deliberative assembly deserving to be described as a politics. It was under the influence of Arne Rasmusson's *The Church as Polis: From Political Theology to Theological Politics* (Notre Dame: University of Notre Dame Press, 1995) that I used the subtitle *The Church as Polis* for *In Good Company*. I suspect it never occurred to Yoder it might be necessary to choose *polis* or mission as primary images for the character of the church. For Yoder,

> the Christian faith is a missionary faith. Where people in particular positions embraced the faith, it was not because they were recruited for those social slots but because Christian witness reached them there. People are won to a new religion mostly where there is the greatest mobility: conversion appears more in town than in the country, more in the trade classes than in the artisan classes, more among the mobile generation than among older people. Where the greatest social movement is, there the most Christians were to be found. (Yoder, *Christian Attitudes to War, Peace, and Revolution*, ed. Theodore Koontz and Andy Alexis-Baker [Grand Rapids: Brazos, 2009], 52)

38. Paul Minear's important book *Images of the Church in the New Testament* (Philadelphia: Westminster, 1960) always bears rereading.

Kerr may well be right, however, that the characterization of the church as *polis* does not adequately suggest the necessary dispossession of the church correlative of the missionary imperative.[39] Thus Kerr's claim that "the question of Christian political action with respect to the eschatological New Jerusalem" must be reconceived as a work of exile; but I should like to have some concrete exemplification of what that might look like.[40] Kerr has recently helpfully drawn on de Certeau's work to suggest how Yoder's understanding of the church can avoid the politics of establishment, but there remains an abstract character to Kerr's position that betrays his stress on the particular.[41]

For example, I think it would be helpful if Kerr dealt with how Yoder understood the necessary interrelation of the missionary character of the church, the quest for Christian unity, and nonviolence. From Yoder's perspective the unity of the church and mission are inseparable. Thus Yoder's claim that "the unity of Christians is a *theological* imperative first of all in the sense that its reasons arise out of the basic truth commitments of the gospel and the church's intrinsic mission."[42] Therefore, for Yoder, "where Christians are not united, the gospel is not true in that place," which means the witness of the church cannot help but be compromised.[43] So mission, at least on Yoder's ground, is tied essentially to the church's catholicity.

For Yoder, therefore, the admonition in Matthew 18:15–20 is not only constitutive of the mission of the church, but it is the necessary definitive mark of the church's catholicity.[44] The practice of binding and loosing embodies the nonviolent character of the church because for it to work it must be presumed that Christians cannot kill one another. As a result, Christians discover through mutual correction that they are united in a manner that Christ has made possible. Binding and loosing is, therefore, the necessary condition for the church to be in mission and in unity in a world fractured by difference.

Locality and Mission

I call attention to Yoder's understanding of binding and loosing because, as he observes, "the only passage of the Gospels where Jesus speaks of the church, the Spirit works through a local procedure of 'binding and loosing.'"[45] Accord-

39. I should like to think the title *Cross-Shattered Christ: Meditations on the Seven Last Words* (Grand Rapids: Brazos, 2004) might suggest that "dispossession" is not a foreign theme in my work.

40. Kerr, *Christ, History, and Apocalyptic*, 184.

41. Nathan Kerr, "Communio Missionis: Certeau, Yoder, and the Missionary Space of the Church," in *The New Yoder*, 317–35.

42. Yoder, *Royal Priesthood*, 291.

43. Ibid.

44. I am indebted to Nathaniel Jung-Chul Lee for this way of putting the matter.

45. Yoder, *Royal Priesthood*, 317.

ingly, Yoder understands such a practice as the definitive mark of catholicity. As he puts it:

> The process of binding and loosing in the local community of faith provides the practical and theological foundation for the centrality of the local congregation. It is not correct to say, as some extreme Baptist and Churches of Christ do, that only the local gathering of Christians can be called "the church." The Bible uses the term church for all the Christians in a large city or even in a province. The concept of local congregational autonomy has, therefore, been misunderstood when it was held to deny mutual responsibilities between congregations or between Christians of different congregations.[46]

Yoder claims, therefore, that his emphasis on the local congregation as the source of radical catholicity "gives more authority to the church than does Rome, trusts more to the Holy Spirit than does Pentecostalism, has more respect for the individual than humanism, makes moral standards more binding than Puritanism, is more open to the given situation than the 'new morality.' "[47] He can make these claims because he sees the work of reconciliation in binding and loosing as the necessary mode to find unity amidst the differences created through mission.[48]

So catholicity and mission are interdependently bound together, through the presence of a people whose very existence is determined by the worship of God.[49] That is why it is a mistake to send out *a* missionary. Two, at the very least, have to travel together because otherwise those to whom they go would not be able to "see" the gospel.[50] For the gospel is just that—a seeing of a communion between people that the world cannot otherwise know.

The church is mission because it is catholic. The catholic character of the church means it is in mission. The church may be everywhere, but it is able to be so because to rightly worship God means it is always somewhere. That is why the catholic character of the church names a quite different geography than the current language of globalization. Kam Ming Wong observes that the

46. Ibid., 352.

47. Ibid., 325.

48. Yoder develops this interrelation especially in *Royal Priesthood*, 329–30.

49. For Yoder's understanding of the relation between Christian unity and mission, see his "The Ecumenical Movement and the Faithful Church," in *Radical Ecumenicity: Pursuing Unity and Continuity after John Howard Yoder*, ed. John C. Nugent (Abilene, TX: Abilene Christian University Press, 2010), 193–221. Yoder argues that there are good grounds for saying that the Anabaptists were the first ecumenical movement not only because they were truly international but because "they insisted that the church is essentially missionary, and that she must be separate from the world, even if that world has been Christianized" (215). Yoder suggests that this is an idea put forward in our time by Lesslie Newbigin.

50. Jesus's sending of the disciples in Matthew 10 strikes me as a good place to begin to rethink mission. See for example my *Matthew*, Brazos Theological Commentary on the Bible (Grand Rapids: Brazos, 2006), 105–12.

global perspective assumes that phenomena can exist simultaneously anywhere in the world and unite locations anywhere instantly. Wong continues:

> In contrast, rather than relying on technology to move from one place to another, the catholicity of the church collapses spatial barriers of the world into the local congregations, by gathering and uniting all its believers in a particular town or location regardless of any natural or social divisions. The power of transcending boundaries not only of space and time makes the local church truly catholic.[51]

But surely that means no challenge is more important for the mission of the church than Christian unity. I can find no better way to conclude, therefore, than to call attention to Lesslie Newbigin's description of "the unity we seek," drafted for the 1961 World Council of Churches conference in New Delhi:

> We believe that the unity which is both God's will and his gift to his church is being made visible as all in each place who are baptized into Jesus Christ and confess him as Lord and Savior are brought by the Holy Spirit into one fully committed fellowship, holding the one apostolic faith, preaching the one Gospel, breaking the one bread, joining in common prayer, and having a corporate life reaching out in witness and service to all and who at the same time are united with the whole Christian fellowship in all places and all ages in such wise that ministry and members are accepted by all, and that all can act and speak together as occasion requires for the tasks to which God calls his people.[52]

The church, therefore, can only be the alternative to war if Christians refuse to kill. Such a refusal may seem a small gesture given the reality of war. Yet we believe it is a gesture, a truthful gesture, that beckons a future otherwise unimaginable. And so, I end with a beginning:

A Modest Proposal for Peace:
Let the Christians of the World Agree That They Will Not Kill Each Other

51. Kam Ming Wong, "Catholicity and Globality," *Theology Today* 66 (January 2010): 465–66.
52. Quoted by Wainwright in Newbigin, *Signs amid the Rubble*, x.

Index